BEYOND ARARAT
A Journey Through Eastern Turkey

Since Bettina Selby discovered the worth of a bicycle in exploring the wilder places of the world, she has pedalled thousands of miles. Her latest journey takes her to the cradle of civilization, where the Tigris and the Euphrates rise. Beginning along the Black Sea coast of Turkey, her way leads south. Riding through Kurdistan only weeks after the end of the Gulf War spells danger: kidnapping is rife, comforts few. It is a hard journey through some of the most magnificent scenery in the world — and some of its least predictable people.

Books by Bettina Selby
in the Charnwood Library Series:

RIDING NORTH ONE SUMMER

I've travelled the world twice over,
Met the famous: saints and sinners,
Poets and artists, kings and queens,
Old stars and hopeful beginners,
I've been where no-one's been before,
Learned secrets from writers and cooks
All with one library ticket
To the wonderful world of books.

© JANICE JAMES.

BETTINA SELBY

BEYOND ARARAT

A Journey Through
Eastern Turkey

Complete and Unabridged

CHARNWOOD
Leicester

First published in Great Britain in 1993 by
John Murray (Publishers) Limited
London

First Charnwood Edition
published March 1994
by arrangement with
John Murray (Publishers) Limited
London

British Library CIP Data

Selby, Bettina
    Beyond Ararat: a journey through Eastern
    Turkey.—Large print ed.—
    Charnwood library series
    I. Title II. Series
    915.6604

    ISBN 0–7089–8756–7

Published by
F. A. Thorpe (Publishing) Ltd.
Anstey, Leicestershire
Set by Words & Graphics Ltd.
Anstey, Leicestershire
Printed and bound in Great Britain by
T. J. Press (Padstow) Ltd., Padstow, Cornwall

This book is printed on acid-free paper

This book is dedicated to
Xenophon and the Ten Thousand
who also had a tricky time
in the mountains of Eastern Turkey

BULGARIA

BLACK SEA

GREECE

Edirne

Bosporus

Amasra

Zonguldak

Bardin

Teskopt

ISTANBUL

Sile

P O N T

Kastromonu

Yesilçay

Sea of
Marmara

Adapazari

Bursa

Kizil Irmak

Balikesir

Eskisehir

ANKARA

LESBOS

CHIOS

Izmir

F   U   R

R. Menderes

Konya

Denizli

Bodrum

Antalya

RHODES

N

CYPRUS

MEDITERRANEAN   SEA

0   100 Miles 200   300

0   160 Kilometres 320   480

Heights of mountains and passes are in feet

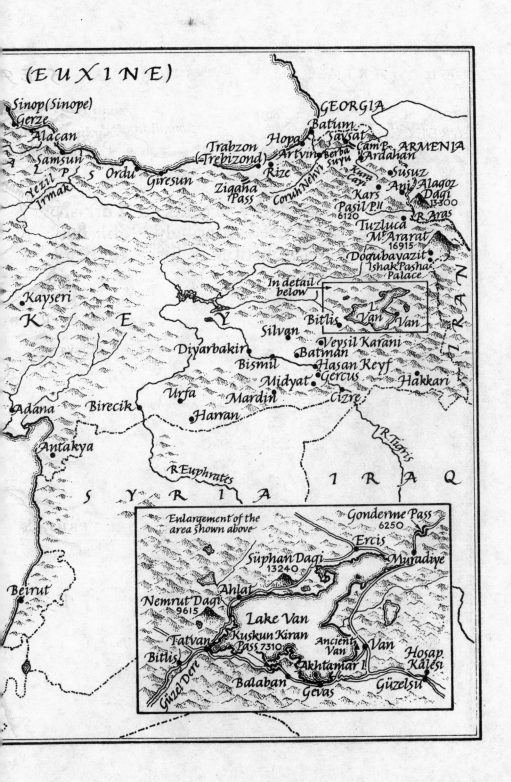

(EUXINE)

Sinop (Sinope)
Gerze
Alaçan
Samsun
Yezil Irmak
Ordu
Giresun
Trabzon (Trebizond)
Hopa
Artvin
Rize
Zigana Pass
Çoruh Nehri
Berba suyu
Camp.
Ardahan
Kars
Pasil P. ll
6120
Susuz
Ani
Alagoz Dagi
13300
R. Aras
Tuzluca
Mt. Ararat
16915
Doǧubayazit
Ishak Pashas Palace

GEORGIA
Batum
Tavsat
ARMENIA
Kura Çayi

In detail below
L. Van
Van

Kayseri
Y
Silvan
Bitlis

T
U
R
K
E
Y

Diyarbakir
Bismil
Urfa
Mardin
Harran
Birecik
Adana
Antakya
Beirut

Veysil Karani
Batman
Hasan Keyf
Midyat
Gercus
Cizre
Hakkari

R. Tigris

IRAN

S   Y   R   I   A
R. Euphrates
I   R   A   Q

Enlargement of the area shown above

Gonderme Pass
6250
Erciş
Süphan Dagi
13240
Muradiye
Nemrut Dagi
9615
Ahlat
Lake Van
Tatvan
Kuşkun Kiran Pass 7310
Bitlis
Güzel Dere
Balaban
Ancient Van
Akhtamar I.
Gevaş
Van
Hosap. Kalesi
Güzelsu

In the interest of clarity accents in Turkish words have been used sparingly. 'Sh' has occasionally been substituted for ş to help with pronunciation.

Acknowledgements

All travellers are dependent upon the goodwill of the people of the countries they pass through. Although Eastern Turkey presented dangers in plenty, the kindnesses I received far outweigh the hostility. I therefore owe a debt of gratitude to a great number of people who cannot be named in this book.

I would like to thank Jock Murray for the introduction to kind friends of his in Istanbul, who have now become valued friends of mine also.

Travellers are lucky if they have a partner who does not resent their being away for long periods. I would particularly like to thank my husband for his patience and forbearance and for keeping everything going in my absence.

I would also like to thank all those who have enjoyed my books and written to say so. Their encouragement has helped tremendously when the going was hard.

1

An Idea Takes Shape

'AND God remembered Noah ... ' These words lodged in my mind long after I had outgrown the charm of stiff little pairs of wooden animals going neatly two by two into a fat-bellied overcrowded ark. Such wonderfully portentous words, 'And God made a wind to pass over the earth, and the waters subsided ... And the Ark rested in the seventh month, on the seventeenth day of the month on the mountains of Ararat ... '

The spark that fired the idea of making a long journey towards the mountain where Noah's Ark was supposed to have come to rest, however, came about as a result of chancing upon a particular passage in a book by a nineteenth-century explorer named James Bryce, who had actually climbed Ararat:

Below and around, included in this single view, seemed to lie the whole cradle of the human race, from Mesopotamia in the south to the great wall of the Caucasus that covered the northern horizon, the boundary for so many ages of the civilized world. If it was indeed here that man first set foot on the unpeopled earth, one could imagine how the great dispersal went as the races spread

1

themselves along the course of the great rivers down to the Black and Caspian Seas, and over the Assyrian plain to the shores of the Southern Ocean, whence they were wafted away to the other continents and isles. No more imposing centre of the world could be imagined.

Reading this I felt a familiar shiver of excitement as the first glimmerings of the idea took root. Kaleidoscopic images began to flicker through my mind — great primal rivers rushing and tumbling through gorges, blue inland seas, towering shaggy mountains, and the thousands of years of layered history and legend: Hittite and Urartian ruins from the dawn of civilization; Lake Van and the Garden of Eden; Jason and the Golden Fleece; Amazons; and Homer's Greeks in their high-prowed boats; Selçuk mosques and palaces; Kurdish robber castles; Xenophon's Ten Thousand fighting their way back through Kurdistan after their abortive attack on the Great King; Trebizond and the last whispers of the Byzantine Empire. I realized at once that it was a journey I had long wished to make.

A first glance at the atlas revealed a tempting route. Beginning at Istanbul — of all cities the most evocative — I could follow the fascinating Black Sea coast right round to Trebizond. From there, or perhaps even nearer to the Russian border, I could make my ascent up to the Eastern Anatolian plateau and begin the long sweep towards Ararat. And why stop at Ararat?

Beyond lay the great mountain-locked Lake of Van and the beginnings of the ancient land between the Tigris and the Euphrates, the cradle of biblical history. Through Kurdistan, with its cities of almost legendary antiquity, the way led southwards to the Arab borderlands, to Harran where Abraham had sojourned after leaving Ur of the Chaldees, before finally setting out for the Promised Land. Names rose from the map like siren calls.

A more detailed study of larger-scale maps was somewhat sobering, as I began to realize the distances involved and the difficulties of the terrain. At the age of forty-seven, I had made my first very long bicycle trek through Pakistan, Northern India and Nepal, weaving in and out of the Himalayan valleys to Kathmandu. The soaring passes I'd toiled over on that journey had been only just within my powers. How then, ten years later, would I manage to cross these endless ranges of Turkish mountains, many of which seemed very little lower than those I'd tackled in the Himalayas?

And what of the fierce dogs which roamed free in Eastern Turkey guarding the great flocks of sheep from rapacious wolves and bears? Most dogs given half a chance, delight in pursuing bicyclists and sinking their teeth into whatever part they can get at. 'The herd dogs of Eastern Anatolia', I read, 'are half-wolf, the bitches being sent up into the hills to mate, and thus maintain the ferocity of the breed.' They were also armoured with spiked collars, according to this account, so that wolves couldn't grip

3

them by the throat in a fight, and these collars carried a medal for each wolf the dog killed. 'Unfortunately,' it continued, 'they are not trained to limit their attention to four-legged predators, and will attack anything that moves' — especially cyclists I had no doubt!

My route would also be taking me very close to the borders of Russia, Iran, Iraq and Syria, four of the world's least peaceful frontiers where wars were a frequent occurrence, and where the hills were currently full of disaffected and armed Kurdish guerillas. How, I wondered, would they react to a lone female on a bicycle?

There are two possible choices for a person contemplating a difficult or potentially dangerous journey — either to be hopeful about what cannot be changed, or to give up the idea altogether and stay at home. Like all travellers, I am an optimist by nature, but that does not preclude making what careful preparations I can. Only after I have convinced myself that I have done all that is possible to ensure my safety am I happy to leave the rest to Providence.

In spite of the mountains, I was still set on making the journey by bicycle, for this unique and, to my mind, sadly underrated means of travel remains for me the perfect way to see the world and to meet people. I am never happier than on my own two wheels, but if necessity forces both me and my bicycle to become temporary passengers on alternative transport I don't object. Buses, trains, planes, mountain porters, camels, dug-out canoes — all have at one time or another helped rider and

4

machine over difficult or forbidden ground, and I expected this trip would prove no exception. But even so, if I was to have any chance of making the Turkey expedition under my own steam I would need a very special bicycle — one that was both lightweight and strong, and whose main virtue was its ability to climb. My trusty Evans which had carried me across the rough deserts of Africa had been stolen from outside the British Museum some months before, but even had it still been with me it would not have been suitable for this journey. For those who are not cycle enthusiasts, and who think all bicycles are much of a muchness, and that what makes one go faster and further than another is largely the rider's strength and determination, let me assure you that you are not altogether wrong. Good design, however, can and does make a surprising difference, particularly on hills.

I consulted one of the fast-vanishing breed of British bicycle craftsmen who operate from small premises in back streets, turning out hand-made machines that resemble ordinary bicycles only as far as a thoroughbred horse is like a hack. After an afternoon's discussion centring around such matters as weight-to-strength ratios, the angles of the frame, the number of teeth on cogs and sprockets and other such matters, all deeply rivetting to anyone involved in getting around the world on two wheels, I went away to await events.

What finally emerged from Mr Roberts' workshop was a splendid-looking hybrid machine, part-touring, part-mountain bike. It had mountain bike wheels for strength, sealed bearings for keeping out damaging grit and water, lightweight tubing and very low gears for taking the effort out of steep gradients. The frame had a very short wheelbase and angles almost as steep as those of a racing bicycle. It wasn't a smooth ride, and going fast downhill with loaded panniers it proved to be a touch 'twitchy' in the steering and needed careful handling, but as by now I am far steadier in a saddle than I am on my feet this did not worry me. What mattered most was that the bicycle climbed superbly, and because of this marked ability to propel me upwards where lesser cycles would have failed, and because of the classical lands we would be travelling through, I considered calling my new companion Pegasus. When I tried out this name, however, it didn't come naturally, perhaps it was a touch too exotic, even for so uncommon a bicycle. So, as I had done with its predecessor, I took to calling it by the name of the maker, emblazoned on the down tube — Roberts — a name with a fine Scottish ring to it, at once chivalrous and dependable.

The worry about Anatolian dogs was resolved quite by chance during a casual conversation at the Royal Geographical Society. Had I not heard of an ultra-sonic device called the Dog Dazer? I had not, but very soon I was the owner of one. It was an unimpressive looking small grey plastic rectangle, weighing about four ounces; and a tiny red spot that lit up when I pressed a button was the only indication that it worked, for the sound it was supposed to emit was above the upper level of human hearing, and discernible only to dogs, cats, horses and any other creature sensitive to the ultra-sonic range. I was quickly given proof of the effectiveness of this device. Unknown to me Bootle, our aged slow-moving cat, came into the room as I was showing the Dazer to my husband. When I pressed the button the cat was about twelve feet behind me and the business end of the Dazer was pointing in the opposite direction. Possibly the sound bounced off a radiator, but however it reached him, the effect was spectacular. I swung round at my husband's shout, just in time to see poor Bootle leap several feet into the air, his face wearing the sort of expression associated with meeting a particularly horrid ghost. As soon as he landed he beat a hasty retreat, moving considerably faster than he had in months. Sorry though I was to have been the unwitting cause of such a fright, Bootle's reaction to the Dazer boded well for encounters with ferocious dogs, and the manufacturer's claim that the experience left no permanent damage was borne out by his speedy return to normality.

I rather wished I could find something equally effective against ill-disposed humans, but short of a gun (which is illegal and which anyway I probably wouldn't be much good with), there was nothing. My personal safety was, as usual, one of the things I would have to leave to Providence, helped out by common-sense precautions.

The rest of the time before departure was taken up with assembling my kit and equipment, and organizing it into four pannier bags and a handlebar bag, in such a way that it would all be perfectly balanced on the bicycle, and come to hand instantly. Readers who are interested in the details of this equipment will find it listed at the end of the book. Knowing where each item is stowed is important, not just for being able to make camp in the dark, or get out the first aid, or the Dog Dazer in a hurry, but also to avoid a lengthy exhausting search every time any item is required. One of the chief pleasures for me in travelling as I do is the freedom it gives me. To have all one's material possessions reduced to what can be carried on a bicycle is a joy in itself. The aim after that is to be as little aware of them as a snail is of its shell.

Even after years of packing for expeditions, however, I still agonize over items I feel I cannot do without (usually books) but which I know that, in the interest of keeping the weight at an acceptable level, I must resist. This, together with obtaining 'jabs', tickets and last-minute necessities, so absorbs my attention for the final week or so before departure that the journey itself tends to get pushed into the background.

So it was almost a surprise to find myself sitting in an empty Istanbul airport at three o'clock one hot July morning, waiting for a more suitable time to ring the people with whom I was going to be staying for the next few days. I could have got out my self-inflating mattress and sleeping bag, and curled up in a corner. But now that the adventure was at last

8

afoot I felt too keyed up for sleep. Only a short distance away, cocooned in one of the largest urban sprawls in the world, was the lovely wraith of a Byzantine city, a city I had fallen instantly in love with when I'd first seen it seven years before. Had Roberts not been in pieces in a large bag at my side, I could have been there in an hour, standing once more in front of Haghia Sophia, or gazing down from the gardens of the Süleymaniye Mosque over the Golden Horn.

2

Sailing to Byzantium

Nor is there singing school but studying
Monuments of its own magnificence;
Therefore I have sailed the seas and come
To the holy city of Byzantium.
    W. B. Yeats, 'Sailing to Byzantium'

NO other city possesses the haunting magic of Istanbul nor, anywhere in the world, could there be a more superb position for the capital of a great empire. I came to it the first time by ship, sailing in across the Sea of Marmara in the late afternoon when the domes and minarets of a hundred mosques were softly gilded by the setting sun and the ruins of the great Byzantine walls of Theodosius were stained rosy red. Having seen it like that, I find that I still retain something of the sense of wonder and excitement I felt then, in spite of the accelerating depredations of the last seven years.

But even in the first excitement of being back in this wonderful city, I was at once reminded of Rose Macaulay's Aunt Dot in *The Towers of Trebizond*, and her pronouncement of, 'Abroad isn't what it used to be'. Istanbul is currently the world's fastest growing city, having more than doubled its population in the past seven

10

years. On the drive in from the airport I had already seen that the perimeters of Istanbul had become one vast bulldozed building site, with raw ugly blocks of uniform flats swallowing up the ground like a rapacious army on the march. The tailback of vehicles night and morning crossing the Bosporus to and from these expanding suburbs lasts for many hours.

If the numbers of Istanbul's inhabitants had doubled, tourism appeared to have increased forty- or fifty-fold. With the medieval streets clogged with traffic and with pedestrians jostling for space on the crowded pavements, it seemed as though the city was drowning under a double tidal wave of humanity and traffic. Where previously vehicles had been driven with anarchic abandon, now they were so densely packed they hardly moved, and the exhaust fumes were terrible. The substance was still there, but now it had a veil drawn over it; it didn't overwhelm you all at once any more, especially not in the baking heat of early July.

I was fortunate in that I was staying with a Turkish family on the Asian shore of the Sea of Marmara. My hosts lived in a house of great charm, surrounded by a pretty garden inhabited by a family of superior grey cats, and set on the very edge of the sea with romantic views across to the Princes Islands where once over-ambitious or unruly members of Byzantine dynasties had been confined.

But even here there was little peace. Fifty yards or so out from the shore a causeway was being constructed parallel to the land, which would eventually carry an eight-lane highway. Not only had this scheme been denied international aid on the grounds that it was environmentally damaging, but it had also been declared illegal by the Turkish courts. In spite of this, the contractors were working around the clock in order to make the project a *fait accompli*. What tortured ramifications of bribery and corruption had brought about a state of affairs where a private company could flout a court's directive I could not begin to understand. Perhaps with elections approaching and a possible change of government, they were hoping for a change of policy. When the causeway was completed and the land between it and the shore had been drained, the Sea of Marmara, already threatened by excessive pollution, would have suffered a massive shrinkage. It gave a macabre twist to Yeats' 'That dolphin-torn, that gong-tormented sea'.

A great advantage of staying on the Asian shore was that I could come into Istanbul by boat, avoiding the horrid road congestion and recapturing something of the magic of that first approach. Arriving by ferry, where the wide waters of the Sea of Marmara meet the narrow Bosporus, and the Golden Horn flows off to the left under the Galata Bridge, was all still much as I remembered it. A great clamour and bustle arose from the tugs, barges, trawlers, ferries and liners, all sounding their horns imperiously as they passed within a few yards of one another, and little dinghies weaved suicidally in and out amongst them. Gulls swooped and screamed and fought for scraps around the heads of the fishermen calling out their assorted catches at the quaysides. The swaying bouncing Galata Bridge was also unchanged, though it was soon to be torn down and replaced by the less exciting structure nearing completion just upstream from it. But for the moment the old Galata had its row of rod and line fishermen on the upper level, its fish restaurants on the lower deck, and vendors anywhere they could find a spot to sell anything, from fried fish to re-packaged cigarettes.

Once across the Golden Horn, it was straight into the maelstrom of mixed traffic and humanity battling up the hill, to fetch up at last, breathless, in the sanctuary of the great open space at the heart of Constantine's city, where the Blue Mosque of Sultan Ahmet faces Haghia Sophia across the ancient Hippodrome.

All this area had been considerably cleaned up since I had last seen it, and with its perimeter of brash air-conditioned tourist coaches it had lost much of its romantic, slightly down-at-heel charm. The ancient marble capitals which had once served as useful resting places for glasses of tea and coffee had been replaced by swathes of plastic chairs and tables. The hotel whose roof I had once slept on, and from where it seemed I could almost touch the roof of Haghia Sophia, had been pulled down to make way for something less individual and much more expensive. The importunate carpet-sellers who had pressed their pretty glass 'evil-eyes' on any likely-looking clients had given way to touts selling illustrated guide books in all the major tongues to the streams of tourists alighting from their coaches. Even the gloriously unhygienic and much-loved Pudding Shop had been refurbished to a state of shamefaced respectability. But it was Haghia Sophia itself that proved the biggest shock.

Since AD 548 Haghia Sophia, the Church of Divine Wisdom, has stood on its hill overlooking the shining sweep of the sea. For over fourteen hundred years it survived earthquake and fire, conquest and sacking. Again and again it was patched up, buttressed, and refurbished. The Ottoman conqueror Mehmet's first action on taking Constantinople in AD 1453 had been to come bare-headed to Haghia Sophia to pay homage to so great a building. After a further few hundred years of service as a mosque, with a mihrab to point the way to Mecca set annoyingly off-centre in the apse, and with Arab calligraphy inscribed on huge black disks suspended so as to ruin completely the soaring lines of the great piers, the denuded shell was relegated to the status of museum. Yet none of this had succeeded in changing the essential genius of one of the most glorious Christian edifices in the world.

When I had first walked under the great central dome it had appeared to be hovering there, suspended between earth and heaven without visible means of support. Filling the four pendentives of the dome were the swirling feathery masses of vast terrifying seraphim which further enhanced this effect of ethereal lightness.

14

Below, in magnificent contrast, massive porphyry columns, with capitals like fretted marble lace, emphasized the immense weight and the extent of the venerable battered structure. From apse and galleries restored fragments of gold mosaics gleamed from the ravished walls like Yeats' 'Sages standing in God's holy fire'.

Now I found the interior of Haghia Sophia half filled with scaffolding towering clear up to the ceiling of the dome, which in consequence no longer appeared to hover. Large coach parties of diverse nationalities seethed about the remaining spaces, above and below, like ants in a nest. The great structure boomed like a tower of Babel with tour guides haranguing their charges in a score of competing languages, and camera flashes blazed out of every dim recess. If the unrepentant spirit of Henricus Dandalo was anywhere near the place, I reckoned it would be rubbing its hands in glee. Dandalo, the evil Doge of Venice, a blind old man of eighty, full of spite, had been largely responsible for this city losing many of its priceless ancient treasures and for this magnificent church being looted and desecrated by a Christian army two and a half centuries before the Ottoman Turks overran the Byzantine Empire. The Fourth Crusade had been on its way to free Jerusalem from the infidel in AD 1204 when Dandalo had managed to subvert it from its purpose and set it instead against Constantinople. Through a series of disastrous circumstances, due largely to the political strife endemic in Constantinople, the Crusaders had succeeded in getting through the impregnable defences and had taken the city, sacking it in a three-day orgy of destruction; Christians decimating Christians while the Turks tightened their grip ever more closely around the Christian world. Dandalo was buried in Haghia Sophia, but eighty years later, after the Latins had been ousted, his tombstone was set into the floor so that the Byzantines could vent their feelings about him by walking over it. That at least remained unchanged, except that now the treading was purely accidental, for it was hardly possible to see one's feet in the crush. Only by concentrating on the marvellous remaining mosaics like the Deesis and the Mother of God in the conch of the apse was it possible to recapture a sense of the awe and wonder I had previously felt, and I left the Church of the Divine Wisdom quickly before I should lose even that.

I escaped across the road into the cool dim depths of another of Justinian's great structures, the Basilica Cistern, which until recent times had been an important part of the city's elaborate water system. Considering that these cool vaults were the best place to be in the sweltering heat of July, they were wonderfully and echoingly empty. Someone had been having fun installing green lighting since I had last seen it which gave the place something of the appearance of a fairy grotto. The catwalks had been repaired and extended too, so it was possible now to explore it fully. A forest of columns, about three hundred and fifty of them — all re-used material taken from pagan temples — supported

16

the street above for a length of a hundred and fifty yards. For a purely practical underground water storage tank, the cistern is amazingly elegant, the lovely classical columns carefully paired according to their varied capitals, and with the vast sheet of water lapping around their bases. It is one of the most evocative Byzantine monuments in the city, because it cannot have changed since it was built around AD 525. Nor was it any surprise to learn that it was popularly known as the 'sunken palace'. I wondered if adventurous Byzantines came down here after a party to swim in and out among the columns, as I would have loved to do had the water been a little deeper. At the far end I came across two colossal plinths supporting some extra unseen weight above. Each block was carved with a gigantic head of Apollo, and like the rest had been taken from a classical temple. The blocks had been positioned so that one head was on its side and the other upside down. As every other detail in the place had been executed with such care I couldn't believe this was accidental, and I wondered if the builders had positioned them like that because Apollo was a pagan deity, unsuitable for a Christian city, and turning him the wrong way round showed that he wasn't being worshipped.

I stayed down in the cool damp vaults for a long while, mulling over the changes that had overtaken my favourite city. It seemed to me that Istanbul was far too hot and far too crowded, and it would be best to leave as soon as I could for the Black Sea coast. There were some remembered places I couldn't leave without seeing again, like the little mosque which had been the exquisite church of SS Sergius and Bacchus, the magnificent frescoes and mosaics in St Saviour in Chora, the grim quarters of the harem in the Topkapi Palace and the sublime Süleymaniye mosque. The rest of Istanbul would have to wait until I passed through on my way home, when hopefully it would not only be cooler, but might once more be a joy to wander haphazardly through the narrow streets near the Golden Horn discovering scraps of ancient Byzantine palaces and cisterns and old Turkish timbered houses.

Both my hostess, Feride, and her husband Irfan were university teachers, and spoke such fluent English that I quickly forgot we were of different nationalities. Only at times was there a distinct dissimilarity, such as when I was reassembling Roberts. It went so against the grain for Irfan to see a woman wielding tools, that after hovering for a while offering unnecessary advice, he actually took the spanner from my hand to do the job himself. At that moment I could see why Feride called him 'the tribal chief'; and I thought that if the gentle urbane Irfan had such pronounced attitudes to what he considered a woman's role, how much stronger would be this stance further east.

Bicycles are rare in Turkey which, considering the mountainous nature of most of the country's terrain, is not really surprising. Also Turks, particularly men, consider unnecessary exertion to be contrary to their religion. The idea of anyone choosing to travel by bicycle, especially around the east of the country, where very few Turks who don't actually live there have ever ventured, intrigued Irfan and Feride's friends, and many of them visited in order to view this phenomenon. One acquaintance, who worked on a national newspaper, thought the undertaking so unusual that she came to interview me and to write a piece about it for the *Çumhuriet* which is the only 'serious' newspaper in Turkey; all the others devote at least two full-colour pages to rows and rows of photographs of Turkish football heroes. In addition, a further two or three pages are filled with row after row of full-colour snapshots of European-looking girls disporting themselves nude or semi-nude on sunny beaches. I gathered that this enormous daily ration of titillating female flesh is obtained by an army of Turkish photographers armed with telescopic lenses who haunt the many nudist camps and beaches on the Turkish Mediterranean coast, popping up like so many rabbits from their holes every time a likely looking subject comes within range. Obviously all these richly coloured offerings left little space for news, except in the *Çumhuriet*. Turkish readers however, being predominately male and pleasure-loving, seem to prefer soft porn and football, and the prestigious Istanbul *Çumhuriet*, whose back page Roberts and I were to adorn in a large but humble black and white photograph, has a comparatively small circulation.

The photographer wanted Roberts fully equipped with pannier bags and water bottles,

19

and I had to ride it up and down a hill to demonstrate how easy it was. By the time I'd done this twenty times under the blazing midday sun, it felt more like sweated labour.

One thing that had greatly surprised me on arriving in Istanbul this time was to see women and girls wearing shorts. Seven years before no one, including the men, would have dreamed of exposing their legs much above mid-calf level. Turkish men used to hang around touristy places like Ephesus expressly to stare at all those exposed Western thighs descending from coaches. I had cycled in long voluminous trousers so as not to attract too much attention or to give offence. The female Turkish population, at least in Istanbul, has at last caught up with Western fashions, and the women who now stood out from the throng were those who belonged to a devout Muslim sect and who went about in floor-length grey coats, with their heads and most of their faces covered.

I gratefully accepted the loan of a pair of Feride's decent knee-length shorts, for in the light of my previous experiences in Turkey I had brought none. The difference they made to comfort in that climate was considerable. Feride couldn't see why I shouldn't wear them on the cycle too, and I thought I would do this for as long as I felt they were acceptable. The further east I went the more conservative people were likely to be, and the more likely to react unfavourably towards someone they considered to be immodestly dressed. I must have mentioned this business of shorts to the journalist, for she featured it prominently in her article, which was to prove helpful later on.

Between making preparations, meeting people, and giving interviews I also fitted in visits to Istanbul making good use of Justinian's cistern to cool off between sites. On my last day Feride accompanied me to the Süleymaniye Mosque. So confusing were the crowds and the traffic, even to someone who has lived in Istanbul for years, that we had to ask the way several times, working our way gradually through the bazaars and the narrow streets until suddenly we passed out of a mean little alley straight into one of the city's large oases. Most of the great mosques were built as cities in miniature, with infirmaries, schools, libraries, dining rooms, kitchens and gardens and cool marble courtyards. It is the exteriors of mosques which I enjoy, and especially the deeply shadowed and highly embellished courtyards. To someone brought up in the rich drama of the Christian liturgy with its colour, music and ritual, the interiors of even the grandest mosques seem very austere, designed as they are so that nothing should distract the heart from prayer. Most of the skill and artistry of Muslim craftsmen has been lavished on the exterior stonework — the lovely stepped domes of the roof, the soaring minarets, the arches, the fountains and ritual washing places, and the tombs. Muslims seem to use the courtyards as outdoor drawing rooms, to read in, teach, meet friends, sell things, or simply to relax.

Feride and I nearly got into serious trouble at the Süleymaniye because we were so tired with the heat and the long walk that we lay under the shade of a tree in the gardens. We had nearly fallen asleep when an irate gardener came and made us get up, shouting at us in Turkish (which of course Feride understood) that he would have kicked us to our feet had we been men. Apparently sitting on the ground is perfectly alright, but lying down implies disrespect, or worse. I was rather alarmed. If a well-brought up Turkish woman could get caught out by these niceties of behaviour, what hope had a foreigner?

3

Coming Down to the Black Sea

WHEN the day arrived to leave Istanbul, Feride would not hear of me braving the maelstrom of the city's traffic on Roberts. She borrowed Irfan's car, into which the bicycle could easily be loaded, and spent over an hour driving me around the worst of the early morning's rush hour jams. But even after this helpful start it was no easy matter getting clear, and I spent a frustrating hour or two finding my way through the suburbs.

Once I had finally won free of the terrible northern sprawl of Istanbul I felt like bursting into song. Nature had not been totally obliterated after all. The grimly-uniform barrack blocks of flats and the littered bulldozed earth, which I had begun to think would go on forever, had at last given way to steep-sided hills, shaggy with pine trees, with bright green fields at their feet. The tarmac was deformed and pot-holed, and I had to watch the path of my front wheel more than I would choose, but otherwise life was once more a thing to be enjoyed.

I stopped several times at small wooden shacks with rustic tables and chairs set out beside them under shady trees, where I could buy glasses of *ayran*, the salted yoghurt drink which is so wonderfully refreshing in the heat. On this and

23

nothing else, for nothing else was available, I cycled on and on towards the Black Sea.

By late afternoon I had reached it, and stood gazing entranced over a wild and treacherous-looking coastline, with waves breaking white over the numerous submerged reefs, and green breakers crashing in against the whitish-grey cliffs. The sun was still hot and bright, although only an hour before a tremendous downpour had soaked me to the skin before I had time to don my waterproof jacket. The high humidity made distances hazy, particularly out across the water. There was a feeling of unreality about being on the edge of this almost land-locked sea, a sense of legend and geography coming together. I thought of the first Greek explorers, navigators making their cautious way through the narrow passage of the Bosporus to burst suddenly upon this great wild expanse.

It was not difficult to imagine a high-prowed black ship out there in the blurred middle distance, with Jason at the helm and his fellow Argonauts bent over their long oars, pulling hard to keep her off that perilous shore. Not that they had needed to worry over much about shipwreck, for according to the legend, one of the heroes Jason took with him was Orpheus, King of Thrace, and the music of Orpheus's lute proved to have the power to move rocks from the Argo's path, and to calm the sudden squalls of the ill-omened Euxine — as the Black Sea was called in Greek times. Colchis, where Jason and the Argonauts were headed in search of the Golden Fleece, lay far to the east, in

the direction I was going, and the thought of
the Argo ghosting along on a course parallel to
my own made my journey seem that much the
richer.

A little further on towards the small seaside
town of Sile, the low cliffs gave way to brown
sandy beaches, where men and boys were hurling
themselves through the surf with great skill and
abandon. The few women who wore bathing
costumes were timidly keeping to the shallows.
Other women were disporting themselves fully
clothed, even to the scarves tied around their
heads and pulled well forward to hide their
faces. Where a few of these bundled-up females
ventured out, or were playfully dragged out to
deeper water by their male companions, their
many layers of skirts billowed out around them,
threatening to topple them over on to their faces,
or to drag them down beneath the waves.

There was an almost continuous line of camp
sites along the edges of these beaches, but
although I was proposing to spend the night
in my tent, this was not quite what I had in
mind. It seemed as if camping was a return to
ancestral roots for these Turks. Their tents and
crude home-made shelters were erected cheek
by jowl with hardly space to walk between
them. All around them lay a welter of litter
and the remains of cooking fires, and in spite
of the shining sea beyond, the scene could
only be described as squalid. Apart from the
myriad children and the sounds radiating from
scores of ghetto blasters it could have been the
halting place of an invading nomadic army on

the last stages of their march upon the city I had just left.

A little nearer to Sile I found a much nicer site that was some way from the beach, among trees, where there was a little wooden restaurant and pension that could supply dinner. The round, mustachioed patron rushed out to capture my custom, a warm, enthusiastic man, and voluble, I gathered, in any language. 'Good camping; many coming German; you like; toilet clean, shower clean; all time plenty water.' Clearly he knew European priorities, and his claims were at least half true. I certainly liked it. Compared with the communal beach colonies it was an excellent place, clean and rubbish-free, with flowers everywhere, some in the ground, but most bursting out of old oil drums and petrol cans neatly placed all around the site. The extended Muslim families of at least four generations, whose women remained all bundled up in layers of garments and head coverings, preserving their air of segregation in spite of being under canvas, more than made up for the non-existent Germans. As for the failure of the promised water in the showers, I assumed the burgeoning flowers had claimed priority, for in this heat they needed a constant supply, as did the many trees. With the sea only a short walk away, lack of water was not the disaster it might have been.

Before I was allowed to get on with putting up my tent and taking my swim, however, I had to satisfy the patron's curiosity about what a lone female with a loaded bicycle was doing down by the Black Sea. Knowing that Turks have a lively curiosity and are never tired of asking questions, I had come supplied with a letter in Turkish which outlined my proposed journey. After this had been read aloud by the patron to the twenty or so males who had gathered around us, I was made to feel fully accepted. My hand was shaken by all present, and I was invited to come to the little café to drink tea.

In my turn I thanked everyone, and said how much I liked Turkey. One of the most useful phrases in Turkish, and one I had already committed to memory is '*Çok gezel*' (pronounced 'chock gazelle' and meaning delicious, very nice or very good). '*Turkey çok gezel*' was the perfect, indeed the only answer to the question most frequently put to visitors — 'How do you like Turkey?' It was never a good idea to enlarge upon those three words, particularly not with a 'but', for example, 'Turkey is lovely but there is an awful lot of litter about', or 'Turkey is very nice but I wish there was less noise . . . less pollution . . .' or, 'If only drivers wouldn't blow their horns quite so vigorously'. Such sentiments produced a genuine sadness in the Turk, and I was always sorry when I had expressed them. Deep down they knew they lived in the best country in the world, and wanted only to hear an endorsement of this belief. And actually most people feel like this about their own country, and while it is quite alright for us to run down our own government, our own economy, or whatever, when foreigners presume to do this it annoys us.

The reception concluded, my small blue tent was up in a trice, and my few bits and pieces stowed. I locked Roberts to a tree, and with the aid of a few signs, I abandoned all my other worldly possessions to the care of the neighbouring extended family and set off for the sea. Behind the camping field I came to a wide swathe of very soft sand, and had to go back for my flip-flops as it was too hot to walk on. Buried to their chins in this waste of burning sand were two elderly Turkish ladies, still, as far as I could see, completely muffled up in all their clothes, and with a tattered black umbrella set on a pole high above them so that it cast a shadow over their heads. I supposed the idea was for the hot sand to relieve rheumatic or arthritic limbs, but as their hands and forearms had been left unburied, and the ladies were busy knitting, with the work held close to their seemingly severed heads, the effect was extremely bizarre.

The sand of the long straight beach was hard and vendors pushed barrows across it filled with all sorts of eatables — kebabs, fried fish, ice cream, cold drinks. Family groups sat around on cloths, the children, young girls and men in bathing suits, mothers with scarves around their heads and muffled up to their chins — really a very odd combination. There was lots of litter about too, but what made it all look so drab and dirty I decided was the colour of the sand, which was a dark uninspiring brown. I wouldn't have fancied a picnic on the beach, but the green and white sea was wonderful. I had to work hard to get out beyond the battering waves, which knocked me down and washed over me many times before I won free. Beyond this breaking surf I could float at my ease, delightfully rising and falling on the heaving green expanse, watching puffy little clouds flushing to pink and red as the sun dipped into the hazy west, thinking what a strange mixture of the squalid and the beautiful Turkey was so far proving.

I ate dinner on the verandah of the little restaurant, washing down the rather dull but healthy vegetable stew, rice and salad with excellent Turkish beer. As soon as I had eaten the apple that concluded the meal, a youth who spoke English was sent by his family to sit with me, bringing a gift of tea in the standard small tulip-shaped glass. He ran through his repertoire of English, telling me about his school in Istanbul, his hopes and his aspirations in a series of statements that needed very little response from me. I thought how very kind and polite Turks are. They had sent the youth over not just to practise his English but because they thought that being alone I must be lonely.

Music played all night from the café, but I was pitched far enough away for it to be no more than a background murmur. I woke often because of the novelty and the excitement of sleeping out under the stars again in a strange country.

By half-past five I was up and taking a shower in the deserted rustic toilet block, where the promised water was at last running cold and clear and almost too invigorating. Breakfast was yesterday's chewy bread, with cheese, almonds, grapes and a cup of instant coffee. I was still at the stage of the journey where preparing a meal in the open was as enjoyable as the food itself. The simplicity of life with no more chores to face than rinsing a single cup and plate enhanced my sense of freedom. It remained only to dismantle the tent, pack up the panniers, all of which need take no more than ten minutes, and the day was my own. I could have been away well before six o'clock had I not decided to let the dew dry from the tent first, and this gave me time to read a chapter of Xenophon while I waited.

One of the serious deprivations of a travelling life for me is how little reading matter I can take because of the restrictions of weight. I can't hope to be able to exchange or replace books as I go, so I choose the few slim volumes I allow myself with great care. Because poetry is in a sense condensed literature, that is what I usually rely upon. I had with me this time some T. S. Eliot — principally 'The Wasteland' and 'Ash Wednesday' — for I find these poems are what I miss most when I don't have them. I also had a selection of W. B. Yeats, because I so love the richness of his imagery, and for this journey his Byzantium poems seemed particularly appropriate. In addition I had Xenophon's *Persian Expedition*, a contemporary account of a Greek army's retreat across two thousand miles of hostile territory, following more or less the route I would be travelling, only in reverse. Although the events described in Xenophon took place in the early part of the fourth century BC, many of the towns he describes are still identifiable, their Greek names changed only slightly. I thought I would enjoy reading his wonderfully lively prose in the places he was writing about, and see if any of it was applicable to today's Turkey.

By the time I'd finished the account of how Xenophon's Greeks had attempted to wrest supplies from a reluctant peasantry in these parts, the sun was already high, and with the tent dry and stowed I set off, Jason's emerald-green Euxine on my left. Very soon the narrow road turned inland and headed north, climbing and twisting ever upwards, over cratered surfaces and gradients that were manageable only in the lowest gears. After a very hard fifteen miles I rode into the first of the day's villages, sweating copiously and badly needing refreshment. It was an unspoilt little hamlet with lots of old-fashioned small wooden houses. The men, as is the Turkish custom, were taking their ease under the pergola of the village café, and called out to me to come and drink *çay* with them. There wasn't any *ayran* at the cafe, but one of the men sent a young girl to his house for some. In the meantime he and the other men found me a seat, and satisfied their curiosity about me with the aid of the letter.

When I tried to pay for the *ayran*, which had been a cool brown jugful, it was as though I had committed a painful social gaffe. In that wonderfully minimal gesture of the Turk, eyes almost closed, eyebrows raised slowly

31

and deliberately, the unmistakable 'Yok' was pronounced soundlessly, except for a slight click of the tongue against the roof of the mouth; not a mere 'No' but the absolute negative — literally, 'It does not exist'. But they waved me on my way with friendly smiles, so clearly there were no hard feelings.

Having gained height so painfully the little road now plunged downwards, squandering all my sweat and effort in one long cooling swoop, mile after mile, until I was back again at the sea, which was now a brilliant cobalt blue. There was a newly built small white hotel beside a pretty sandy bay backed by dazzling white cliffs, all as yet unspoiled. I was the only customer, and the cook came to escort me to his kitchen to show me what was on offer. Not a lot as it turned out, but never did omelette, salad and yoghurt taste so good, though I couldn't decide whether this was because my appetite had been so sharpened by the morning's work, or because of the superlatively lovely setting in which I was eating it. I felt so happy there that I would have been tempted to stay, but for the thought of the day being still so young and of the many hundreds of miles that lay before me.

I rode through the burning heat of afternoon, out of sight of the sea, through a landscape where the harvest was already in, and the fields were dry and bare, and I too felt baked and dried out. Just as the sun was beginning to loosen its grip on the day the road again brought me down to the sea, to the small fishing port of Yesilçay, which was in the throes of becoming a Turkish seaside resort. There were a number of raw new hotels and restaurants, half-constructed roads and all the general litter of expansion, but it was a nice place for all that. Young holiday makers from the cities were riding up and down a new sea front boulevard on mountain bicycles; perhaps Turkey was changing even more profoundly than I had thought in Istanbul. The camp site was cramped and uninviting, so I stayed instead at a brand-new simple little *pansyon* that faced on to the front. Across the road was a grove of very beautiful pine trees, and beyond that the sea, and all around were piles of building rubble and a general scattering of rubbish.

It was in this *pansyon* that I acquired a useful addition to my travelling documents. The friendly young woman, Stafl, who managed the place, spotted the account of the interview I had given to the *Çumhuriet* in that day's edition. The photograph was not particularly flattering, not even of the dazzling Roberts, and the translation I was given of the article sounded rather odd too, and full of inaccuracies, as newspaper articles so often tend to be. But Stafl thought it was all very prestigious and exciting, and she particularly enjoyed the bit about wearing shorts. She asked me to autograph the copy, and add a line to say that I had stayed in her *pansyon*. Another copy was obtained for me and put into a clear plastic envelope. I used it subsequently to explain myself to Turks who wanted to know more about me, and I suppose because it was in print, it seemed to impress people more than a mere letter.

Stafl sent me on my way the following morning with a magnificent breakfast of boiled eggs, cheese — both hard and soft — melon, olives, tomatoes, cucumber and honey, served with fresh crusty bread and coffee — just the sort of foundation needed to give a cyclist the strength for the extreme Turkish terrain.

The day soon became a series of fights to stay by the sea, all of which I lost. Turkey is quite the worst-mapped country in the world, and even the expensive German map I was using was often no more than an approximation. There were roads marked hugging the coastline, albeit very minor ones, but when I tried to find them it was always 'Yok'; they didn't exist, or they had been swallowed up, washed away, or had never existed. I had a most frustrating time, making endless detours, using up precious energy but making very little eastward progress. Xenophon's troops had had much the same problem all those hundreds of years before. In fact at one point they stopped for a conference about it, and decided to make the 'natives' repair the roads before they proceeded any further!

The grain of the land in Asia Minor runs mainly east-west along great river valleys, and only in a few places do the towering mountain ranges open up to provide a natural passage down to the Black Sea. Great stretches of beetling cliffs and marshy river estuaries have made the construction of a continuous coastal route extremely difficult; and until the existing goat tracks meandering across crag and marsh have been upgraded, one mile gained in these parts can mean going at least half a dozen in some other direction. While this might not matter so much in a car, with the energy provided by a human motor I found it difficult at times not to feel that the dice were loaded against me.

In one place where my proposed route was again '*Yok*' it meant making a huge one-hundred-mile detour around a vast river estuary, climbing through mountainous terrain, to a town I had no wish to visit. The men who gave this piece of unwelcome information were entertaining me to tea at a roadside café, and they roared with laughter as I pointed out on my map the coastal road I had been hoping to take. 'Not even a tractor could make it,' they said in German, nearly splitting their sides at my expense.

I had covered very little of this latest detour, feeling perfectly happy once I had accepted the inevitable, for the pretty countryside looked rather like a Constable painting except for the tortoises which occasionally trundled across the road, when a truck swerved in and stopped in front of me, almost knocking me from the saddle. And there were my erstwhile hosts of the tea house leaping out and hauling Roberts aboard. I could not have argued had I wanted to, it was just like Irfan seizing my spanner. They had decided I needed a lift and a lift I was going to have! I was firmly tucked into the cab between three of the men, while others supported Roberts in the back and we sped on at what seemed to me a sickening speed after my gentle amble.

The road where they set me down was very busy, for it came from the large town of Adapazari and ran down to the sea through a well-watered plain, continuing on around the coast to the coal-mining town of Zonguldak. Imperious drivers with no concept of the rights of cyclists made me feel threatened and wary. I could see no likely place to spend the night. Villages pressed hard upon one another, but none of them had a pension or hotel. I rode on, while the day lost its heat and it grew later and later. In one village a stout boy on a small bicycle rode beside me on the pavement, making repeated signs for me to give him a cigarette. The fact that he could so easily keep up with me made me realize just how dog-tired I was. There would be nowhere to stay, it seemed, until I reached the coast forty miles further on. It was already dusk and I had no lights. I simply had to find a spot to put up the tent.

Most of the villages seemed to be made up of rows of smallholdings, just simple detached houses fronting the road, with long gardens behind running down to fields. I stopped at one where a young woman was talking to her neighbour. She gave me a beaming smile as I pulled up, but grew shy as soon as I tried out my Turkish, and called a young man out to speak with me. Soon several members of the village had gathered round and were considering my request for a corner in their garden. Hospitality was offered in several houses, but I stuck to my

36

guns and said I wanted only a small spot to put up the tent, and eventually a place was found for me behind the house of the young woman's mother, who lived next door.

All the family came to watch me set up camp. There were about thirty or forty adults and children living in several households in the village. They all stood around in a semicircle making me feel like an event. The oldest male, to whom everyone deferred, thought I would not be comfortable with my thin half-length self-inflating mattress, and sent some of the girls to fetch rugs and cushions. These they brought, giggling with excitement, and stuffed them into my small tent, until I began to doubt whether I would be able to fit in too. Now that the ice was broken everyone wanted to contribute something and soon my camp was very grand, with a chair and table alongside, on which was placed a glass, a jug of *ayran*, and a bowl of fruit.

The garden, or rather rough orchard, was full of interest. There was a duck pond, a couple of working horses, a tethered cow, hens, a well, a few sheep, and all sorts of agricultural implements which I would have liked to have examined more closely. But I had little chance to do so, for my young benefactress invited me by signs to come and take a shower in her house, after which I was drawn into the rich social life of the village women, and stayed there until I could no longer keep my eyes open, and was led off by torchlight to my tent.

The house I was taken to was far more modern than its rather ramshackle exterior had led me to expect, and it was equipped with both electricity and television. It was furnished traditionally, with raised seating all around the rooms, and with Turkish carpets on floors and seats. Glass-fronted cabinets held modern glasses and china. Everyone left their shoes outside the door, and sat comfortably on the benches with their feet tucked under them. The water for the shower was heated by lighting a small wood fire under a tall thin cylinder, which was so efficient that it took only ten minutes or so for the water to reach the required temperature. Afterwards I sat with a group of women, girls and babies, exchanging a surprising amount of information, considering that they knew no English and my Turkish still consisted only of a few basic words. But I had with me two small Turkish/English dictionaries, and these we took turns to thumb through, finding approximations of the words we wanted, and then eking these out with gestures. It was not unlike an expanded session of charades.

The children were dressed in European-style clothes, the young girls in elaborate frilly dresses, but the women, young and old alike, wore large headscarves and traditional shapeless all-concealing garments which came down to their ankles. All, that is, except my young hostess, who was married and had one baby son. It was her free upright stance and bared head that had first attracted my notice. She said that as her husband did not mind, she chose to be modern and leave her face exposed; she would also like to wear trousers as I did, but must wait a while for that. Her sisters all laughed, and said they would not want to follow suit even if they had been allowed, but they were sure their daughters would be just like me, for times were changing very fast in Turkey.

While all the talk had been going on, other women had been busy cooking in the kitchen. We ate very casually, anyone who felt like it sitting down at table and helping themselves from various dishes of spaghetti, stewed meat, olives, cheese and melon. As soon as anyone left the table someone else took her place and continued eating whatever was on the plate. I was the only one not allowed to drift off, but was pressed to course after course, until my pleas of being unable to manage even one more olive were accepted, and I was at last permitted to depart with my torch-bearing escort to the over-full tent, where I fell almost instantly into a deep unbroken sleep.

4

Getting to Grips with the Pontic Alps

THE further east I travelled, the higher soared the mountains, and the more closely the humidity settled over me like a warm, all-enveloping blanket. Turkey has several distinct climatic zones, and that of the Black Sea coast is akin to a tropical rain forest. My clothes would become saturated with sweat in the first hour of riding, and stay wet all day. The air either did not contain the quantity of oxygen a bicyclist needed, or else had too much, and I gasped and panted on slopes that normally I would sail up quite easily. And yet, in spite of the effort, there was something wonderfully carefree and undemanding about the country itself, that was ideally suited to the life of an active tramp; something that was also slightly bizarre and inconsequential like Edward Lear's 'Coast of Coromandel where the early pumpkins blow'. Just as on that imaginary shore, food here was also 'plentiful and cheap', and although in the small towns and villages where I ate, it tended to be the same fare of either stewed aubergines or kebab and salad, it was nearly always available when needed. And fruit was so abundant that I was seldom allowed to pay for it, but had it pressed upon me as a gift.

There was no sense of hurry because I was

enjoying the country I was passing through, and the frequent halts I needed to regain my breath gave me all the more opportunity to savour the views. The upper parts of the mountain ranges were seldom visible in the steamy haze that hung over them, but just occasionally I caught brief exciting glimpses of towering dark shaggy masses where I had expected to see only sky. The shagginess of these great mountains, so densely covered with bristling pine trees, far above what would normally be the upper limit for them, and clinging thickly even to the most precipitous slopes, added considerably to the bizarre character of this coast. My route meandered in and out of the lesser hills, and the sea appeared and disappeared on my left, sparkling and shimmering, a scintillating sapphire blue. As the day wore on, the sea gradually darkened, until by evening it could become as sombre and mysterious as if a dense purple pall had been laid over it.

Sitting before my tent in the late afternoons, or drinking a beer on some rickety terrace overlooking a soiled and littered beach, I watched the daily drama of the setting sun. There was very little that was pristine on this coast, few places where man had not left scars; even the fishermen's jetties and harbours were nothing more than rough unsightly strips of loose rubble. But as the golden light gilded the swimmers, the wave tops, hovels, cattle wandering along the beach and the littered beach itself, it transformed the scene into something timeless and heroic. It was like a

41

glimpse into another country, or perhaps the same country as it had once been, for there was also the sense of other ages, other worlds impinging upon the present. Later, as I lay in the tent falling asleep, with the sound of the surf eternally thundering on the shore, I wondered if I was being influenced by reading too much of Yeats' poetry. He had the sense of history being something other than merely linear, of it eternally invading the present. T. S. Eliot's poetry is also full of the sense of past and future being present in the moment now. And whether or not it was because of Eliot and Yeats — 'Those images that yet fresh images beget' — or the magic woven by this legend-rich coast, when I slept it was of Jason, Xenophon and the Byzantines that I dreamt, and it was something of a surprise to wake to the world of late twentieth-century Turkey.

The contrast could not have been greater. Turkey I could see was leaping into the late twentieth century with helter-skelter abandon. There was a positive rash of rebuilding town centres and widening roads. Nothing ever seemed to be finished, but brickwork was left unfaced or unpointed, and depressing piles of rubble mixed with general litter lay all around. Massive schemes of electrification, and the installation of a modernized telephone system had resulted in swathes of wires being draped across anything that could support them. Everything looked gimcrack and temporary, and there appeared to be a total absence of any sort of town planning, so that wherever there was any sort of human settlement on the coast, large or small, the wonderful natural beauty gave way to squalor, side by side with an easy undemanding comfort. The marble splendours of which I dreamed had gone forever, but there was no shortage of cafés and restaurants and places to stay.

Where attractive nineteenth-century Turkish houses still stood, they had usually been allowed to fall into a ruinous state, as though they were waiting their turn to be supplanted by something in breeze block and concrete. The same wholesale destruction in the name of progress has taken place in many towns and villages in Britain and the rest of Europe over the last few decades, and always with subsequent regret; for the convenience of the new buildings never quite compensates for the charm and harmony of what has been torn down. It seemed to me a great pity that Turkey couldn't benefit from the mistakes of others.

One redeeming and individual feature of these otherwise anonymous blocks was that often on their flat roofs a little hovel would be perched, cobbled together from cardboard and plastic sacks. Whether these were the temporary nests of nomads or lodgings for night watchmen I never discovered.

The only new buildings that showed a high degree of care were mosques, of which there was also a great spate. Even in very small poor villages which already had one mosque, but no school of any kind, a large elaborate mosque would be nearing completion, resplendent with marble cladding and gilded crescent and finials. Many people told me that the money for these mosques came from Iran, others said it was Saudi Arabia, but whoever was footing the bill, the superabundance of new centres of worship was a strange anomaly in a country that Atatürk, the father of modern Turkey, had established as a secular republic, and in which there were already so many fine historic mosques awaiting repair and restoration. Apparently a lot of money could be made in bribes by allowing these new mosques to go up which was not the case with patching up the old ones.

Apart from this profusion of new mosques the casual visitor to Turkey could easily be mistaken for thinking that the national religion of the country was Atatürk worship, for his image is everywhere, even to the extent of being portrayed in lights from the tops of innumerable citadels. His portrait hangs in every office in the country; and every town and village has at least one statue of him in their main square, and often several more scattered about in gardens and in front of public buildings. Like religious images, these representations of Atatürk also follow certain strict conventions and portray him in set roles: there is the soldier in 1920s uniform, off or on horse; elder statesman in a sober Western suit; suave party-goer and ladies' man in white tie and tails. Later I came across a yard outside Istanbul in which these statues were made. There were thousands of them, a great army of small, medium and large Atatürks.

Before I left London, the Turkish Tourist

Office had given me a pamphlet which included a section about what visitors were forbidden to do in Turkey on pain of dire consequences. Heading all possible offenses (worse even than drug-running) was the crime of insulting Atatürk. This seemed such an unlikely thing for anyone to want to do, especially since the man has been dead for over fifty years, that I wondered just how one would set about it. The more I thought about this the more worried I became, in case it was something that could be done accidentally, or in one's sleep, without at all meaning to. In the light of all the thousands of statues I passed it wasn't a worry that ever receded, and I found myself quickly smothering my spontaneous laughter on seeing all those cloned Atatürks; the thought of languishing in a Turkish jail was not a pleasant one.

Xenophon's advisers had told him that this part of the coast was made up of beautiful plains and quite dreadful mountains. 'All land routes', they said 'were very difficult, while others were quite impossible'. On their advice Xenophon decided to go by sea and accepted a lift for the Ten Thousand on a fleet of Greek ships. But when I capitulated and sought alternative transport for myself and Roberts, there was no boat to take us. In Xenophon's day the Greek towns in Aegean Turkey and those on the Greek mainland itself were busy establishing colonies all along the littoral of the Euxine. Trade soon followed, and because of the difficulties of travel over the intractable land, everything and everyone was shipped in and out. Boats continued to provide the only sensible way of getting around the Black Sea coast until the motor car revolution reached Turkey a decade or so ago. Had I been here even ten years before I would have found steamers calling regularly at all the historic little ports, but now, except for a once-weekly cruise from Istanbul to Trabzon, in a car ferry far too large to stop at any but three of the deep water ports along the way, there is no passenger sea transport at all. Trade still plies its paths across the Black Sea, but maritime disasters are no longer lost cargoes of wine jars, pottery, statues, gold and the like, but oil spillages that wreck marine life and raise the price of fish to the point where the ordinary traveller in Turkey and the Turks themselves can no longer afford to eat it.

I felt I needed a spell of alternative transport at this point, not because of the excessive ups and downs of the route, but because industry had become somewhat intrusive. I had reached the outskirts of Zonguldak, a town which, in its role of supplier of low-grade sulphurous coal to the capital, had spread itself over all the lovely surrounding hills, and was spilling out a dark stain far into the blue sea. One look was enough to convince me that I wanted to get through this area with all possible speed, and since there was no boat to whisk me away I thought I would try to find a bus.

In this I was helped by several men who rushed up to me the moment I rode into the bus terminus. Buses are plentiful in Turkey and several companies compete for custom in any one area. Within seconds the company 'agents' had discovered where I wanted to go, sorted out who should have my custom, and had slid Roberts sideways into a capacious luggage compartment beneath one of the buses. That done I was helped to buy my ticket, entertained to a glass of tea, and finally escorted to my seat.

The cleanliness of the bus was remarkable; it was the most immaculate thing I had seen so far in Turkey. Upholstery and carpets were new and luxurious, and showed not a speck of dust. Each seat had a snow-white cover on the head rest, and there were neat clean curtains to draw against the sun. It was, in a sense, a shrine, for the driver had a wealth of 'sacred objects' such as blue glass eyes for averting evil, various dolls, beaded strips and artificial flowers dangling around his windscreen. The impressive console in front of him was also equipped with a tape recorder which was in constant use, though each new tape sounded to my Western ears exactly the same as the syrupy confection that preceded it.

The acolyte who served at this altar to comfort and progress was kept very busy and was constantly being summoned from his place at the rear of the coach by means of a telephone link from the driver's seat. He made the frequent small adjustments to the window blinds and ventilation that the driver considered necessary, brought him glasses of tea or water, supplied a light for his endless cigarettes, or simply sat beside him to provide an ear for the stream of talk that most male Turks enjoy.

When not attending upon the driver, the conductor also saw to the needs of the passengers, loading and unloading their luggage, bringing them paper cups of ice-cold water, and sprinkling lemon-scented cologne on to their hands, which the passengers then rubbed over their faces and necks. When we stopped at a filling station for petrol, the passengers wandered off for refreshment and the conductor swept out the interior of the bus, while two other men, armed with hoses fitted cunningly into the heads of brooms, washed down the exterior to remove the all-pervading dust of the Turkish roads. The contrast between this almost clinical cleanliness of the buses (cars too I was to discover), and the general mucky and littered state of the streets, beaches and other public places was remarkable. Even in the poorest and most remote places where hose pipes were unknown, there were always cars and lorries to be seen standing in the shallows of rivers and lakes, being washed down.

The other passengers were very kind and friendly. Those who sat near offered me cigarettes, apples, sweets, bubble gum, biscuits, nuts and other confections with which they sustained themselves between refreshment stops. The favourite nibble was sunflower seeds, which Turks can devour at great speed, splitting the small black and white seeds between their front teeth and extracting the tiny kernel in a single swift movement. Try as I might I never learnt this skill, and could only gaze in admiration as they made a reasonable snack in the time it took me to unshell four of five.

The one distressing feature of the journey was the cigarette smoke. Since Turkey grows large amounts of very good-quality tobacco, there is inevitably a conflict of interests in discouraging smoking. Balancing profit against an escalating health bill for smoking-related diseases has not yet resulted in any significant anti-smoking campaign, and I do not think that the average Turk has any belief that smoking damages health. Cigarettes, particularly those made from the coarser type of tobacco, are cheap enough for anyone to afford, and every male over the age of twelve smoked in this bus, as well as one or two of the younger women. The air conditioning helped to disperse it, but when we were halted for some time by road works, the concentration of fumes became such that I was overcome by uncontrollable coughing, and my eyes streamed. The woman beside me at once seized my map case and vigorously fanned me with it. Concerned males brought their offending cigarettes even closer as they leaned over to see what the matter was. As soon as the cause was diagnosed however, all cigarettes were extinguished immediately, the driver opened the automatic doors, and yet again I was overwhelmed by the courtesy and kindliness of Turks.

The bus having first made a great sweep into the hills, arrived at the town of Bartin, where I descended with something of a sense of jet lag, having covered about sixty-five miles in

49

just a few hours, a journey which in that heat and over such terrain would have taken two days by bicycle. Bartin was an example of how very pretty a Turkish town can be with its dark unpainted wooden houses, the balconies and window sills bright with flowers, the perfect foil for the white minarets and domes of mosques and the marble street fountains. But it was already becoming badly congested with the increase of traffic, and winding cobbled streets were in the throes of being dug up and widened. I could only hope that someone would appreciate how very attractive it all was before it was entirely swept away and replaced by featureless concrete and rubble tips.

The conductor carefully unloaded Roberts and then held him upright for me while I replaced the panniers. Half my age, he nonetheless took a paternal interest in my welfare, and wanted to know where I was going to spend the night. When I told him I was cycling on to the little seaside town of Amasra he looked very dubious, and said I should take a taxi. I thought he was merely being Turkish and did not understand that I enjoyed cycling, and thought nothing of a ten-mile ride. I was in fact looking forward to riding away the cramps and fumes of the bus journey. He indicated that there were steep climbs between Bartin and Amasra, but again I misinterpreted his concern. The bus had been going upwards ever since Zonguldak, and it hadn't appeared to lose any of this height, so surely I could anticipate a downhill run to the sea? And indeed I could, eventually. But first came a four-mile climb up and over an alp of such unrelenting steepness that had I known how long it would continue I should certainly have hired a taxi, or anything at all that could have carried Roberts and me up to the summit.

No ascents, not even the steepest Swiss passes or the Himalayas, exacted the degree of sweat and toil as did these Pontic Alps. The people who first built roads over them clearly hadn't heard about gradients. Even the Romans, who always favoured direct routes, would never have dreamed of following so vertical a course. But in Roman times, of course, access to the important port of Amasra would have been by sea. Indeed one of the main reasons the Greeks were able to establish their colonies on the littoral of the Euxine, and to hold them for so long, was because it was so difficult to get at them by land. While the rest of Anatolia was under Persian domination the Black Sea coast remained virtually independent.

There was no question of my being able to ride; I could barely manage even to push the laden Roberts up, bent almost double and panting fit to burst with the effort. Stints of a hundred yards or so were all I could manage, and I needed long rests in between to down pint after pint of water. Fortunately, in true profligate Turkish style, there was drinking water at every corner, running to waste out of fountains, tanks, taps or just plain rusty pipes — and no less welcome for that. I trusted that at this altitude it was probably clean water. Perhaps it wouldn't have mattered had it not been, since

I immediately lost it all in sweat. On eventually reaching the summit (whose existence I had long since ceased to believe in) I could hardly straighten up because of the pain in the small of my back.

The transformation from this state of abject misery to one of sheer delight was achieved the moment I began to coast down the other side through great sweeping hairpin bends. There are few physical pleasures that can hold a candle to a long descent by bicycle, especially on a hot day, after a particularly tough ascent. The quality of the day changes instantly in the sudden remembrance that there is more to life than mere brute effort. It was as though I had been blind, deaf and incapable of feeling until that moment. Birds which doubtless had been trilling away unheard by me, suddenly burst into song; the restricted view of a grey patch of road beneath my wheels gave way to a kaleidoscope in which images stood out briefly from a rapidly passing blur. The abrupt revelation of the broad sparkling sea far below made me catch my breath in wonder, making me want to shout '*Thalassa*' like Xenophon's Greeks when they had their first glimpse of the Euxine after enduring the rigours of Kurdistan.

But it is the body itself that feels the greatest joy in these descents. The rapid cooling down is pure hedonism as the sweat-soaked hair lifts and blows back from the forehead, and a wonderfully relaxing stream of soft warm air plays over hot flushed skin and tired limbs. Most of all, there is the lovely sensation of effortless physical mastery, especially coming so soon after the hard plodding ascent; rider and bicycle, one perfectly poised entity, flying down the steep bends with no more effort than a slight pressure on the brakes, and an inclination of the body to right or left.

The only shadow on this perfection was having to choose between pursuing the joyous swooping descent, or stopping frequently to take in the tremendous views before they were gone for ever. The atrocious surface also cast something of a blight, as did the sharing of it with a Turkish wedding party. This last is an unfortunate modern version of the ancient Turkish custom of celebrating nuptials by a procession around the villages of the bride and bridegroom, on foot or on horseback. The practice is now followed on the highway in an enormous cavalcade of highly decorated nose-to-bumper cars, whose drivers sound their horns with the constancy and power of so many Joshuas intent on bringing down the walls of Jericho. Given that the procession also halts at frequent intervals for the male members to refresh themselves with raki, it is not a force to be trifled with. This particular family group was squashed into twenty-four vehicles; I had several opportunities to verify the number as they kept stopping and overtaking, always on a blind bend, and always with a frenzied blaring of horns and a jolly waving of hands. They nearly had me over the edge each time, though I'm sure no harm was intended; they were just being friendly.

In fading light I swept around the last steep bend, and came to an abrupt stop where great fissures and craters in the tarmac announced the final approach to the town, making me realize, as usual, how good the road really had been until that point. The last of the sunset had spread a red path across the still water of the inner harbour of Amasra, a place that I recognized at once as being far more antique and exciting than anything I had encountered so far on this coast. But my enthusiasm had to be contained until morning. There was no time then to look at anything in detail; with night fast closing in, the first thing was to find shelter.

Just where the road had made its last right-angled bend to skirt the harbour front was a very small camping place, with space enough for no more than three or four tents, and with an excellent view out over the water. But it was also very exposed to public view, and a rather ripe smell put me off. This was just as well as it happened, because it turned out that I had damaged my back getting Roberts over the Pontic Alps, and I would have found camping in my small low tent very difficult. This left the town's two hotels, and tossing up between them (since there seemed no way of deciding which was better) I plumped for the Kapitan Pasha Oteli where a tiny room was found for me, and a spot for Roberts where it could be locked to the balustrade.

A kindly plump Greek lady who spoke excellent English and Turkish interpreted for me during the inevitable bartering over the price of the room. She afterwards put me further in her debt by initiating me into the intricacies of the hotel's bathing arrangements. About these she was very knowledgeable, having taken her holidays in the Kapitan Pasha Oteli every August for the past twenty years. If I left my bath until after my evening meal, as I was planning to, it being so late by now, and I being ravenous after the day's efforts, then she informed me, every drop of hot water would have been used up in the evening rush. It was the English she said. English? I queried. Yes indeed. Like her, the English loved Amasra. They came every year for their holidays, enough of them to keep the hotel's two showers occupied until the hot water ran out.

Abundant hot water is one of life's luxuries for a travelling bicyclist. In many countries I frequently have to wash myself, my hair and my clothes in a half-bucketful of cold water. The method I have evolved for this bucket bath cum launderette is first to remove all my sweaty clothes and place them on the floor beneath my feet. Cupful by careful cupful I slowly pour the precious water over my head, keeping as upright as I can so that it trickles over as great an area of skin as possible before soaking into the clothes (wonderful sensation this when the water is hot, agony when its cold). Once I am damp all over I apply the shampoo and soap, and the sudsy water also trickles down on to the clothing. Stamping and dancing about on the washing as I continue to pour cupfuls of water over myself, body and clothes get clean at the same time. The last drops in the bucket are reserved as a final rinse for the garments. I then dress in my clean set of clothes and hang the wet garments on a line that I string from convenient projections in the room, or tie from bicycle to tent if I'm camping. If they are still damp by morning, I safety-pin them to the rear panniers where the sun soon bakes them or the wind blows them dry.

I had not so far found the erratic showers of Turkey any great improvement on my half-bucket multi-purpose bath. For one thing, I hadn't yet come across a Turkish shower unit that did not suffer from some serious malfunction; shower heads were always falling off, dealing me painful blows; water would suddenly stop in mid-flow just as I was covered all over in soap; or it would run in such thin pathetic trickles that it wasn't worth waiting for. And as for hot water! That proved elusive even in quite good hotels. So although I seldom had to go unwashed, it wasn't always as pleasurable an experience as an African or Indian bucket bath could be at its piping-hot best. My first night's ablutions in Amasra under an ample, warm and trouble-free deluge was therefore a rare treat.

As I was leaving the Kapitan Pasha, clean and shining and in search of dinner, a great number of children and adults (clearly 'the English') were trying to squeeze through the tiny lobby where some of them had caused a bottleneck by stopping to admire Roberts. I stopped too to explain about the altimeter which greatly intrigued young people, and almost at once the oldest of the girls asked if I was Bettina Selby, because, she said, she had read some of my books and recognized me from my photograph on the jackets.

As this proved as good as an introduction, we were soon exchanging information about what we were all doing in the Turkish seaside resort of Amasra. I found that I had fallen in with an archaeological party from Warwick University led by Dr Stephen Hill and Dr Jim Crow. They came to Amasra each year in order to map the extensive Byzantine walls, and as both were family men, and it was the summer holidays, their wives and children came too. Altogether, with the eight children and various colleagues who were experts in coins, inscriptions and the like, they numbered sixteen, and took over more than half of the Kapitan Pasha Oteli — no wonder there was a run on the hot water!

Like most archaeologists, they were full of enthusiasm for their project, and made it sound so fascinating that I longed to hear more. I was also very glad to learn that my initial response to Amasra had solid foundations, and that it had once held an important position on this coast. They in turn warmed to my enthusiasm and promised to take me on a guided tour in the morning, and in the meantime they kindly provided an escort of young people to show me the way to Amasra's best restaurant. As we walked there — the children, Tom, Emma and Theo, plying me with more information than my tired brain could hold at one time — I was aware that beyond the insignificant little buildings lining the dimly lit streets, high ancient walls shut out patches of the velvety

57

star-filled night, and again came that frisson of delight I'd felt when I'd first come down to the harbour. It was not recognition exactly, but more a feeling of kinship with the place — the sort of feeling that reminds me of why I travel.

5

A Byzantine Naval Base

THE Kapitan Pasha Oteli was not the ideal place to nurse a strained back, or indeed to find any sort of rest. Although it was superbly positioned on the edge of the ancient harbour, with a long clear view across to the walls of the ancient city, it was flanked by the modern town, and, as always in Turkey, this meant noise. All night long traffic roared up and down, stopping and starting with a great slamming of doors and a wild cacophony of horns. Turkish music competed with Western-style pop, whining and throbbing from every building, each source competing to drown out the others, until the sounds began to blur and fragment. With the windows shut fast against the noise, the little room was like an oven, but the noise was not much less and sleep quite impossible. I thought longingly of my cool airy tent, and the soothing thunder of the surf on the beach. Eventually I raised the energy to heave myself painfully upright and find the wax earplugs I carry for such emergencies. These however magnified the sound of my heart beats until I could no longer bear the booming inside my head, and had to take them out again. At about four a.m., with the pale streaks of the false dawn, there came a brief lull when the weary insomniac could at last drop into an exhausted dreamless insensibility, before the town awoke at around six a.m. to begin a new throbbing day. It says a lot for the attraction of Amasra that I stayed on there for two more nights.

I thought it said a lot for Turkish stamina that they could manage on so little sleep. Later however, I modified this view, finding that it was not so much that Turks needed less sleep, but rather that many of them were able to make it up at different times, sleeping late, taking siestas and the odd short nap. Most found the starry cicada-loud nights so pleasant after the hot humid days that they could not tear themselves away and go indoors. Even in villages the old men sat on in mosquito-filled gardens playing cards or tric trac, drinking tea until well into the small hours. But it was also true that noise never seemed to worry Turks, and that those who did go to bed at a reasonable hour because they had to rise early, could sleep through all the hullabaloo that invariably kept Westerners awake. I never found a satisfactory solution to the problem, except that when I had to sleep in a town I found a hotel in what seemed to be the quietest street, and insisted on a room on the top floor where the sounds, like the air, were usually more rarefied.

As the Kapitan Pasha did not provide meals, I was invited to share the alfresco breakfast of the archaeologists. It was ten-year-old Lucy who pressed me to accept, as was her right, since it was she who was first up and went out to buy the freshly-baked bread. Most of the others slept late having, like me, been kept awake most of the night. The archaeologists had the whole of the top floor to themselves, and as this had a very large balcony overlooking the western harbour, it was ideal for eating, drying clothes and assembling all the various pieces of equipment that the expedition needed. It was also an ideal place for the children to play games and spread out their things. All of this had induced the archaeologists to come back to the Kapitan Pasha each year in spite of its shabby rooms and the dreadful noise. But as they said, there wasn't really any choice, the other hotel with its on-site disco was both noisier and more expensive.

One good thing about Amasra as far as the parents were concerned was that all but the youngest children could be left to roam the town in the certain knowledge that they would come to no harm. Turks seem to love all children, not just their own, and if anything, the Hill and the Crow children felt they suffered from over-protection. Everyone in Amasra always knew where any one of them was at any time; and any adult would intervene if they thought the children needed help or were doing anything dangerous. The younger children complained that their cheeks were permanently sore from Turks lovingly pinching them, but that apart, they appreciated the freedom.

The older children spent a lot of their time swimming from the seaward end of the harbour. They took me along with them when my back had recovered a little, and I found the bathing excellent, with the additional thrill of a submerged Roman pier beneath the turquoise water, which twelve-year-old Tom, the eldest Crow boy, claimed to have discovered. Tom was an excellent guide, having absorbed a lot of information about ancient Amasra from his father. He already had an archaeologist's eye, and in addition to locating the sunken pier, had spotted several ancient artefacts and part of a stone anchor which were now in Amasra's tiny museum. 'Under my father's name,' said Tom, 'not fair.'

The adult archaeologists were currently experiencing a most frustrating period. In spite of limited time and a tight budget, they were forced to twiddle their thumbs in idleness because archaeologists are not allowed to pursue their work without a Turkish minder to oversee their activities, and their's had just been called up to do his military service. Although a replacement was daily expected, no one knew when he would appear. I had arrived at just the right moment to benefit from this enforced inactivity. Two days later, just as I was leaving, the new minder arrived, and there would have been no time for guided tours after that. Once again my traveller's luck had served me well.

I couldn't have understood the place without their help, since my guidebook didn't even mention Amasra, as it was off any usual tourist track. The walled town, I learnt, had been a defended site since the Bronze Age, and remained so throughout its subsequent history. But during various peaceful periods following its colonization by Greeks, the city had spread beyond the walls, occupying the narrow plain between the sea and the steep mountainside. It seems to have reached its greatest extent around AD 83 when Pliny was doing a tour of administrative duty there. The river which accounted for the ripe smell I'd noticed in the harbour must have been particularly obnoxious then for Pliny wrote to Rome about it, describing it as a 'foul sewer, in name a river which flows down the main colonnaded street to the sea'. Pliny strongly advised that it should be covered over at Rome's expense. But now that the extensive Graeco/Roman city has almost entirely disappeared, together with the colonnaded street, the condition of the 'foul sewer' has improved somewhat and is in the process of being contained within concrete banks, for coming down from such great heights, it must often flood quite devastatingly. Just then it was in a very shrunken state. We followed it quite a long way up and found quantities of fat frogs tenanting the reed-fringed shallow pools, with huge dragon-flies hovering above them on navy-blue lacy wings.

After about half a mile we came to an enormous roofless ruin, thought to be a Roman shopping arcade, the Harrods of its day. Isolated now in the middle of green fields it looked vast and imposing and at the same time highly improbable, like a film set. The fact that it was still standing when all about it had long since vanished, was because its hugely thick walls were built of brick, and brick cannot be plundered and re-used as stone can. Only one further fragment of antiquity remained *in situ*, and this was up against the steep mountainside where a single supporting arch of a Greek theatre was concealed behind a romantically overgrown Muslim cemetery. On the flat platform where the stage and the orchestra had once stood, turbaned headstones rested under canopies of brambles and trees.

Walking the circuit of the walled city with two such enthusiastic archaeologists as Jim and Stephen was to have it come to life in a way that would have been impossible had I been alone. The walls were extensive, completely encircling the elevated neck of land, and had been kept up as defensive bulwarks almost to the present day. Russia, Turkey's old implacable enemy, was less than a day's journey across the Black Sea, and had invaded this coast on many occasions within living memory. Part of the fortress was still manned by the modern Turkish army, as were many historic castles and walled cities in Turkey, continuing in commission as defences to counter the ever-present threat of invasion from Russia. With the sudden dismantling of the Soviet Union I wondered what would now happen to these ancient monuments, or where Turkey would now look for a new enemy.

One particularly unusual feature of the walls of Amasra was that they had been extended to incorporate the off-shore island of Boz Tepe, which had been linked to the town by means of a heavily fortified bridge. It would have been well worth coming here just to see these walls, so impressive were they in their completeness, and so interesting in the varying handiwork of different ages. Some sections had clearly been built, or repaired in times of crisis, using any material to hand. The seating from the Greek theatre had gone into one part, and throughout their circuit they were punctuated with re-used stones from the vanished antique city, many of them finely worked marble pieces, such as columns, funeral stele, and in one place a head of Medusa. Beneath the hurried cobbling could be seen the finely cut regular stone blocks of earlier, more peaceful times.

The walls also carried a number of Genoese inscriptions, and because of these it had been generally assumed that the later elaborate fortifications were constructed in the turbulent period following the fall of the Byzantine Empire in the fifteenth century. It was to disprove this theory that the work of Jim Crow and Stephen Hill was directed. They had first come to Amasra while they were on a touring holiday of Turkey and were almost immediately convinced that the Genoese theory was false, and that the inscriptions had merely been stuck on to existing late Byzantine work. Archaeology by its very nature tends to be full of romance and chance encounters. But only very occasionally are there the sort of dazzling discoveries — such as uncovering the site of Homer's Troy, or finding the treasures of Tutankhamun's tomb — that fire the public imagination. Slow painstaking detective work accounts for most of the archaeologist's time, as was the case here, but the romance remains for all that as, piece by small piece, the tapestry of history expands. With their work almost complete Stephen and Jim reckoned that what they had hit upon here was an extensive Byzantine naval base; that from the port of Amasra regular patrols had set forth to quarter the waters of the Euxine, repelling the attacks of Vikings and Russians, at a time when the coasts of Europe and Britain were also being harried by similar raids. They felt that this was the only possible explanation for the enormous work and cost of extending the fortifications around the island of Boz Tepe. The town itself would have been too small to contain all the activity and personnel, and they thought that the remains of huge stone structures they had discovered on the island must have been naval barracks; but until money could be found for a large dig that would have to remain supposition.

The greater part of the modern Turkish town sprawled at ease outside the walls, and within was quite another and more peaceful world, wearing the tatters of its former glory. The main street followed the spine of the hill close to the sheer western wall, as it must always have done, with narrow lanes and alleys leading down steeply from it towards the sea walls. Several fine old Turkish houses and a mosque which had formerly been a Byzantine church lined the sleepy shaded street, but for the rest, the Turkish town merely perched on the solid foundations of the Byzantine city, with no more permanence than a tented camp. At the highest point were unroofed walls of squared masonry built out from the curtain wall twenty feet or so high. Where once Byzantine guards had rested from their watch over the unquiet sea were now hollow spaces where lean-to hovels with hens scratching in the dirt, a mangy dog or two and piles of bric-a-brac made a strange contrast to the substantial solid stonework. It was as if a nomadic band had moved in on the heels of a victorious army, and might tomorrow be gone again, leaving no trace.

Further down the hill was my favourite building in Amasra, the ruined gem of a small Byzantine church. It was unusually constructed with alternate courses of brick and stone laid in varying chevron and lozenge patterns, and it stood out from its surroundings of hovels in a way that made me catch my breath each time I saw it. It was my good fortune to see it at all: another year or two and it will be quite gone. Already it was no more than a ruined shell, and nothing was being done to preserve it. Pigeons nested among the crumbling bricks in the conch of the apse, half the roof was gone, and ominous cracks in the fabric heralded the final collapse. There were still scraps of plaster on the walls inside, and on them, so faint that I could only make them out in certain lights, were the ghost-like frescoes of saints and the Mother of God holding the Christ Child.

By the end of the second day in Amasra I could straighten up again with hardly a twinge, and thought that as long as I did not have to push Roberts back over the Pontic Alps, I could safely move on. It was something of a wrench to leave so many new friends all at one swoop, and I knew I would particularly miss the evening meals I'd shared with them. Eating alone in restaurants at night is the only time I consciously feel lonely on a long journey.

I had dined more adventurously in Amasra than anywhere since Istanbul. With so many at table the *metze* with which meals usually began in Turkey could be enormously varied, and we shared between us aubergine purée, vine leaves stuffed with meat and rice, marrow stuffed with rice and pine kernels, white beans in vinaigrette, cigar shaped flaky pastry stuffed with cheese, and brown beans with onion, tomato and garlic. We had followed this with locally caught fish which was not ruinously expensive, because on this part of the coast there were no oil spillages and fish was plentiful. We had eaten them with chips freshly fried in olive oil, and although 'fish and chips' can never perhaps be made to sound like a superior gastronomic experience to English folk, these were like none I had previously encountered. If anyone could manage a pudding we had a choice of yoghurt, semolina cake in syrup, shredded wheat with pistachio nuts and honey, rice cooked with saffron and a great variety of fresh fruit. We drank local wines, also delicious and cheap, and a great treat, for when alone I had always to stick to beer because a whole bottle of wine — they seldom had half bottles — was too much for me.

The children ordered far more conservative fare, such as boiled eggs, hamburgers and chips, and Coke, and they claimed that the reason their parents often caught tummy bugs while they did not was because the adults were more daring in their tastes.

Quite a number of the sixteen members of the expedition came to see me off and to make sure that there was no difficulty about getting Roberts aboard a bus. On Jim's advice I was taking an inland route to Sinop, my next significant port of call. The coastal route was so precipitous in places as to be all but impassable, and certainly no buses went that way. Xenophon's army had done the same stretch by ship, and I wished I could have done so too, and seen the beach where Jason was said to have landed. It was strange to read in Xenophon the words, 'was supposed to have landed' and to realize that even then, more than two thousand years ago, Jason was a distant legend. The inland detour sounded equally exciting, however. Just behind the Pontic Alps an ancient trade route followed a rich river valley guarded by a town called Kastromonu, which Jim said was well worth visiting for its splendid Byzantine citadel and fine Selçuk buildings. But first I had to retrace the dizzy route over the Pontic Alps.

6

Through the Mountains to Sinope

IT seemed to me that I had reached an excellent compromise with the Pontic Alps, and I could now thoroughly enjoy the ascents. All morning I sat at my ease being transported up and over towering passes — the most elevated of which was far higher than anything in Britain — and very pleased I was not to be toiling up them on Roberts. Only small buses, which did not have a luggage compartment large enough for a bicycle, travelled these routes. So keen were the bus crews to help, however, that Roberts would be manhandled inside, and placed along the rear seat. I would be charged (quite rightly, I considered) for four places: one for me and three for Roberts. But once the bus had filled up Roberts was moved to the aisle, where it was a perfect nuisance, blocking all passage up and down the bus, and with the handlebars and pedals sticking into unfortunate passengers who happened to have chosen the wrong seats. Everyone was amazingly good natured about the discomfort and inconvenience, and adapted to the situation by resting their arms or feet on any bit of the bicycle that impinged upon their space. Even the conductor, who had to squeeze past again and again on his rounds with the lemon-scented cologne, made a point of smiling reassuringly as he did so (he might also, of course, have been smiling at the thought of the price of those three seats paid for twice over).

The anointing of hands with lemon-scented cologne was invariably performed in all the buses I travelled in, even the small local ones, and also in private houses when a guest came, and I assumed it was a form of welcome. I didn't care for the over-sweet smell of it, but I enjoyed the ceremony. The act of holding out the cupped hands, the careful sprinkling, with cloth held ready to mop up spills, and the slight bows that both parties exchanged imbued the ritual with solemnity and significance, rather like the ablutions after High Mass. It also created an atmosphere of unified harmony in the bus so that it was impossible to imagine anything like a fight breaking out.

The last thirty miles to Kastromonu I bicycled, rejoicing in the mountain air unadulterated by tobacco smoke, and in moving again under my own steam. The dark shaggy hills of the first steep ascent from the sea had given way to a dry undulating plain, grazed by small herds of horses, from which a wide river valley led off eastward, closed in on either side by a wall of mountains. The broken varied landscape was reminiscent of Provence, with slender poplars taking the place of cypresses. It looked very fertile and green, even with the harvest gathered and the fields bare. Any army travelling through this valley would have had no trouble living off the land I thought, and I wondered if it was in order to prevent Xenophon's Ten Thousand doing just this that the colonists at Sinope (now Turkish Sinop) had helped to organize ships for the sea route. I was glad I had been persuaded to do the opposite, for it was a completely different world up here between the mountains. Being much higher it was also cooler and less humid, which made cycling very much easier.

I was thinking what a delightful ride it was proving, when the sky suddenly clouded over and released a great deluge of water. I arrived at Kastromonu soaked to the skin, and with my sights set only on a hot bath and dry clothes. No town looks attractive behind a grey curtain of rain, with mud underfoot and everyone scurrying for shelter, and had the clouds not cleared again before sunset, I might well have been left with an entirely false view of this charming, little-known town.

Like all such towns in this part of the world, Kastromonu had been there since earliest times, when a small band of people had built a settlement on top of a free-standing hillock, an acropolis that could be easily defended against marauders, principally because any attacker was forced to fight uphill. Anatolia is liberally provided with suitable hills possessing very steep sides, tops flat enough to build upon and a good permanent source of water. Later, more advanced civilizations ringed the simple hill forts with solid fortifications capable of repelling an army. As populations increased, however, they were forced to build outside the confines of the walls, and the cities spread on to the flat ground at the foot of the acropolis. In the event of attack people and their livestock could retreat uphill behind the protection of their walls.

Kastromonu had a splendidly tall acropolis, completely dominating the modern city. It was circled with ancient walls, many times rebuilt, and the remains of the Byzantine citadel, like all such places, was crowned with the red Turkish flag and a huge outline head of Atatürk in neon tubing, which I felt rather spoilt my photographs. Narrow cobbled alleyways wound their way almost vertically up to the foot of the walls, each lined with little lathe and plaster Turkish houses, raised above their station by the addition of beautiful lintels and thresholds of antique stone plundered from ancient ruins. Groups of women and girls, all bundled up in layers of skirts and headscarves sat talking and knitting at their carved doorways, enjoying the last of the sunlight, while young boys kicked footballs about the few flat places. I was stared at frankly as I passed, which made me feel very self-conscious about how I was puffing and panting over the steep ascent. None of the local people seemed to experience such difficulty. The stoutest of the women, and the old men with cigarette drooping from the lower lip, walked upwards with little sign of effort, whereas I found it difficult even to spare the breath to respond to the friendly greetings.

The climb was well worth it. Just standing on the walls looking out over a landscape that so many and such diverse cultures had also gazed upon gave a sense of history more tangible than could be gleaned from any book. Not for the first time I wondered about the people of the land, those referred to by Xenophon and Pliny as 'the natives', people who, no matter which new conquering race had taken over, had always been there, getting on with cultivating the land and other pressing matters of daily life. Hittite, Phrygian, Greek, Persian, Roman, Byzantine, Selçuk, Mongol and Ottoman had all held sway here in their turn. But the numbers of each new wave of conquerors had always been relatively small. The native population could neither be assimilated nor destroyed overnight, and probably each new change of power made very little difference to the daily life of the majority.

Apart from the unifying spread of Christianity, followed by the equally unifying spread of Islam, the greatest changes in rural Turkey have occurred in the last few decades with the advent of mass media, the motor car and the nationwide electrification scheme. Increased awareness of the Western world has been accompanied by a huge and accelerating urban drift and a headlong race to become industrialized as quickly as possible, so as to accomplish in a decade or two what has taken the West several hundred years. The further east I went the less obvious were the changes, particularly in the matter of dress. In this little backwater of Kastromonu, women's dress remained as conservative as ever, and I was glad that I had not arrived wearing shorts.

Darkness fell as I walked back down the steep slopes, past layer after layer of Roman-style red-tiled roofs. Ruined and re-used Byzantine buildings rubbed shoulders with Ottoman and Selçuk mosques. On the valley floor near my hotel was what had once been a Greek and then a Roman agora, cut off and left high and dry now by present-day traffic. In the centre of this island was a particularly beautiful ruined Selçuk hammam, its roof all gentle swelling domes. With the coming of darkness it was the only thing in Kastromonu that could be described as feminine, for all the women had vanished. There were only men in the restaurant where I ate, and in my hotel foyer every chair was occupied by a man watching television, the air blue with cigarette smoke. As I made my way to my room, through open doorways I could see still more men in trousers and singlets, sitting on their beds eating kebabs out of greasy papers, and washing it down with raki. The only visible member of my sex, I had to endure a battery of stares everywhere I went, and was glad to turn in early and make up for lost sleep.

Pedalling on towards Sinope the next day, enjoying the downhill drift of the land, I suddenly remembered the need to replenish my supply of Turkish currency and turned off the highway to the next small town. Inflation was currently running at a staggering seventy per cent so it didn't do to convert much money at any one time. Nevertheless, I was living so cheaply that this was the first time I had needed to change money since Istanbul.

Teskoptu had several banks, none of which expressed any enthusiasm for changing my travellers' cheques. But at the Is Bank my request was not immediately rejected out of hand. Instead, all four clerks gathered round to examine the American Express travellers' cheque I presented, passing it from hand to hand, all of them saying they had never seen one before! Huge reference books containing facsimiles of bank notes were taken out and consulted but without any result. With the aid of my two small dictionaries I was at length able to put across the idea that travellers' cheques are not bank notes, after which more huge reference books were consulted. This time they featured specimen bank cheques from places as far away as Bilbao and Costa Rica, exotic, but fruitless for my purpose. Time passed. Several glasses of tea were sent for and presented to me. Everyone was amazingly friendly and eager to help, but we were making no progress, except in compiling sentences. Further ledgers were consulted, but not one single travellers' cheque was illustrated. The clerks were still friendly, but it had become clear that their faith in my having negotiable currency was waning. 'Never mind,' I said eventually, 'I'll just write in my book that the Is Bank has never heard of American Express travellers' cheques.' That produced a tremendous reaction; the honour of the bank was at stake! Cries of 'No, no' were followed by the decision to ring Head Office at Ankara.

I could see from the expression on the face of the clerk holding the 'phone that the first enquiries had raised their flagging hopes. My cheque was seized and every detail on it relayed over the phone. My signature was demanded on a scrap of paper. It matched! Relief, joy even, shone on every face. They were, they said proudly, prepared to take a risk: they would change one cheque for fifty pounds. But just then the bank manager arrived and the whole thing started all over again — explanations, deep suspicion, consulting of ledgers, deeper suspicion. I was about to give up and break into my secret reserve of dollar bills when the manager remembered another cupboard, where further reference books were stored, and here, after several false starts, the slim volume containing the American Express facsimiles came to light. There was only one further hiccup over the words 'not negotiable' in place of the 'fifty pounds' written on my cheque, but this detail was magnanimously brushed aside. One of the clerks handed me a ruler and pen, 'To mark out Is Bank is not knowing' she said, spelling it out with the help of my dictionary, and then adding the ubiquitous 'Is Bank çok gezel'. And to show just how good Is Bank really was, I was ushered into the manager's office to be entertained to lunch with him at a low coffee table. It was a royal feast of huge chunks of freshly barbecued sheep, eaten with raw onion and flat bread, all spread out on the paper it had come wrapped in, and washed down with bottles of Pepsi. A delicious pudding of cracked wheat soaked in milk with dried fruits and nuts

(Noah's pudding) followed. Later I found out that this dish was so called because of an old legend about the state of the Ark's larder towards the end of its time upon the waters of the Flood. Finding everything running low, Mrs Noah, it was said, tossed all the remaining food together in a large bowl and served it to her menfolk. While we were eating it, the triumphant smiling bank clerks came in to get my signature, give me my money and shake my hand. As they went off for their own lunch, they each called 'Goodbye' shyly, having just learnt the word from my dictionary. I began to wish I had a supply of dictionaries to leave as gifts; I can imagine nothing that would have been more welcome.

As a result of this lengthy financial transaction I was forced to pedal to some purpose in order to get to the turn off for Sinope before the last infrequent bus arrived there from the other direction. It seemed important not to miss it as a huge Pontic Alp lay between me and the sea, and I had no wish to strain my newly mended back again. The meaty lunch was not best suited to such efforts, but fortune smiled on me, and the bus and I both reached the spot at precisely the same moment. The long haul up to the Damaz Pass was over the worst road I had yet encountered. In one place workmen were patching up a stretch where there had been a landslip, and it looked doubtful that we would get through; a lorry had already tried and gone over the edge. But the bus moved on with only half the width of its offside tyres on the soft unprotected edge, and although we made it, I felt sick and fervently wished that I was back on my own two wheels.

The scenery was very wild and beautiful, and the higher we climbed the more Alpine it became, with primitive wooden chalets set in rough meadows among magnificent beech and fir forests. We came over the Damaz Pass as the light was fading from mauve to purple, and the immensely long peninsula on which Turkey's most northerly town stands was a dark pointing finger on a pewter sea. It would be a race as to whether darkness or the bus reached Sinope first, and night won by more than an hour.

Sinope was once the most important town on the Euxine, having an even more favoured site than Amasra. Under the Greeks it was the supreme naval base and dominated the entire Euxine. Successive powers, including the Selçuk Turks, continued to maintain it as an important trading port. But the Ottoman Turks shortened its name to Sinop and turned their backs upon it, preferring to develop nearby Samsun, and most of the great walls have been allowed to fall gradually into ruin. There was still enough of their bulk left to impress a tired traveller, however, even coming to them at night and seeing them half illuminated by dim street lighting. A great citadel loomed on my left, a venerable mosque on my right — barely more than impressions in the hot still air that smelt of spicy dust and the sea. It appeared a strangely exotic and far more cosmopolitan place than Amasra. The inner harbour was lined with cafés, bars and restaurants, with chairs and tables set out under awnings by the water's edge. Rows of small wooden fishing boats were moored along the quays, and beyond them were large trawlers converted to excursion craft. I cruised the narrow streets near the waterfront looking for an hotel, and found that I was too late. Sinope was a popular holiday resort and everywhere was full. The last hotel I tried was right on the waterfront and it too was full, but the owner, with typical Turkish hospitality, offered me a berth on one of the excursion boats moored across the harbour against the sea wall. Two uniformed boy waiters, both about fourteen, helped me to manhandle Roberts across several other boats to the Omar Baba. Kind, competent boys, they fixed me up a bed in the wheelhouse and made sure I had water to drink and a candle to find my way to the boat's amenities — quite the most spotless I had yet encountered.

It wasn't a quiet berth. Sounds of music and gaiety came wafting across the water all night, and small fishing boats passed in and out with slow chugging engines. But from my narrow bunk on the unlit seaward side of the harbour I was high above it all, with a view out over the moon-raked sea as well as across to the neon-lit cafés. And I felt the same comfortable sense of detachment and safety that I experience in my tent, and lay there supremely happy, drifting in and out of sleep until morning.

I liked Sinope so much that I stayed on for a further two days, with the vague idea that I would make up for lost time, and avoid what seemed like a boring stretch of modern development by taking the car ferry to Giresun. In the event there was no ferry, but I had no regrets about staying on. The hotel repossessed their wheelhouse and found me a room with a balcony overlooking the harbour, from which I could watch the brightly painted wooden fishing boats coming and going, day and night, and the old men who sat watching them round the clock, drinking tea daintily from tiny tulip-shaped glasses, and spitting reflectively into the water. The charm of Sinope was that it was a working fishing port first, and only incidentally a seaside resort. The foreign visitors stayed mainly at modern five-star places outside the town. Within the walls, around the inner harbour, the town catered for Turks, and the emphasis was on an undemanding, slightly down-at-heel comfort. Mosques, houses, shops, hotels, were all squashed together cheek by jowl. Barrows loaded with fruit and produce were trundled over the cobbles with scarcely room to pass one another. Unaccompanied dogs trotted nonchalantly about their affairs; old men washed their feet at a fountain in a small dusty square shaded by plane trees, before going in to midday prayers. This fountain had a dedication plaque written in Turkish with an English translation underneath. It read:

FOUNTAIN OF MARTYRS

> Before the Ottoman Russian War
> On November 30 1852 Wednesday
> Russian fleet had a sudden attack
> To Sinop This fountain was built by
> The money picket up from the
> Martyr Turkish soldiers pockets.

It seemed a touch cavalier that a nation should finance their 'martyrs' memorial by picking the said 'martyrs' pockets, rather than sending the small change home to the bereaved families.

The walls of ancient Sinope are nowhere near as complete as those of Amasra, though they pre-date them, and must once have been even more impressive. They had at one time certainly enclosed a more substantial and impressive city according to the geographer Strabo, who described it as it was during the reign of the Pontic king, Mithradates Eupator, when the city was at its most splendid:

> Mithradates was born and raised at Sinope; and he accorded it special honour and treated it as the metropolis of his kingdom. Sinope is beautifully equipped both by nature and human foresight; for it is situated on the neck of a peninsula, and has, on either side of the isthmus, harbours and roadsteads and wonderful fisheries . . . The city itself is beautifully walled, and is also splendidly adorned with gymnasia, marketplaces and colonnades.

In 73 BC Mithradates overreached himself, setting forth from his splendid port with a great armada, in order to attack Bythnia. It was an ill-planned scheme that succeeded only in bringing down upon himself the wrath of the all-powerful Roman Empire. Within a few years Rome had annexed Pontus and brought most of Anatolia within the Empire.

The most complete part of the walls was that to the south side of the city where they still stood at the original height, and were full of all sorts of re-used classical material — a history book in stone. They were also still in use, sheltering a contingent of the modern Turkish army, and a sentry on guard at the top of the wall regarded me with suspicion as I examined them and began to take photographs of the more interesting pieces. Photographing military installations was included amongst the 'don'ts' in my Turkish tourist booklet, so my fear about inadvertently infringing Turkish law was not so far-fetched; I wouldn't have dreamed I was doing anything wrong until a head topped by a helmet and flanked by a rifle appeared suddenly over the parapet.

There were also some impressive remaining sections of the defence wall and towers built across the neck of the peninsula. These could be climbed, and I wandered along them enjoying the stunning views eastward and northward beyond the harbour and the curving bay, imagining I could just make out the Russian shore. But it was the northern sea walls that I found far the most evocative. They had been built on the sea's edge and great jagged segments of them lay overturned on the black rocks, the embodiment of colossal ruin.

Apart from the walls and the endless domestic drama of the waterfront, Sinope's museum was my favourite place, not so much for the exhibits (I don't remember seeing anything of significance there) as for the ambience. It had once been the site of a pagan temple, and the foundations of this, as well as the small museum building, were surrounded by a fenced garden in which stood all the marble pieces for which there was no room inside — Asia Minor suffers from a superabundance of marble, because of having so long a history, with so many successive cultures determined to leave a permanent record in stone. Archaeologists are unearthing still more of this marble all the time, so that it is small wonder that Turkish curators have a different scale of values to British ones. No stern sterile display for them. Both within and without it was the plants that took pride of place. Ferns, potted oleanders and other burgeoning greenery provided decorous privacy for the indoor statuary, and added a little colour and movement to the inscriptions and tombstones. Climbing vines used the larger pieces as a jumping off ground *en route* for the upper balcony, from where they hung in a great obscuring veil. In the garden, roses rambled and tumbled over classical columns and a wealth of Ottoman tombstones; sturdy young trees gently eased other memorials and classical columns out of boringly symmetrical positions, and no piece of marble was left unadorned. It seemed to me like a Turkish version of a seventeenth-century English folly, and made an excellent place for the curator and his friends to sit and play cards and drink tea.

I also found a pair of shorts in Sinope to replace the pair my friend Feride had given me in Istanbul, which by now had quite worn out in the seat. I was surprised that I had been able to continue exposing my knees so far east without feeling I was giving offence to the populace. Perhaps it was because bicycling was so unusual in these parts that people could accept a rider being oddly dressed, and in any case I changed into longs the moment I arrived anywhere. I was determined to carry on riding in shorts unless positively forced to give them up, because they made such a difference to comfort, particularly on hills. A seaside resort like Sinope was inured to bizarrely dressed foreigners which was why I had been able to purchase this particular pair of dark brown, discreetly long and, I hoped, hard-wearing shorts. They came from an international franchise that clearly was a little ahead of its time outside Istanbul, for everything in the shop was reduced to half price, and the owners still open to bargaining.

7

Amazons and Hazel-nuts

THE road to Samsun runs high above the sea, threading a path across the lower slopes of the great wall of mountains. Traversing dense woodland, it passes modest farms hidden among the trees, the small cabins almost disappearing under the rampant greenery of their gardens. Every household seemed to keep one pretty and diminutive black cow, a good many of which I met, all wearing brightly coloured woollen necklaces, and trotting eagerly along the roadside, an old woman racing along behind them, waving a stick to try to make them slow down. There were occasional small clearings where the hay had just been cut and put to dry in the same charming little beehive stooks that they make in the Outer Hebrides.

From the densest shade boys sprang out to offer baskets of freshly picked blackberries and hazel-nuts to the rare passers-by. Ragged little boys, they were nonetheless self-possessed, curious and friendly. The ones I stopped to trade with were eager to barter their wares for cigarettes, but when I said '*Yok*' (I don't have any), they would have made me a present of their fruit. The men in the small villages along the way were equally friendly; in fact, whenever I passed a house, and people working or resting in their gardens saw me, there would be shouts for me to come and join them, and gestures of drinking tea, all of which reassured me that shorts were still acceptable wear. I think I would still be on the road to Samsun if I had responded to even half these invitations.

All morning the sea kept appearing and disappearing, a sparkling turquoise behind a fringe of dark green trees. And after Gerze, cape after shaggy cape dropped dramatically to the sea with deep inaccessible bays between, and the road twisted and plunged more than ever. From some of these headlands a rocky spit extended seaward beneath the waves, and I wondered if these were sunken antique jetties where slim black galleys had slid ashore, full of warriors with bronze swords and plumed helmets. So strong was the image that I found myself straining my eyes to see if anything moved on the shimmering water, but in spite of the clear blue skies, visibility was limited to a few miles because of the permanent mist that hangs over these mountains.

Alaçam marked the descent on to the flat ground of the delta of the Kizil Irmak — the River Halys of antiquity. What I had previously considered fertile land seemed almost barren in contrast with this area of the most intense cultivation I had yet seen. It was mostly tobacco, acre upon close-set acre, and every house had its lines of long golden leaves strung out in front of it, drying in the sun. The hot level plain felt oppressive. There were no views at all, the sea was far away, and ahead lay the smoke and noise of a bustling modern city.

It was easy to see why Samsun — ancient Amisus — had eclipsed Sinope. Lying between two rich river deltas, and possessed of a well-sheltered port, it stood at the head of the easiest land route from Central Anatolia down to the Euxine. Mithradates had embellished it with splendid walls and buildings, just as he had done with Sinope, and according to the classical writers it was all most magnificent. But of this antique city not a trace was left. Nor was there anything of interest from the early Turkish period. Only the geography remained; modern Samsun was simply a commercial centre with nothing to persuade the traveller even to pause there. Before I knew it, I was out the other side, crossing the eastern delta over the Yesil Irmak — the ancient River Iris — and once I had done that, and been restored by the sight of the wild ravine through which the Iris flowed down to the sea, I had crossed into the land of the Amazons.

Whether there really was a race of warrior women living in these Anatolian mountains, no one can say for certain, though many ancient writers, including the historian Herodotus, and the geographer Strabo, who was born in Pontus, believed implicitly in their existence. Strabo wrote of them:

. . . The Amazons spend ten months of the year by themselves performing their individual tasks, such as ploughing, planting, pasturing cattle, or particularly in training horses, though the bravest engage in hunting on horseback and practise warlike exercises. The right breast of all are seared when they are infants, so that they can easily use their right hands for any purpose, and especially that of throwing the javelin. They also use bows and arrows and light shields, and make the skins of wild animals serve as helmets, clothing and girdles. They have two months in spring when they go into the neighbouring mountains which separate them from the Gargarians. The Gargarians, also in accordance with ancient custom, go thither to offer sacrifice with the Amazons and also to have intercourse with them for the sake of begetting children, doing this in secrecy and darkness, any Gargarian at random with any Amazon; and after making them pregnant they send them away; and the females that are born are retained by the Amazons, but the males are taken to the Gargarians to be brought up; and each Gargarian to whom a child is brought adopts the child as his own, regarding the child as his son . . .

Whatever anyone today might think of such an arrangement, it certainly gave the Amazons more autonomy than most women have enjoyed since! And if we believe the account of them written by Herodotus, the Amazons themselves were certainly aware of the value of their freedom. His anecdote is about some Amazons who were captured by Greeks and taken off in a ship. They had managed to kill their captors, but being unskilled with boats, had drifted to the northern shore of the Euxine. Here some young Scythian men became enamoured of them, and wanted to marry them and take them home. Herodotus has the Amazons reply:

We and the women of your nation could never live together; our ways are too much at variance. We are riders, our business is with the bow and the spear, and we know nothing of women's work; but in your country no woman has anything to do with such things — your women stay at home occupied with feminine tasks, and never go out to hunt, or for any other purpose. We could not possibly agree.

Since the Scythians were still keen, however, Herodotus reports that a compromise was reached, and Amazons and Scythians went off together towards the Caspian Sea where they founded a new nation. 'And to this day,' claims Herodotus (which takes us only to around 440 BC), 'the women have kept to their old ways, riding, to the hunt on horseback, sometimes with, sometimes without their menfolk, taking part in war and wearing the same sort of clothes as men.' Which, in what is so often the universally sad lot of womenkind, could be described as having one's cake and eating it.

After Samsun the way was a good deal easier for bicycling, but considerably more dangerous. A narrow riviera allowed for a road to run close to the sea, a road that was, for the most part, fairly level and well surfaced. With the prevailing westerly wind propelling me towards Trebizond, it could have been a cyclist's idea of paradise. But the road also carried a heavy weight of traffic, certainly too much for its width, and, as is so often the case with motor vehicles, they exerted a disagreeable influence upon the people driving them. The Turk, I soon decided, was a decidedly pushy and not particularly skilful driver, and distressingly heavy on the horn. Bus drivers, especially, had an inflated idea of their own importance, and expected bicyclists to take to the rubble at the side of the road at the first imperious note of their approach. There *were* Turkish bicyclists in this area (though few in number, and all of them male), so I was not the only two-wheeled road user who resorted at times to shaking a fist. Unless there was an imminent risk of collision I was not prepared to be bullied off the road (particularly when I was riding through the historic land of the Amazons), working on the premise that no driver would wantonly mow me down and be delayed by all the palaver with the police that would ensue. It was often touch and go, however, especially crossing bridges, where time and time again I would look up in alarm to find a grinning driver watching me in his wing mirror high above, as he nudged me ever closer against the rail. But the favourite ploy was simply to keep a hand on the horn from the moment they sighted me until they were well past. Horn does not adequately describe the instrument that was fitted to most of the larger vehicles; it was more like a high-pitched siren heralding the Day of Wrath, and produced a volume of sound so dreadful that I am sure it would be banned in Europe. I noticed with a certain grim satisfaction that Turkish cyclists were even more intimidated by this appalling noise than I was, but then I had taken to wearing my wax earplugs for protection.

The area is famous for cherries and hazel-nuts. Indeed, cherries are believed to have originated here, and to have been taken from here to Europe by the Romans. The cherry season was well past, so I had no chance to sample the native variety, but the hazel-nut harvest was in full swing. Every town I passed through had the promenade along the sea front covered in plastic sheeting on which the nuts were spread to dry. There were miles and miles of nuts; thousands upon thousands of tons of them, with more being brought down from the mountains all the time. Dealers sat around on kitchen chairs doing business, cracking the nuts between their teeth and showing the fat white kernels to their customers, adopting a bored expression as they did so and glancing in the other direction — as if to say 'I don't need to look, I know the quality of my wares; you won't find better than this anywhere.' In appearance and taste the nuts were very like the English variety, so perhaps the Romans had introduced them along with the cherries.

The tremendous amount of building work I had noticed further west was also happening on this stretch, and the narrow coastal strip was filling up fast. Towns had no room to expand except upwards and lengthwise, and a ribbon of tall development was spreading from village to village, town to town. I thought that it would not be long before the Black Sea coast resembled the continuous urban sprawl that blights the southern coast of Britain. But I had only to lift my eyes to realize that it could never really be like that. The unique savagery of this landscape, with its huge rough densely-forested mountains, mist-shrouded and sea-lapped, would surely prevent it being entirely ruined; it would be so difficult, and ruinously expensive, to build on those precipitous slopes. No matter how much raw new building there was, or how unharmonious it appeared, or even how much litter and rubble lay around, all these works of man paled into insignificance beside such a rampant and implacable display of nature.

I camped each night if I could, loath to spend time in the noisy towns when I could be under the stars; also I needed the peace and quiet to recover from my days amongst the blaring traffic. Quiet however, being alien to the Turkish nature, was never guaranteed, even in a tent. Camping hadn't yet caught on along this eastern end of the Black Sea, and places that advertised themselves as such were usually no more than an area of rough ground around a beach restaurant, with a cold tap to wash at, if you were lucky. The owners usually claimed to have plans for developing the site into a tourist beach resort — it just hadn't happened yet. In the meantime it served as a hang-out for local males who came there to drink beer, or just to sit by the sea watching television. If I pitched my tent too close, I could be kept awake until two or three in the morning.

At one such place, near the town of Ordu, a sinister family descended upon me. Earlier, a boy had spotted me on the stony beach, and had come running to discover my nationality and whether I was planning to stay there. As soon as it was dark he returned with his mother, father, grandmother, an older brother, several cousins, and his sister, a girl of about sixteen. Apart from the very few words the boy knew, only the sister spoke English. She had come on a begging mission, 'for friendship' she said, but also for books, money, a trip to England, help to continue her studies, and for many other things which I have forgotten, but which she thought I might be persuaded to supply, and the tribe was there to provide support. On the face of it, they were an ordinary extended peasant family, except that somehow they lacked the normal inhibitions that one would expect, even in this overtly friendly country. They sat down all around me on the café balcony, leaning forward expectantly, their stolid and unusually Slavic faces wearing beaming smiles, and their small narrow eyes disappearing into slits. When they thought they were not observed the smiles vanished, and the eyes opened to reveal a range of calculating expressions. 'O yes, I am loving England,' began the girl, without preamble. 'But I am not having the books. I want to going to college, and working in the bank. Turkey very difficult. You will give me books?' No writer could remain totally unmoved by such devotion to the written word, and had she left it there, I might well have found myself committed to sending her a parcel of books when I returned home. But she persisted with her catalogue of wants, and with accounts of apocryphal kindnesses showered on her by other travellers, setting off one nationality against another — a Belgian had given her a bicycle, a French lady had given her dresses, others had given money, and on, and on, until even her watchful family appeared to lose interest, and turned their speculative glances elsewhere. I had bought them all tea or soft drinks, and considered I need do no more. The girl's heavy importuning began finally to bore me, and I said goodbye and sought the privacy of my tent, which was some way off.

Half an hour later I heard the zip of the tent door being slowly opened, and saw a head appear in the opening against the star-filled sky. Even if shock or fear is my first reaction at such moments, I have learnt that anger is the best defence, and usually I take the offensive automatically. 'I am wanting your address,' stammered the girl, as my fierce words broke over her head. Behind her I could see the dark shapes of her back-up group, and I shouted all the louder, so that anyone on the café terrace would hear. It was enough; they all made off with remarkable alacrity, and I saw no more of them. Perhaps it had all been perfectly innocent, and I had over-reacted; travel is often punctuated by misunderstandings. But I was glad that the café owners set their guard dog loose to patrol the area for the remainder of the night.

The last hundred miles to Trebizond took twice as long to cover as previous stretches because much of the way was so beautiful that I had to keep stopping. Around the most dramatic capes the coastal strip narrowed to no more than the width of the road, newly blasted from the cliffside. By climbing down over the edge and finding a rock to perch upon, I could sometimes enjoy an hour of complete privacy, a rare luxury in Turkey. Eschewing the strong brown native tea, I would brew up a kettle of the Lapsang Souchong that I had brought from England as one of my permitted luxuries, finding it the most refreshing of all teas in hot weather. The act of preparing it in these superlative surroundings, watching gulls flying over the broken remnants of Byzantine fortresses, or cormorants fishing from rocks that were named for Jason and the Argonauts, made me feel wonderfully Victorian — the wagons-lits of Europe, and the private sitting rooms of respectable hotels from Calais to Rome had once hummed with the spirit lamps of English lady travellers — no foreigner could be trusted to produce a proper cup of tea!

But rarely did I have the shoreline completely to myself. Even in the most inaccessible of places there would usually be a few young boys playing among the boisterous waves, as much in their element as otters or seals. They could have been from any age, any race — Greek, Persian, Roman, Byzantine, or those that Xenophon called 'native'. Even without a dolphin or two, these brown carefree boys, pitting their strength against the waves in an ancient magical sea, seemed potent symbols of a less complicated age.

Tea plantations were now beginning to make their appearance as the humidity grew daily ever higher, and the rain became more frequent, splashing down in sudden heavy thunder storms that turned the beetling capes into shadows. The climatic conditions were now such that I could have imagined myself in Darjeeling, or some other hill station of Northern India, with vapour rising thickly from the moist mountain sides whose lower slopes were now covered in acres of neat low glossy bushes.

One evening when I was soaked to the skin, and there was not a hotel until Trebizond, fifty miles on, I found myself the subject of civic concern. I had taken belated shelter under the roof of a village fountain, and was soon surrounded by what must have been most of the village males. Several tried out their store of foreign phrases on me, while I resorted to my dictionary to gather replies. The problem with these multi-lingual conversations is always that, although a simple idea can be put across, no one understands the other person's answers; and really the dictionary is much more reliable because the appropriate words can be pointed to, and then enlarged upon with mime. The village men thought I ought to find somewhere to get dry and change my clothes, a sentiment I fully endorsed. 'Would I care to be a guest?' I cautiously thought I might. Some sort of Dutch auction then took place, with several men putting in their claim, and one, whom I later discovered to be the baker's delivery man, proving successful. Roberts was picked up, complete with baggage, and stowed in the back of the winner's estate car. I was ushered into the passenger seat, and we took off almost vertically up the mountainside. At once we were in quite a different world, intensely green and agricultural. But I had no opportunity to observe it in any detail as we bumped and slewed and thudded over a broken cobbled path hardly wider than the vehicle, and so barbarous that it must have spelt ruin to any car's suspension in a very short time. It would also have spelt disaster to us had anything been coming down the mountain! Cobbles gave way to dirt, and still we shot upwards, and I began to wonder a little about my host? . . . abductor? I had, after all, no idea who he was, or where we were going, or whether I had understood what was being offered. But before such vague fears had time to take root, we had stopped at a small clearing in the wall of greenery, in front of a very new, unfinished house. A strangely urban building it seemed, to find miles from anywhere, a concrete no-nonsense structure, three square boxes on top of one another, more like a very small modern block of town flats than a house. Later I learnt that it had been constructed like that with the idea of adding on more floors as the family grew, and money permitted, and that this was now standard practice all over Turkey. I rather liked the idea of a rash of little Turkish towers dotted about the mountainsides and housing whole clans; it would be something like the brochs the Celts used to build along the western coasts of Scotland.

I had no time to think about any of this just then, however, because I was overwhelmed by the enthusiastic welcome of what seemed to be dozens and dozens of people. Had I been the returning Prodigal I could not have been received more warmly. I was embraced and hugged and kissed by all the females, while the men shook my hand, and everyone said '*Hos Geldeniz*', (Welcome) over and over again. My shoes were unlaced and removed, and I was brought into what seemed to be the master bedroom, complete with double bed. The women were all for staying and dressing me up in the flowered Turkish trousers and dress they had taken from the wardrobe. But one of the men, who perhaps realized that Western women are shyer than Turks, ushered everyone out, and I was able to don my own spare clothes (quite dry, thanks to my habit of packing everything in plastic bags).

A little later, I sat in a comfortable, well-furnished room of no particular character, while a man sat beside me shelling hazel-nuts for me to eat, and helping me to work out who everyone was. There were four generations present. The oldest couple were about eighty and retired, and lived in the original farmhouse at the other end of the extended allotment. Their son was the head of the house, but he was at present working in a factory in Germany. The new building and its furniture had been paid for with the money he sent home. His wife was a woman of about my own age, but 'acting tribal chief' was her son, a man of thirty, and father of the three or four small infants who were crawling about trying to get at the nuts. It was their mother, Gülperi, who was the kingpin of the house, and she adopted me as her special charge, her 'friend'. There were younger brothers, sisters and cousins too, far too many to sort out all the relationships in a single evening's visit. Gülperi had a tremendous capacity for showing affection. Although she was rushed off her feet between preparing the dinner and getting the children ready for bed, she stopped to give me a hug each time she passed between kitchen and storeroom, and seemed absolutely delighted that she had an unexpected visitor to look after. When she could snatch a moment to come and sit beside me, it was to repeat her request that I stay with them for at least a week.

As usual, the dictionaries were in continuous use, people taking it in turns to share one, while I was kept busy finding answers with the other. The television in the meantime played on in the background, showing the inevitable foreign film dubbed into Turkish, which seems to account for three-quarters of what is shown on Turkish television. No one was watching it, and the infants squabbling and fighting on the floor had to bellow all the louder to be heard at all, at which their father shouted for cheerful over-worked Gülperi to come and remove them.

Dinner was remarkable for the number of different dishes, all the produce of the farm except for the meat. There were tiny brown trout that had been 'guddled' from mountain streams, omelette, olives, salads of cucumber and tomatoes, melon, stewed meat with aubergine, stewed aubergine with onions and tomatoes, cheeses, grapes, hot peppers, and little brown-fleshed pears which looked rotten but were perfectly sound and which were a speciality of the region. People ate very casually, coming to the table in ones and twos, while Gülperi made sure I had more than my fair share of everything and kept finding special titbits to tempt me.

Gülperi's small son Hüseyin ate with me, the most remarkable young trencherman I had ever seen. He was about three and as broad as he was high. He looked like a miniature Sumo wrestler, a circumstance entirely due to the amount of food he put away: far more than anyone else present. He glowered every time his mother passed me anything, and although he was given his own plate heaped high, he still reached out his fork to spear up whatever he could get at. Everyone roared with laughter at his efforts, which did nothing to distract him. In the end he was carried off from the table bawling with fury at not being allowed to eat more.

For any corners that might be left there were more nuts, for the wealth of the farm was founded on hazel-nuts. Sacks of them were stored in every room, even under the children's cots. And while we cracked nuts and drank coffee, a young man demonstrated the sound of a home-made, two-stringed mandolin against the eternal background of the television film. But the dictionaries were still the big attraction, and with their help we sat and talked, mostly about life on the farm and gathering the hazel-nuts, work that fell mainly on the women and the young girls. They showed me in mime how they plucked them in bunches from the trees, with a two-handed pulling motion like milking a cow. They wanted to know about my life too, and here the newspaper article helped a little, but my town-based Western existence was too far outside their experience to be comprehensible. All the time I was plied with more food and drink, coffee from Germany, more of the brown pears, peeled and cut up for me, yet more shelled nuts. And the sweet-natured Gülperi sat by my side trying to make me promise to come back next year with my husband and children and grandchildren. So pressing was she that I had to say I would, even though I doubted it, and each time I was made to promise I added a pious Muslim 'Insh'Allah', God willing, to cover myself against the lie.

All evening, behind the chatter of our voices and the eternal droning of the television, was the rumble and crash of tropical thunder storms rolling around the mountain sides. And all night, as I tossed and turned in the large double bed, trying to escape the attacks of mosquitoes, trying to find a softer spot on the rock-hard pillows, and stifling under a heavy quilt, the rain beat down on the canopy of leaves, so that for once, in spite of all the minor irritations, I was very thankful not to be out there in the tent. But in the morning when I looked through the bedroom window, the sun was shining on a world that looked newly created, and more wonderfully fresh and green and altogether more riotously and improbably abundant than I would have thought possible.

Before the baker's car came to take me down to the road again Gülperi took me around the small piece of land on which the family grew everything they needed. A few yards of maize yielded a year's supply of flour. There were aubergines, peppers, tomatoes, cucumbers, grape vines, banana plants, all sorts of fruit trees, all manner of vegetables. Two wells which never ran dry supplemented the abundant rain. So densely cultivated was the little shelf on the precipitous mountainside, that there was even room for a cash crop of tea to supplement the nuts from the hazel groves. Gülperi took a pair of shears that had a small bag attached along the length of one of the blades. When she snipped at the tips of the tea bushes, the pieces fell automatically into the bag. Such a simple idea, yet remembering how I had watched Indian women laboriously plucking the leaves by hand, how very ingenious.

I left one of the dictionaries with Gülperi, as it was the only thing I had that I knew

she would value. Often in the months that
followed, travelling among less happy people, I
would think of her bustling about in that green
secluded little paradise, so happy and contented
with her lot.

8

An Emperor's Garden in Trebizond

TREBIZOND, of course, does not exist. For more than five hundred years it has been Trabzon, a run-down Turkish port, recently grown prosperous on oil, and currently host to half a million itinerant Russians hawking their mixed bag of shabby goods along the littered front. But as my guidebook stated: 'The English-speaking world still thinks of Trabzon as Trebizond, a remote and romantic outpost.' And I am sure this is right, at least in my case it is, for the name Trebizond (and even now I cannot think of it as Trabzon) conjures up the very breath and fibre of romance. From earliest times it was the gateway to Armenia, and the place where the trade route from Persia and the East descended to the shores of the Euxine. When Xenophon's Ten Thousand had fought their way through Kurdistan and survived the terrible ice-bound crossing of the mountains, it was to this spot, already a flourishing Greek town, that they came. For two thousand years it continued to be the principal port on the Euxine, an urbane and gilded city, host to kings, ambassadors, and such travellers as Marco Polo. But the most illustrious period — and the reason for its remaining Trebizond in the hearts of not only 'the English-speaking world' but the Western world in general

105

— was the two hundred years that followed the scandalous occupation of Constantinople by the Latins. Then, as Trebizond, it housed the brilliant world of the Comneni dynasty, and kept alive the genius of the Byzantine Empire. In the fifteenth century, after the Ottomans, under Mehmet the Conqueror, had finally taken Constantinople and seemed poised to sweep on, through Europe like a tidal wave, Trebizond was all that remained of the Byzantine Empire, and had held out in the lofty citadel of the Trapesus Rock, surrounded by a sea of Islam, for eight further desperate and heroic years. And although some historians are fond of pointing out that cruelty and corruption characterized the Byzantine Empire quite as much as brilliance, I can only agree with Rose Macaulay who wrote in *The Towers of Trebizond*:

. . . like most empires, they no doubt deserved to go under, but not so deeply under as Trebizond has gone, becoming Trabzon, with a black squalid beach, and full of those who do not know the past, or that it ever was Trebizond and a Greek empire . . .

So although I had been forewarned of what I should find, I still rode through the ugly spreading suburbs of crumbling concrete with a great sense of expectancy, which could only result in disappointment.

I rather wished I had arrived by ship, for of all the stagey settings enjoyed by cities along the Black Sea coast, that of Trebizond in its

106

great sweeping semicircular bay, with the cliffs and the ravines of the citadel rising up behind the modern town, and the shaggy mountains beyond, was by far the most dramatic. The colonists from Miletus who settled there in the eighth century BC named their settlement Trapezus because of the extraordinary Trapesus Rock soaring up between two riverine chasms, as distinctive and improbable as any Turner painting of castles on the Danube. Shelves of land at different heights had allowed for the succession of cities — Greek, Roman and Byzantine — to spread out over the mountainside and to flower with splendid temples that gave way to churches, and later still to mosques. And all this would have been best appreciated from the sea, without the dirt and tackiness of modern Trabzon getting in the way.

The shoreline became more and more noisy and bewildering as I rode on looking for the way to go up into the city. I could not look too hard for it required all my attention just to stay alive, so pushy and dashing was the traffic. The harbour and docks extended in a grimy smoky mess behind high fencing on my left, and on my right was a sort of market that ran parallel to the road and appeared impenetrable.

Eventually I found a place where I could turn right round and come back on the other side of this market, and discovered that it was the area given to the itinerant Russian traders in which to sell their goods, an area that stretched eastwards for at least half a mile. And what goods! One woman would be offering a couple of bunches of safety pins and maybe a few cheap torches; another would be selling a half bottle of brandy, some rudimentary plastic toys, ties, paper flowers, playing cards. It was a jumble of anything and everything that could be got into a suitcase or the boot of a car. That anyone should want to search through such an ill-assorted disarray when the same things could be purchased for very little more in Turkish shops seemed madness. Why people were prepared to put up with the rudeness of the Russians traders was also beyond me, for they mostly seemed to adopt an arrogant and hectoring manner with the Turks as though they despised them. Five years ago Russia was still the number one enemy of Turkey, as it had been from time immemorial. Few Turks could even utter the word Russia without spitting in the dust or shaking a fist in the direction of that country. Yet here they were welcoming them in droves, with a completely open border policy. The authorities were expecting there to be three million Russians in Trebizond by the turn of the century I learnt, when finally I found my way up the hill to Atatürk Square and the tourist office. What was more, the country was in the process of being physically bound to Russia by a pipeline carrying natural gas direct to Ankara and other major Turkish cities.

Various Turkish friends in Istanbul had attempted to explain Turkey's complicated and changing international politics to me, but as no two of them ever seemed to hold quite the same views, it remained for me a cloudy and ambiguous area. If there was a consensus of opinion, it seemed to be that with the break up of the Soviet Union and the changes in the Middle East, Turkey saw increasing opportunities to become once again a great power, the crossroads of the world and the controlling link between Asia and Europe. They felt that with Turkey's unique position in NATO, and what they hoped was her imminent acceptance into the EEC, the countries of Asia and the Arab world would increasingly look to Turkey to represent their interests in any disputes with the West. The Gulf War, and Turkey's decision to allow American forces to operate from her territory, had alienated the Arab world, however, so at present Turkey was looking far more towards her links with Asia, and particularly the Russian Turkic states, like Azerbaijan.

But not all Turks were in agreement with this extreme form of *perestroika*, not in Trabzon anyway. Various city dignitaries I was invited to meet expressed grave misgivings about the Russian connection from the point of view of morals, economy and security. Prostitution, they claimed, was rife for the first time since Mehmet had accepted the city's surrender in AD 1461; indigenous traders and shop keepers were being put out of business, and who knew how much useful military information was being gathered for the future? Sides of noses were tapped knowingly. 'Only hotels benefit; they squash the Russians in three to a bed. Russians smell, they don't wash. They drive all other tourists away.'

Whether the Russians did sleep three to a bed I did not discover, but it was certainly true that the hotels were overcrowded as well as more expensive than elsewhere on the coast. But as Trebizond was an idea I had to pursue, and since there was nowhere to put up my tent, I rooted around until I found a fairly clean and reasonable little place overlooking the littered harbour with its forest of cranes. All night the traffic roared along the waterfront, doors banged continuously, Russian prostitutes strode up and down below the windows soliciting noisily, and above it all came the canned and distorted muezzin's call from several mosques, competing with each other to wail that prayer was better than sleep — a sentiment with which I was unable to agree. Since there was no possibility of sleep and I did not feel like prayer, I read and re-read my three books and tried to learn some more Turkish, while I waited for the dawn. There wasn't any point trying to find somewhere quieter, because all the city was like that.

The reason I stayed even one night was because I wanted to see if the ghosts of Trebizond's brilliant past that Rose Macaulay had glimpsed when she came here in the 1940s were still to be discovered. The place had clearly gone down even further since then, but one advantage I enjoyed was that the most glorious building the city boasted — the thirteenth-century church of Haghia Sophia (which was a ruin when Rose Macaulay made her visit) — had

110

since been restored, and was now a museum. As soon as I had booked into my modest lodging house and chained Roberts to a newel post, I boarded a cab in the excellent little shuttle service that plies a fixed route between Atatürk Square and Haghia Sophia, two miles away. There was just five minutes to view the place on that first evening before the gates were locked for the night, and even had there been nothing else for me in Trebizond, that brief glimpse would have been quite enough to convince me I had to stay on for a day or two.

I breakfasted each morning in the little garden that surrounds Haghia Sophia, arriving there as soon as the gates opened at eight a.m., when I could count on having the place to myself for an hour or two, and could doze off for a while if I felt like it. The church had the most superb setting on a terrace overlooking the sea, and at that still hour of the morning, under a gentle sky, the creamy-yellow building was at its loveliest. A greater contrast to the rackety steamy nights could not be imagined.

The ground plan of the church is cruciform with equal sides, and with four magnificent marble columns supporting the central dome, which is raised up on a high drum. It is a totally different concept from the much earlier Haghia Sophia of Constantinople, and much smaller too, but many scholars have considered that it marks the acme of the Byzantine achievement. Three great barrel-vaulted porches extend the north, south and western ends, all supported on beautiful re-used classical columns. But it is the

111

south porch that immediately rivets the attention with its superb sculpted frieze depicting the story of Genesis, with the single-headed eagle of the Comneni forming the keystone above it.

The inside walls and ceilings of the porches, the narthex, and the body of the church were once completely covered with wonderful frescoes, the real purpose of which (leaving aside beauty, art, and the glorification of the founder) was a statement of faith — to tell in pictures the story of God's redemptive acts towards mankind, from Genesis, through Old Testament prophecy, to the birth, life, death and resurrection of Christ, with the lives of the saints thrown in for good measure. Thanks to the painstaking work of Professor Talbot Rice and his team from Edinburgh University, many of these paintings, together with the crumbling half-ruined building itself, have been restored, if not to their original splendour, at least to a state where the extraordinary magnificence can be appreciated. So extensive and detailed are these restored frescoes that anyone could spend a month studying them and still find something new. The most awe-inspiring of them, I thought, was the head and shoulders that remained of the Christ Pantocrator in the central dome, with a wonderful frieze of angels around the drum beneath. There was also a long Greek inscription from Psalm 102 on the drum — about the Lord looking down from heaven on those in captivity, doomed to die. It seemed a sadly prophetic text, considering how soon after the building was completed the empire and all its works were to be swept away.

Beside the church was a tall fifteenth-century bell tower which had doubled as a watch tower, and had been built in the desperate last days of Trebizond — just eighteen years before the Emperor, David Comnenus, surrendered the city. This tower was always kept locked, and when I asked the custodian why this was, he said it was because of all the valuable things like ladders and gardening tools that were stored there. The church doors, on the other hand, were never closed, not even at night when the gates to the garden were locked. As a result pigeons flew in and roosted on the ledges and reared their young there, and the first job of the custodian in the morning was to wash away their copious droppings from the battered but still magnificent inlaid marble floor. It was clear that the bird population was doing the building and its priceless paintings no good at all, and the same applied to the young trees and weeds that had been allowed to sprout and flourish among the roof tiles, and which were slowly prising them apart. It must have cost no mean sum to have restored the building to its present state, not to mention the highly-skilled painstaking work, and it made me angry that so little care was being taken to preserve it. But as I had observed in other places, Turks seem not to care much for antiquity. They value gardens above even the most marvellous buildings, which is, I suppose, a perfectly valid point of view, but ironic considering how thickly civilization's treasures are scattered throughout Asia Minor.

There was another Byzantine church that I came upon by accident near to the eastern ravine, and just off an ugly main street. It was the seventh-century church of St Anne, the oldest building in the city, a tiny place built of disproportionately large stone blocks, and with a badly-mutilated marble tympanum over the door that appeared to be a Descent from the Cross. After I found it I kept going back, but to my annoyance it was always locked, and its sole purpose, as far as I could see, was to provide a useful point for anchoring hanks of electricity and telephone cables. On my last visit I sat for a while on the steps of St Anne's to write in my journal about what I thought of this state of affairs, and a boy from the teashop opposite came over with a little stool for me to sit on instead. Once again the disparaging thoughts I'd been harbouring melted away before the kindness of the Turk towards strangers.

Turkey is certainly the place for mood swings. On the first afternoon, I retired to my room to escape the heat, and tired out after the previous sleepless night, fell asleep on the bed. When I awoke it was to find a dozen or so giggling men on the hotel roof opposite ogling me through the open window. My sole comfort was that I had removed only my shirt and trousers, and not my underwear also. After that I confined my daytime naps to Haghia Sophia and took to spending the hot afternoons wandering through the winding alleys that led down to the port, where the sun entered only briefly at noon. Here the Turkish shopkeepers sat in front of their open-fronted stores spitting in contempt after the departing back of some buxom Tatiana who had tried in vain to beat down the price of their blue jeans to below cost. For there was a two-way trade between Turks and Russians I discovered, apart from natural gas. The one thing the Russians wanted to take back with them was American-style denim clothes which Turkey now manufactures in ever-increasing quantities. As has been the case with traders since long before Marco Polo, the aim was to buy cheap and sell dear. On the whole I thought the Russians, particularly the stout, dyed-haired, brash, aggressive matrons, were more than a match for the slower more passive Turks.

I talked with several of the Russian traders in the little cafés which they frequented. The ones who knew English tended to be less rough and bellicose than the average, and since they seemed to regard me as a 'neutral', they were prepared to talk quite openly. Some were teachers or students; one quite young woman, who seemed not at all to mind confessing to being a prostitute, said she was a nurse in Moscow, but found that six months in Turkey could earn her enough to live on for a couple of years. Many claimed it was cheaper just to stay in Turkey even if you didn't sell anything because food was practically given away. The picture of life in the former Soviet Union that emerged from these conversations was horrific. Salaries frequently were not paid, and even if they were, inflation and the price of basic commodities was such that they often could not buy sufficient food for survival. It sounded exactly like the total economic collapse I had witnessed in Uganda after that country's twenty-five years of mayhem under Amin and Obote. Nonetheless, the sight of all these hordes of Russians, from what was until so recently a world power, trying to make money out of the Turks — who could hardly be described as rich, and who certainly were less sophisticated — seemed bizarre in the extreme.

There clearly were rich Turks in Trebizond, however, and also a smarter side of town, which the Russians did not frequent, consisting of a few streets where Western designer goods were sold. I had an introduction to a man called Erol who owned a clothing shop there, a franchise selling the sort of expensive casual 'in gear' that could be found in most major cities of the West. There were five or six such shops in the immediate vicinity, and Erol was in the process of opening yet another across the road, to sell the clothes of a different franchise. Every time he tried to sign the lease on the property, however, the owner put the price up he told me, in order to beat the inflation. Erol and his wife worked a ten-hour day in the shop while the grandparents looked after the two small children. When he wasn't working he was a radio ham, and also a keen hunter. It was because he regularly went east to shoot bears (also eagles, wolf and anything else that moved I gathered) that mutual acquaintances had thought he might be able to advise me on the route ahead.

Erol and his wife took me out for a meal

at an expensive seaside restaurant where we ate excellent fish beside the lapping waves; but neither the waves nor the stars were visible because of the cold bright glare of the blue neon lighting that created an atmosphere more appropriate to an operating theatre. The conversation lagged because Erol's wife knew no English, and my Turkish was never to progress beyond one- or two-word utterances, no matter how many sleepless nights I suffered. And although the food was so good, the evening became more and more depressing because of the long awkward silences, and because Erol's advice about Eastern Turkey was not to go there. He said that even though he had just bought two new rifles which he was eager to try out, he was giving his autumn hunting trip a miss this year because of the activity of the Kurdish dissident groups, the PKK in particular. There was not a day without someone being kidnapped or shot, he said, and the Kurds didn't care who they zapped as long as it drew international attention to their grievances. He thought I would be foolish to go on, but nevertheless agreed to look after any of my things which I might want to leave behind.

Spartan though my luggage was, I knew I had to shed more of it if I wanted to continue under my own steam. I had already left my spare tyres in Istanbul with the idea that they could be sent on to me at need. Now I went through every item that remained, discarding anything I could possibly do without. I seriously considered abandoning the camping gear, but the seven pounds saving in weight this sacrifice would have made seemed not worth it compared with the freedom a tent, mattress and sleeping bag gave me. Instead I sacrificed some of my medicines, spare clothing, my other pair of shoes, fuel for the stove, and the like. Even my swimming costume was left behind, since female bathing was becoming increasingly frowned upon the further east I went. Altogether I was able to dispense with eight or nine pounds and stored the things in the basement of Erol's shop to be picked up on my return, for I planned eventually to take the car ferry back through the Black Sea to Istanbul. A quick check that all was as it should be with the trusty Roberts and I was ready to be on my way again. Only one thing remained to be done.

I had left the heart of ancient Trebizond until last, fearing I would be disappointed, that the ghosts would all have fled. But now that I was myself ready to depart, I could delay no longer. Between the eastern and the western gorges rise the famous walls of Trebizond, snaking up towards the summit of the Trapesus Rock. The Byzantine fortified inner city consisted of three separate *enceintes*, one above the other, the lowest being bounded on its northern side by the sea. It was in the upper citadel, protected by the steepest part of the precipices, and all but impregnable, that the Golden palace of the Comneni had stood. Only the western wall and a scrap of the citadel are left, but the wonder was that I found this last remaining fragment almost exactly as Rose Macaulay described it. I

118

walked up there on a sunbaked afternoon, with the ancient broken walls to my right hidden behind mean houses that threw back the heat and made the steep going harder still. Near the summit was an opening, and there suddenly I was in a high green place among slips of gardens planted between the grassed over mounds of ancient collapsed masonry. Lean-to hovels were built against the hoary outer walls of the citadel, and the only place to walk was along the top of the walls themselves, a few inches wide with an airy drop of a thousand feet or so on the outer edge. From this spot a Comneni princeling is said to have fallen to his death from a palace window. As I made the traverse I wondered if he had really fallen, or if, tyrannical and unchildlike as such imperial infants tended to be, he had goaded his nurse beyond endurance, so that for one awful moment she had lost control and pushed him over the edge. It was not a pleasant thought, and although I am usually unmoved by heights, I was happy to climb down again.

Eight pointed windows flush with the edge of the precipice and a few arches are all that remained of what is thought to have been the banqueting hall of the Comneni Palace. A brooding stillness lay over it, for there was no one about, certainly not the sorcerer whom Rose Macaulay had encountered. In spite of the hot sun, it felt an eerie and a melancholy place, until suddenly the quiet was broken by two young boys and a female dwarf who came bounding into what I thought might once have been the Emperor's garden. The dwarf could

have been any age from fifteen to fifty. She had
a scarf wound round her head in no style I had
observed in Turkey. A heavy shapeless dress, far
too large for her, came down to her calves, and
she wore a pair of high-laced boots. She had the
bow-legged rolling gait peculiar to dwarves, and
there was something both touching and sinister
about her as she capered along behind the boys,
trying to keep up with them. She was chewing
a great wad of pink bubble-gum, and when she
came close, she tilted up her chin and began to
blow, puffing out her cheeks until she had made
a large balloon, which she then burst with a loud
report and a great show of satisfaction. The boys
ignored her; they wanted to take me around the
ruins, but as I had seen them already they lost
interest and wandered off. The dwarf, however,
remained, and came and sat beside me on a
scrap of masonry, still chewing and blowing
her bubble-gum, moving when I moved, and
imitating any gesture I made. At first I felt
intimidated, and offered her money, hoping
she would then go away. But she ignored it,
and I soon realized she was entirely harmless,
and simply wanted to be friendly, so I let her
be, and wrote in my journal while she watched
me closely, kicking her feet to and fro. As we
sat there, in what became a companionable,
undemanding silence, broken only by the sound
of insects and the occasional plop of the bubble
gum, lines from Yeats 'Sailing to Byzantium',
by now firmly lodged in my memory, came to
mind:

120

Once out of nature I shall never take
My bodily form from any living thing
But such a form as Grecian goldsmiths
   make
Of hammered gold and gold enamelling
To keep a drowsy Emperor awake;
Or set upon a golden bough to sing
To lords and ladies of Byzantium
Of what is past, or passing, or to come.

Both the presence of a friendly dwarf blowing bubbles and Yeats' poem seemed to me a part of the abiding genius of the ruined Byzantine palace. Mere fragment of stone though it was, it still held something that could reach out across all those ravaged centuries and inspire another and a different age.

When finally I stood up to go, I feared the dwarf might try to follow me, but she sat on, kicking her heels against the stone as though she belonged there; and she called after me the only words she had uttered the whole time: 'Güle, güle', the Turkish for goodbye, which means literally 'Go smiling'.

9

Where Eagles Fly

THE ancient caravan route to Persia turns south from the coast soon after Trebizond, to follow the River Degirmendere up towards the high Eastern Anatolian Plateau. This lovely valley is still the main route into Central Anatolia from the Black Sea, but it was currently a mess because of the recent catastrophic floods that had swept away the road and many of the bridges. I went that way in order to visit the famous Sumela Monastery, and after twenty miles of negotiating the churned-up mud, gravel and craters, I was only too glad to accept a lift in a truck.

Sumela, the Monastery of the Virgin of the Black Rock, is said to have been founded in AD 385 by two monks from Greece named Barnabas and Sophronius. The Virgin had appeared to Barnabas in a dream, directing him to take her sacred icon, painted by St Luke, and install it in a cave which he would find somewhere in the Pontic Alps. Accordingly, after long wanderings through mountain valleys, the monks found a place corresponding to the details of Barnabas' vision, in the verdant Altindere valley, a tributary of the Degirmendere. The cave of the vision was an impregnable, isolated spot, just below the summit of a great black wall of rock, and supplied with a miraculous spring of clear water that never failed. There were also some useful narrow ledges on which a monastery could be built. Of the early buildings, which were deemed splendid enough for the coronation of Alexius Comnenus III, Emperor of Trebizond, in 1389, nothing at all remains. In fact, apart from the cave itself, the outer shell of the eighteenth-century buildings and some badly mutilated frescoes, nothing survived the fire which took place there just after the Greeks were expelled from Turkey in 1923. Nonetheless it was well worth the effort of getting there.

From below, the monastery looks the very stuff of dreams, a remote white edifice like a Tibetan hermitage, clinging impossibly to the sheer wall of rock a thousand feet above the green and luxuriant valley floor. A steep narrow path zigzags up to it through the trees, revealing a fresh view of the lovely valley at every turn. It was my bad luck to be ascending as three hundred members of the Trabzon Police school were running down. Why a trip to a Christian monastery should be considered a suitable outing for three hundred police cadets (I checked the number with their superintendent, who wisely descended last) I cannot imagine, but clearly the high spot of the day was seeing how fast they could all get back down again to the café at the bottom. The compensation for being so nearly and so frequently swept from the cliff face was in not having to share the monastery site with them — though how all three hundred could have been up there at the same time was a puzzle.

A refreshing drink of cold water from the miraculous source had to take the place of the glass of ouzo and plate of goat's cheese and olives I would have been served had the monks not been expelled seventy years earlier — though as a woman perhaps I wouldn't have been received at all, as is the case on Mount Athos.

Close to, the romantic white building could be seen for what it was, a few burnt and mouldering walls carefully held together with scaffolding so as to preserve the impression from below (the Turks are well aware of its value as a tourist site). With the horribly mutilated frescoes, and with every tiny cell, wall and courtyard of the skilfully contrived scheme showing the evidence of wanton destruction, it was a great sadness. And yet the desolation did little to spoil the essential magnificence of the site. The breathtaking idea of it survived, as did the beauty of the outlook over the gracious wooded valley, and a sense of worship still emanated from the little cave church at its centre. I remembered the fierce old man in Trebizond who had told me that Ottoman was the only period that mattered in Turkey. He had met both Freya Stark and Rose Macaulay, and had doubtless had this conversation with them both, and had grown fiercer about his ideas over the years. 'Ottoman overlays everything in this country,' the old man had insisted. 'But you English are besotted with anything and everything Greek. Greeks, Byzantines. Pah!

124

Finished, both! Is Ottoman who matters now.'
But I thought that if we could have stood here
together on this high terrace, beside the ancient
sanctuary, instead of in the busy office in Atatürk
Square, we might both have agreed that what
really mattered lay much further back than either
Ottoman or Greek, and that whatever was the
genius of this place had been here long before
Barnabas and Sophronius had arrived with the
Virgin's icon and with their particular ideas
about the nature of God. I left Sumela feeling
that there was something of significance there,
of which I had only brushed the fringes.

Had I continued up the Degirmendere valley
to the Zigana Pass I would have come to the
spot where the Ten Thousand caught their first
glimpse of the Euxine after all the bitter months
on the long march from Persia:

> . . . they heard the soldiers shouting out
> 'Thalassa! Thalassa! The sea! The sea!' and
> passing the word down the column. Then
> certainly they all began to run, and drove
> on the baggage animals and the horses at
> full speed; and when they had all got to
> the top, the soldiers, with tears in their eyes,
> embraced each other and their generals and
> captains . . .

And I followed their route back down to the
coast because it seemed pointless to continue on
the ruined road up to the plateau, with heavy
plant everywhere. Instead I rode on eastwards
along the coast road towards Rize, intending to

make the ascent to the plateau from nearer the Russian border.

It could have been an entirely different shore to the one I had been following, for the mist had suddenly come right down, and the sea was like a Chinese painting, with boats and rocks suspended in space, and with a sense of timelessness over everything. A grubby little hovel loomed out of the mist, revealing itself to be a restaurant, and I stopped there for a late lunch. It was cooked for me by an amiable man who had lived for two years in a London suburb, and had been homesick for it ever since, because as he said, 'Weather very good in Edgware; here is always raining.' He was one of life's losers. Having been sent to London to do business studies, he found it was all he could do to learn the language, and had dropped out of college and spent his time talking to his Irish landlady and learning to drink English beer at his local. Returning home with nothing tangible to show for his time abroad, his father had disowned him. Now he was a cook in a part of Turkey far from where he had grown up, and in a run-down café that was not even his own. It was difficult to see a brighter future for him, as he was a very poor cook, though wonderfully self-assured about his imagined skill. I rode on suffering a rare bout of indigestion, but even that could not spoil the magic of the day, with the sun coming and going behind the mist like a magic lantern show.

By six o'clock, when I reached Rize, I had cycled nearly seventy miles, but even so I went on. Rize was out of tune with my mood. Where

I had expected to find the pretty seaside town I had read about, I found instead the by now familiar crowds of Russian traders, and tall concrete hotels going up willy-nilly, with builders' rubble all around. Also, after the sleepless nights in Trebizond, I was scared off by the numerous mosques in Rize; every hotel was built next door to one, and all of them bristling with loud speakers. I decided that I must sleep in the tent.

There wasn't much in the way of sites, for once out of Rize the sea came right up to the road again, and a cliff rose on the other side. The first likely spot came after a few miles, where a restaurant jutted out into the sea on a spit of rocky land. It was a ramshackle sort of place, a long low hut built out of bits and pieces, but it had a small fringe of garden around it, with a few straggling roses and leggy flowers, and a pool which was meant to contain fish for diners to select, but which was currently serving only to breed mosquitoes. The half-blind old man who ran the place, with the help of a small army of young male relatives, was quite happy for me to pitch the tent there. He slept in the restaurant at night, he said, and Roberts could be locked in with him. I would only have to shout if I needed help. A plump rat crawling over the low fence from the littered foreshore put me off a little, but I didn't think I would find a better site. Besides, it was almost nightfall, which veiled over the grosser deficiencies of the scene, as well as preventing me cycling further.

I ate my kebab, yoghurt and salad in the

garden, under skies which had cleared and showed a slip of a moon riding among the stars. The younger members of the clan were bathing off the end of the spit, cleaving the black water with blazes of phosphorescence, and the hushed expectancy of the sea had returned. My host grilled me about my journey as I ate, though he knew no English, and we couldn't use the dictionary because of his poor eyesight. He was horrified when he learnt where I was going, and launched into a spate of gruesome stories all about the Kurdish resistance movement, the PKK (pronounced portentously Pay Kah Kah), slaughtering babies and slitting throats. Each graphic description, sketched with gestures rather than words, was concluded with raised hands and an upward turning of the eyeballs. He went over my itinerary, naming each and every town in Eastern Turkey; if I said 'Evet', Yes, I was going there, he would throw up his hands again in horror, exclaiming 'PKK' in a voice of doom, rocking backwards and forwards, as though in prayer. It developed into a litany: 'Kars? Ahhh, PKK! Dogubayazit? Ahhh, PKK! Van? Ahhh, PKK!' and so on and on. Pure drama though it seemed, I felt he was genuinely concerned for my safety, and anxious to instil in me the danger of the situation. The point of it all was to get me to agree that I would not camp out in Kurdish areas unless it was beside a police station. The litany changed tack: 'Kars; camping yok! oteli.' Touched by his solicitude I was happy to respond 'Evet. Kars hotel; tent yok!' But my chief feeling was delight that such

128

a performance could be achieved with so very few words.

Not that I thought his warnings were without substance. While in Trebizond I had heard about a large party of German holiday makers who had just been kidnapped by the PKK on the mountain of Nemrut Dagi, by Lake Van. I had every intention of trying to avoid a similar fate. It would certainly be 'Camping *yok*!' unless I was assured of a safe place to pitch.

So tired was I after this drama and the long day's ride that I crawled into my tent straight after dinner, and slept through the conversations of the other diners and the noise of the passing traffic. But I had not spotted the small mosque just across the road from the restaurant, and both the late night prayers and the early morning invocation came over magnified and distorted through the all-pervasive sound system.

Hopa, some sixty miles further east, was to be my last port of call on the Black Sea coast, and I was twenty-five miles on my way there by nine a.m., so thoroughly had the muezzin's call roused me. The mist was much thicker than the previous day, and so low that I felt I was riding through a grey shroud. In order that the thought should not prove prophetic, I kept an ear tuned for the sound of engines so that I could get off the road before any passing juggernaut mowed me down.

In a small ugly village that was no more than a line of dank concrete buildings on either side of the road, I stopped for supplies. I picked out a bunch of grapes and handed them over to be

129

weighed. Was that all? the shopkeeper asked, and without bothering to weigh them he put them into a thin plastic carrier bag, added a few plums for good measure and sent a small boy to wash them under a tap. My money was waved away; there was no charge, nor were my thanks acknowledged by more than the merest twitch of an eyebrow that said 'It is the custom'.

When the mist had lifted a little I found a perch for my last picnic beside the sea; a sea darker and more mysterious than I had yet seen it in all these long weeks. Behind me an equally dark mysterious land of forbidding mountains appeared and disappeared behind curtains of torn grey cloud. Conditions, if somewhat sombre, were wonderfully appropriate, for I was now in the ancient land of Colchis, where enchantment had once been an everyday affair; where the old could be boiled back to youth in a magic cauldron, and where the blind could regain their sight. It was here, and doubtless on just such a day, that Medea, the sorceress, had outwitted her father and helped Jason to steal the golden fleece. When a cormorant flapped slowly across the sea, it seemed so clearly a bird of portent, that I was surprised it did not turn its head and intone some doom-laden prophecy.

But nothing portentous occurred, only the strange dream-engendering coast itself going on and on with the curtain of mist parting and closing again, until, in the early afternoon, I came to Hopa and my final parting from the Black Sea.

A few miles ahead lay the Russian border, but

130

before that a road took off southward into the hills, towards Artvin, where I hoped to spend the night. I had no intention of even trying to bicycle the first part, for my map showed the road ascending in a series of convoluted spirals to a height of some five or six thousand feet in a very short distance. I could, doubtless, have struggled up somehow, but my experiences further west in the Pontic Alps had convinced me that discretion was the better part of valour. Once up in the dryer air of the plateau climbing would be less of a problem, but down here, fighting the high humidity as well as the ascent would have been too much. Accordingly I went in search of a bus, but discovered that only *dolmuses* (mini-vans) tackled the Artvin run, and although there was an endless conveyor belt of these transporting Russian traders and their suitcases, prices were sky-high. For Roberts and me (reckoning on us occupying five seats), a price was quoted that at normal rates would have taken us the length and breadth of the country. Feeling that I was being taken advantage of, but unwilling to argue with the unpleasant youths who ran the service, I pedalled off along the Artvin road.

I passed several groups of lorries that looked as though they would be making the ascent when their drivers had refreshed themselves with tea, or had finished their loading, and I stopped to see what the possibilities of getting a lift with them might be. The first enquiry was successful, and although I tried to agree upon a price for the ride first, my money was brushed aside. Roberts was swung up on top of the load

131

and roped down, and the panniers and I were bundled into the passenger seat.

We set off straight away, and almost immediately began grinding up terrible gradients with my ears popping at the sudden change of pressure, and my hands gripping the seat in sympathy with the aged engine's efforts to keep turning. I soon realized that I had chosen a truck in the very last stages of its useful life. Somehow it managed to breast the first of the ridges, and then the terrible gradients were downwards for a while. It now appeared that the brakes had failed, for we began to gather speed through the hairpin bends, while the driver struggled desperately to engage a lower gear, and failing to do so, tried instead to ram a very long screwdriver down through a hole in the floor. Whatever the screwdriver hit, it did the trick; with sparks jumping up through the floor and an appalling noise of tortured metal, we finally slowed to a halt. I was quite keen at this stage to continue the journey on Roberts, but the driver ignored me and got down his toolbox, and thinking he had enough to worry about, I didn't like to insist. No sooner had he got himself under the vehicle than a police car appeared, and a terrible haranguing began through a loud hailer. It was an awful racket, quite as distorted and as unbearably loud as the muezzin's calls from the mosques, and it went on and on, until the poor driver, who had crawled out from beneath the truck, began to look quite desperate. After this verbal softening up, a policeman got out, inspected the driver's documents, wrote down all the details in a book, and handing over a copy, he drove off. The driver got back under the truck, and soon another lorry driven by a friend of his rolled up, and together they managed to get things moving again.

Once more we crawled upwards with painful grinding slowness, on and on and on, the scenery quite ignored in the noise and anxiety of it all, until a loud report announced that one of the completely bald tyres had blown. This time the driver himself decided I would be better off on Roberts, and lifted it down. No sooner was I out of the cab, however, and beginning to attach the panniers, than he demanded 'Dollar, dollar'. He seemed suddenly very menacing, his hand out and a nasty expression curling his lip. I had a few dollars for emergencies, but was loath to use them unnecessarily. I offered him the Turkish money which I was prepared to pay, the equivalent of two fares to Artvin by *dolmus*. This he pushed aside, and again demanded 'Dollar, dollar'. At that moment the friend in the other lorry who had been following on behind, joined us, and sizing up the situation motioned me to get going while he fended off my driver. I still had the panniers to attach, however, and by the time I was astride Roberts, and ready to go, my rescuer had changed his mind, and was also demanding dollars. What would have happened had a convoy of trucks not appeared just then I've no idea. I seized the opportunity and rode smartly off, shooting up the remaining hairpins as if I was in my first youth and Roberts unladen, vowing as I went, that I would accept no more lifts in Turkey.

As so often happens with vows, however, I broke this one almost immediately. No sooner had I begun to enjoy the day again, and to note the change in scenery from shaggy rain forests to bare rocky heights, than I was at the top of the pass where the town of Artvin was supposed to be. Thinking I had just made the ultimate in ascents, I was in for a shock. Artvin was built on a series of terraces that hung another fifteen hundred feet or so above the road. After riding only a hundred feet of the vertical goat track that led up to the first terrace, I was only too happy to stop when an old man waved me down to drink tea with him. Afterwards, when he suggested that he organize a lift for me up to Artvin, I did not even go through the motions of needing to be persuaded. Somehow Roberts was jammed into the boot of a car, and with most of it hanging out on both sides we shot up into the clouds, to the square at the very top of the town where Artvin's finest hotel stood amid an impressive panorama of rugged hills.

It certainly was by far the best hotel in town, but my first thought on walking through the lobby was, 'If this is the best what can I expect further east?' Even after fierce bargaining had reduced the original asking price of the room by half, it was still wildly over-priced. But peeling wallpaper, threadbare stained carpets and lack of hot water not withstanding, it was a memorable spot, with storm clouds tearing past the verandah and peeling off the faces of the surrounding crags.

Artvin was very much a frontier town, muddy underfoot, and with things for sale not readily found in other parts of Turkey. It was the first town where I had seen whisky openly displayed. Together with other international drinks, it filled several windows — good Scottish brands too, and quite a bit cheaper than in the country of origin. I hoped this would be the case everywhere in Eastern Turkey, for I consider whisky to be a universal catholicon, especially good for chills and cyclists' aches and pains, and I should be needing to replenish my supply of it before the journey was over. But what made the town even more frontier-like was the number of Russians, proportionately far more even, than in Trebizond. The old man who had found me the lift had already pointed out to me the number of Russian cars, spitting copiously while he did so to express his view of the situation. Later, when I was invited to dinner with a party of British, Canadian and Turkish geologists who were staying in the hotel, and who had seen me coming in with Roberts, I heard more about the Russians, and the effect they were having on the country. This hotel, the geologists said, had been almost as good as the guidebook claimed, but now, with Russian women using it openly for soliciting (it was too cold and wet outside), standards had gone down a long way. Often in the middle of the night they would be awakened by the management trying to make them double up and release rooms for late-arriving Russians, or they would be asked to give up half their blankets to people being bedded down in the foyer. The biggest inconvenience they suffered though, was trying to get their cars out of the car-park in the mornings. The whole square, they said, was jam packed with traders by six-thirty, with stalls erected in any available space. To try to make the Russians move was a perilous business, as they tended to be belligerent towards such requests, and the Turkish police would not interfere. Like me, the geologists were mystified by the situation, for they could not see how the selection of tatty goods the Russians offered could possibly be worth the effort of transporting. And yet a flourishing black market with a dollar economy was in full swing — which explained the lorry drivers' eagerness for dollars.

Before I retired to bed, I washed my sweat-drenched clothing, slung my nylon line from a couple of handy projections and hung up the wet clothes with safety pins. They were just as wet when I awoke, which seemed only a short time later. It was still dark, but the Russian traders were already at work beneath my window, noisily setting up their stalls. The wet cold washing confirmed the feeling I'd had the previous night of having crossed a frontier. Gone was the comfortable easy world of the Black Sea coast, the tea gardens, the lush rain forests, and the shades of Byzantium. Here was quite another country, harsher, more physically challenging. I put on the dank garments and went in search of a good breakfast, so as to be ready for whatever the day might bring.

10

City of a Thousand and One Churches

IT was only after I had cautiously scraped down the precipitous fifteen hundred feet of the perilously distorted and gravel-strewn road from Artvin, and emerged into a flood of sunlight that I realized how the grey clouds, the general dankness, and the hordes of pugnacious Russians had been getting me down. Riding off south-eastwards beside the blue and white tumbled stream of the Çoruh Nehri the day seemed newly made and totally divorced from its beginnings in the crowded muddy square. The river flowed through the centre of a narrow green valley that curved between great cliffs of banded rock. At some stage in the earth's infancy the area had been subjected to cataclysmic forces that had bent and tilted the layered strata of the rock into giant wave formations and, as the sun rose above the canyon walls, all the exposed richly varied bands of colour burst into life.

Halfway along this magnificent ravine I was hailed from one of the wayside halts which are such a pleasant feature of Turkish roads. They are provided with running water, and sometimes, as here, there is a local man or two selling fruit or making tea for passing motorists. Usually, however, it is the travellers themselves who make tea, and it seemed to me that these watering spots had retained something of the atmosphere of ancient caravan halts. Travellers who stopped at them tended to be hospitable to one another, and to exchange news and views about the way ahead, as though they had been out of touch with civilization for some time. At this particular watering place I was invited to drink tea with four French-speaking Turkish philosophy students from Istanbul. They were on holiday and they told me that their friends considered them very adventurous to be travelling so far east. But what their friends would make of a woman being there on her own, and on a bicycle, they could not imagine. 'Was it not too hard?' 'No,' I told them (for the euphoria of the day had made me quite forget the excessive gradients, the humidity, the incident with the lorry drivers, and such things). Bicycling in Turkey was wonderful. They should try it too. It was the only way to really appreciate their lovely country. But they looked unconvinced, and I could see that they were thinking it would certainly be too hard for them, and I did not think I would make converts of them no matter how lyrical I waxed on the subject. I continued on my way the richer by three greengages, given me by the young fruit vendor who had ridden Roberts around the lay-by and pronounced it '*Çok gezel*'.

My next objective was Kars, a town some three or four days journey away. There seemed to be a choice of route, and I chose the minor one, turning north-eastward off the main valley, along the Berta Suyu which flowed through a narrower canyon, even more beautiful than the one I'd left. The sense of joy I'd felt ever since I'd come down from Artvin grew to the pitch where I had to break into song — thankful as I always am on such occasions that there was no companion to be disturbed by my off-key efforts. There was no cause for such complete happiness, other than the loveliness of the surroundings — the bare hills, the sun, the sound of running water and the absence of cars and also, perhaps, the more rarefied air at this altitude, which suited me much better than the humid coast. Very soon the road began to rise, and I needed to save my breath for the cycling.

All morning I climbed steadily, feeling fit and strong, and enjoying it all immensely, in spite of the growing heat. Nine and ten thousand foot peaks loomed up on every side, and ice-blue water ran down from them in deep boulder-filled gulleys to join the brown, silt-rich Berta Suyu. The river had cut a deep narrow bed for itself, and the road mostly ran well above it, or I would have been tempted to stop and to cool off in the swift-flowing water. There were tracks leading off the road to villages high in the hills, and processions with laden donkeys, small children perched on top, wound their way down them; men and women in long bright clothes, walking with the free swinging stride of mountain people.

Small farms on the far side of the chasm were linked to the road by rough home-made rope bridges. These smallholdings, thickly ringed with trees, made densely green oases on the dry ochre hillsides. There was certainly no shortage of water in this part of Turkey, and where there were peasants prepared to irrigate the land, it seems that good harvests could be guaranteed. Grapes grew in profusion and whenever I stopped, a child would be sent running across one of the swaying rope bridges to offer me a bunch. This made for difficulties since far more grapes were pressed upon me than I could possibly eat, and never could I persuade anyone to accept even a little money in exchange. I had to compromise with my conscience about waste, and accept the gift in the spirit in which it was offered, disposing of the excess later.

Unfortunately I didn't jettison the bunch in which a wasp had gone to sleep. It had been given to me ready-washed; the method for this in Turkey being to put the fruit in a plastic bag, and then hold the bag under running water for several minutes — a procedure no wasp is going to take kindly to. Several hours later when the poor creature was probably nearing suffocation in the hot interior of the pannier, I casually reached into the bag and was at once transfixed by a searing agony in the tip of my middle finger. So intense was the pain that I had to dance about for several minutes squeezing my wrist. When I could bring myself to look, the finger had already swollen, and I realized at once what must have happened and was ready to wreak vengeance. But when I opened up the bag and saw the blackened half-drowned little wasp that crawled out, I really couldn't help but feel sorry for it, and shook it on to a bush to dry in the sun. The finger remained very swollen and stiff for several days, and I kept thinking there must be a moral in the incident somewhere, but never quite succeeded in finding it.

By noon the heat was intense, and I was high on an exposed hillside with the river far below. There were few farms now, and no car had passed for a long while. I crawled under the partial shade of some thorny bushes to brew tea, and needing to sleep, I put on long trousers and socks in an attempt to keep the voracious ants at bay, as well as to protect my skin from the desiccating sun. It was to be the last occasion that I felt safe enough in Turkey to fall asleep in the open.

A couple of miles before Savsat, where I planned to spend the night, I came to an impressive medieval citadel, totally unexpected and not marked on my map. Probably it had been built by Armenians, since I was now within that unfortunate country's ancient boundaries. It might equally well have been Byzantine, or Georgian even, for the Georgians had also been important in this area for a brief period in the twelfth century, during the reign of their formidable Queen Tamara, and their architecture owed much to Armenian influence. But whoever was originally responsible for the building, it would have changed hands many, many times in this most fought-over corridor of changing fortunes. It had been kept in good repair until very recently, and a very large red star and sickle was painted on the walls so that whatever its origins, no one now should mistake it for being anything other than Turkish.

Beyond this fortress, the gradient steepened dramatically, and I was only able to ride the last bit up to Savsat because it was hidden behind the side of the mountain and so, like a blinkered horse, I could not see the full extent of what I had to contend with. When I was almost up, dripping copiously with the effort, my clothes and hair soaked, a car overtook me and stopped, and when the driver got out I saw that it was Mark, one of the geologists I had met in Artvin. This turned out to be a fortunate as well as a pleasant meeting, since Savsat was no more than a mountain village with little in the way of accommodation. The one hotel was full, so Mark kindly doubled up with his Turkish assistant and let me have his room. I was to repay this generosity by cycling off over the mountains the following morning with the key to his locked room still in my pocket.

The area I was travelling through, I learnt over supper, was rich in all sorts of useful minerals, and the Turkish government was currently letting off little parcels of it to various foreign companies. Exploitation of these rights, however, was complicated by the Turkish obsession about people other than their own military possessing large-scale maps of Turkish territory. Every geologist had to have them of course, but in theory this meant they were all guilty of a grave offence, punishable by a term of imprisonment. A study of Mark's map brought to light some interesting facts about my route, the main one being that the road ended at Savsat, and the next thirty-five miles (including a soaring six-thousand-foot pass) would be on a dirt track.

Several bottles of good cold beer helped to brighten the evening meal. There was no choice of what to eat, only chunks of tough unidentifiable meat, cold rice and the ubiquitous salad of tomatoes and cucumber that I had eaten every day (sometimes twice a day) since leaving Istanbul. It did seem extraordinary that in a country that could grow such a wide variety of fruit and vegetables, people hadn't considered a little more variety in their salads.

We had eaten our meal on a terrace that overlooked the customary rubbish heap, but as we sat on over our beers, both of us happy to be speaking fluently in our own language for a change, night descended in a blanket of stars, undimmed by the usual light pollution, and it seemed suddenly a very good place to be. Mark said that when he had first arrived in Savsat, his hotel room had to be fumigated and his bedding burnt to get rid of the bugs. No Turkish woman would wash his clothes, because men's shirts and trousers were considered to be items too personal, conveying forbidden sexual overtones. Conditions in general were so primitive that Artvin had seemed a veritable fleshpot in comparison. Even so he was content to remain in the village for the three months his report would take to compile, because in spite of the numerous irritations, there was something about the place and the area that he loved. Having spent the night in his hot airless little room overhanging the noisy village street, and tried to wash in the communal wash basins outside the noisome lavatories on the landing, I knew that whatever the attraction was it had nothing to do with creature comforts.

Mist was peeling off the mountain sides, and smoke was rising from chalet chimneys as I set off next morning on the dirt track to Ardahan. Ahead of me was a climb the equivalent of the highest mountain in Britain. There was no question of riding up; the surface was both too soft and stony, and the gradients too steep for a laden cycle. Remembering how I'd strained myself in the Pontic Alps, I was careful to husband my energy, and to go slowly, stopping often. So typically alpine was the countryside that I could almost have imagined myself in Switzerland a hundred years ago. Lush mountain meadows alternated with thick stands of pine trees. Mountain chalets with the top wooden storey overhanging a lower one built of stone, neat woodpiles alongside, all added to the illusion. The flowers were quite different however; instead of gentians, the roadside was edged with carnations, white hollyhocks and great banks of blue everlastings, and these continued to grow right up to the summit mists. I saw only the occasional old man dressed in close-fitting leggings and sheepskin coat and cap, and assumed that everyone else was indoors, or in the woods, or tending their flock.

After several hours, when I was about halfway up, a very large saloon car stopped. By that time I needed no second invitation to put Roberts in the back of it. Almost immediately I wished I hadn't, for the short chubby little driver, who could barely see over the steering wheel, and who had exchanged not a single word as yet, seemed anything but safe on such a road. When he was not picking his nose, he was playing rhythms on his thighs with both hands, nonchalantly returning one to the steering wheel just in time to swing the car around the next series of linked hairpin bends. To make matters worse we were in thick mist for the last few miles, but that made not a jot of difference to his speed or his insouciance: he just assumed nothing would be coming down the other way. There were in fact two summits, and I was brought over the second one, before the car stopped and the driver lifted out Roberts. He turned the car around immediately and disappeared the way he had come, so clearly, wherever he was headed when he stopped to pick me up, he had gone out of his way to bring me that far — yet one further example of the Turkish custom of disinterested kindness towards strangers.

The pass marked the entry to quite another country. A high plateau of low rolling grassy hills, grazed by large herds of sheep and cattle stretched on into the far distance under huge skies full of wind clouds. It was not nearly so pretty as the land I had just left, but had a wonderful feeling of spaciousness. There were some semi-troglodyte stone dwellings near the summit, the homes of Kurds, and exactly like the ones Xenophon had described in 400 BC, with parts of them buried in the hillside for protection from the winds and snows of winter. They appeared to be occupied though there was not a soul about.

It was at this point that I realized that I still had the key to Mark's room in my pocket, and as soon as I got down to the valley floor, and on to something that was more or less a surfaced road, I began to flag down any transport that passed in an effort to find one that was returning to Savsat. It was not an easy problem to explain in a language of which one has only a few words; waving a key at people can very easily be misconstrued. No one was going back over the pass in any case so I had to wait until I came to Ardahan, and had found the little shack which was the centre of operations for the daily *dolmus* run to Savsat. The driver of the battered wreck that made the perilous journey promised to return the errant key, and several months later I received a postcard informing me that the commission had been successfully carried out.

Ardahan was a town with three distinct parts. The 'modern' town built on a low hill was of no particular architectural style or interest, just a few acres of rusting tin roofs spread along two roads which crossed another and shortly afterwards petered out into the huge plains. The medieval walled town and fortress that guarded the crossing of the Kura Çayi was the only well-maintained part of Ardahan, and this was home to the Turkish army, and

146

not open to visitors. Across the river, on flat meadows watered by the many arms of the Kura Çayi, was another, separate town of black stone hovels and tents, all dotted about anyhow, with thousands of very muddy geese waddling about among them, together with horses, sheep, goats and dogs. It was a Kurdish semi-nomadic settlement on an enormous scale, and extremely squalid looking because of the ground being all churned up into thick black glutinous mud.

I stayed the night in Ardahan because it was another sixty miles to Kars, and already mid-afternoon. There was a place calling itself a 'tourist hotel' and it seemed I could have the choice of any of fifty rooms there for the equivalent of about £1.50, though I wouldn't necessarily call that a bargain. The large three-storey building was slipping fast towards its final stages of disintegration: windows gone in most rooms, and even in the better ones, like mine, the frames had shrunk so far from the brickwork that they wouldn't hang there much longer. The few male guests had all taken interior rooms with no windows at all, except on to the corridor. Just the idea of sleeping in one of these cupboards had my incipient claustrophobia shuddering: I'd choose a howling gale in preference any day. The worst aspect of the hotel for me was the washing arrangement, one tiny cracked washbasin outside the hole-in-the-floor loo at the end of a long corridor. The male guests were clearly not used to having females around, and were completely

147

uninhibited about washing all over at this sink, as required of them by their religion. The Savsat dinner had given me a bad case of Turkey trots, but every hundred yard dash from my room to the loo had to be checked at the final corner to make sure that some man had not reached a delicate stage in his ablutions.

That evening the skies over the vast daunting plain thundered into elemental splendour as huge cloud towers built up and then emptied in torrential rain and electrical discharges. The sun set balefully red through rents in a jagged grey curtain. With the mercifully distant muezzin's call came a muted chorus of baying hounds from the tented plains beyond the town. Sheets of water poured off the tin roof of the hotel and off all the other roofs, unchecked by anything like guttering or drainpipes. In minutes the town was awash, and I was able to rinse out my cooking things by holding them out of the window under the cascade that fell like a curtain. The sense of being within solid dependable walls disappeared. Nature seemed absolutely transcendent.

Between dashes to the loo, while I waited for the medicine I'd taken to begin to work, I read Walt Whitman's poem 'Passage to India', which I'd tucked into the cover of my T. S. Eliot and forgotten about until now. It had come to light just when I needed it, full of the sort of timeless imagery that matched the mood of these vast archaic plains.

Sailing these seas or on the hills,
or waking in the night,
Thoughts, silent thoughts of Time and
   Space and Death,
like waters flowing.
Bear me indeed as through the regions
   infinite . . .

The skies had cleared by the time I rode away from the ugly little town the next morning, along the road to Kars. I was still overawed by the scale of the land, and the relentless wind-filled skies. It was an implacable landscape where there seemed no place to hide, where distances daunted the imagination. Slowly I climbed again to the six-thousand-foot mark, passing infrequent clusters of the half-buried Kurdish houses surrounded by peat stacks, geese, dark fluffy sheep, herds of small horses and the numerous haystacks for feeding all these animals. Near to such settlements I would see small ragged boys repairing their scattered traffic traps. These were two parallel rows of quite large rocks set a few inches apart, so that nothing but a bicycle could get through without stopping and removing some of them. I did not witness an actual ambush, but one small boy stood poised with a stone in either hand waiting for me to come close. I just kept going and spoke sternly to him as I approached, and nothing happened. Soon afterwards a large shaggy dog, snarling ferociously and clearly looking for a mouthful of bicyclist gave me my first opportunity to try out the Dog Dazer. Fortunately it came to my hand without a fumble and one short squeeze on the button as I pointed the device in the dog's direction was enough. He stopped, looked around as if trying to work out what had happened, and then sloped off, tail between legs. After years of being bullied by dogs who take exception to bicycles it was an immensely satisfying moment.

In spite of the climbs and the wind, I had covered fifty miles by lunchtime, and sailed down into the village of Susuz hungry enough to eat anything on offer. Men and boys dressed in baggy trousers and collarless shirts and waistcoats gathered around, subjecting both cycle and rider to an intense silent scrutiny as though we were visitors from another planet. The usual hello, 'Merhaba', was ignored, so I tried 'Salaam Aleikum', the Islamic 'I greet you in the name of God', and this elicited a few grudging responses. At that point a youth was despatched from the restaurant to lift Roberts up the kerb and stand guard over it while I was taken inside, into the kitchen, where lids were lifted off various pots for me to choose what I wanted to eat. I had aubergines stewed with meat and tomatoes, and served with rice. It wasn't ideal for the state of my stomach, but it looked more appetizing than the unidentifiable meat stews. Usually wherever I travel, I take a lot of trouble about the water I drink, but I find I can eat most things with impunity. But in Eastern Turkey my stomach was to remain in a permanent state of revolt, and I can only think that many of the dishes had been standing around for some time, and reheated again and again.

An hour later I was riding into Kars, a drab nondescript town, but rich in history, for it lies on the traditional invasion route between the Transcaucasus and Anatolia. On a steep cliff above the town, still in use by the Turkish army, is the battered citadel built by the Armenian King, Abas I, around the year AD 927. In the thousand years it has stood there it had been besieged by Selçuks, Byzantines, Mongols, Georgians, Turks and Russians. During the Crimean War a British garrison under General Sir Fenwick Williams withstood an heroic siege within its walls for five months, until finally dislodged by the Russian Army. Subsequently Russia held Kars from 1877 until the Turks recaptured it again in 1920. When the Russians retreated all the remaining Armenian population went too, leaving forever the lands they had occupied for well over two thousand years.

The only other memorial in Kars of its Armenian past is the distinctive church of the Holy Apostles, which Abas I also built, and which, derelict though it now is, and sprouting grass from its finely carved roof, still looks bizarrely grand and beautiful, rising above the low Turkish hovels and vegetable gardens in a muddy unmade road. Most of the local people are not aware that it is an Armenian church because the Ottomans turned it into a mosque, and it is still referred to as the 'mosque of the drum' because of the central dome being raised on a high cylinder. Armenian domes were

151

nearly all built with this tall cylindrical lantern, conventionally rounded inside and quite like late Byzantine churches, the two styles borrowing extensively from one another, as well as from Selçuk architecture. Externally, however, the Armenian dome is conical, possibly the better to shed the thick snow of the mountains, and this feature makes Armenian churches unique and unmistakable.

The reason for planning my route through Kars was in order to have a base for visiting the nearby 'ghost town' of Ani, the site to which the royal Armenian capital was transferred in the second half of the tenth century. Ani was probably the grandest of all Armenia's medieval cities, so richly and lavishly endowed that it was known in its day as the City of a Thousand and One Churches. It was also unique in not sharing the fate of most of the other great cities of Anatolia. It had neither been absorbed and built over by successive conquering peoples, nor had its buildings been used as quarries — at least not until recently. Instead, in AD 1319 Ani suffered a catastrophic earthquake, and was abandoned and entirely forgotten, until nineteenth-century travellers stumbled upon its massive walls and towers and its strangely intact churches. Wilbraham, an English traveller, wandering the area in 1837, expresses something of the wonder that even today is felt on encountering the city: 'The shapeless mounds of Babylon are like a skeleton, but the deserted city of Ani resembles a corpse whose breath has fled but which still retains the semblance of life.'

What I saw was not as impressive as Wilbraham's account, for since 1920 there appears to have been a concerted effort on the part of the Turks to eliminate the memory of Armenia from this part of the world. Churches and monasteries that had stood substantially unchanged for five or six centuries, have become no more than heaps of stone in as many years, and the general suspicion is that they have been deliberately used as target practice by the Turkish army.

Even so, Ani is memorable, and would be still if nothing at all remained but the splendid site — a spacious three-cornered grassy plateau, protected on all sides but one by rivers flowing through deep ravines. Beyond the eastern gorge lies the small independent homeland of Armenia, all that now remains of their once vast territories. Only a very short time ago visits to this site, perched on the very edge of the former Soviet Union, were hedged about with restrictions, and all cameras had to be checked-in several miles before reaching Ani. As a reminder of those hostile suspicious decades, the white face of an armed Russian guard was clearly visible in a tall watch tower on the other side of Ani's defensive ravine; and of the bridge that had once spanned the gorge, only the fine abutments remained on either side with a jumble of broken masonry below.

The massive double wall that secures the exposed flank of Ani is studded with huge towers and is still almost complete, conveying a tremendous impression of strength and power.

In contrast, on the inner wall of the gate through which visitors enter the site, is a delicately carved lion as fresh as though the artist had only just finished it. A mosque and a half dozen or so fragments of churches among the many collapsed mounds are all that now remain within, like the stumps of a few decayed teeth in an empty mouth. And yet there is a quality about the reddish-brown stone that the Armenian builders chose, that make these wrecks of walls and gaping roofs look newly fractured rather than decayed. There isn't the soft worn-down look one expects of buildings a thousand years old. The scraps themselves are still sharp as well as beautiful — the line of a roof, the detail of a niche, even the still discernible fragments of coloured frescoes in the church dedicated to Gregory the Illuminator, that perches dramatically on the edge of a high cliff. One of these churches was the Church of the Redeemer, built to house a fragment of the True Cross for which the monarch, John-Sembat III, had sent his son on pilgrimage. It had been laid down that nightly devotions would continue in the church until the Second Coming of Christ.

There is little doubt that it must once have been a most wonderful city. And it was precisely because it had been so magnificent that contemplating the effect of all the destruction and the long dereliction became intensely mournful after a while. It was raining too, which made for an even more funereal atmosphere, so that it seemed only natural that lines from the

Book of Lamentations should come to mind: 'How lonely sits the city that was full of people!'; 'How like a widow she has become that was great among nations!'; 'I have forgotten what happiness is; so I say "Gone is my glory and my expectation from the Lord."'

And sitting there waiting for the *dolmus* to take me back to Kars I thought it was not really so odd to be thinking about Armenians in the context of laments for ancient Israel, for both peoples had shared a very similar history. Armenia, although a powerful nation, whose influence had extended from the Caucasus to the Mediterranean Sea had, like ancient Israel, always to steer a difficult path between greater world powers such as Assyria, Persia, Rome and Byzantium. She had been in AD 301, the first of all nations to adopt Christianity, and having at the same time devised an alphabet, became so assiduous in Biblical scholarship that when original Greek and Aramaic texts were lost, Armenian copies became primary sources. In art, music and architecture Armenians excelled. It was an Armenian, Trdat, who had rebuilt the dome of Haghia Sophia in Constantinople after the disastrous earthquake of AD 989.

Armenians had to be tough and resourceful to survive in an area of the world that was so often a battlefield for the opposing forces of East and West; and they had proved their ability to adapt through all the centuries of varied pressure and persecution. But in the last days of the declining and corrupt Ottoman Empire, they were subjected to a policy of

155

genocide that parallels what the Nazis were to do to the Jews only a decade or so later. Proportionately it was even more disastrous, for one in every three Armenians was massacred in the Turkish pogroms. It was an action deliberately planned, and carried out largely during the First World War when the Western allies were fully extended, and when little general interest could be aroused over the fate of a subject people.

The whole tottering edifice of the Ottoman Empire has disappeared since the frightful events of the Armenian massacres and the equally terrible forced deportations, in which more than a million Armenian women and children perished on the death marches, and on the barren burning plains of Mesopotamia.

Turkey is now a different country, under a completely different constitution. But even so, the massacres have never been admitted by the Turks. The evidence of hundreds of eye witnesses, from foreign consuls (particularly the American Ambassador, Morganthau), to numerous missionaries working in Eastern Turkey, is overwhelming. There were copious accounts written in all the Western newspapers of the day, as well as numerous books on the subject. The photographic evidence in the Armenian archives is also impossible to refute, and archaeologists are still frequently uncovering the mass graves of Armenian victims, all with bullet holes in the backs of the skulls. But the official Turkish policy is to deny that any of it happened. They even make counter claims that the Armenians were the villains of the piece, and a government department in Ankara sends foreign writers a pamphlet entitled *The Armenian Issue in Nine Questions and Answers* to put them straight on the matter. This is a sinister little document, for it is well produced and persuasively argued. It even has what looks like a most respectable bibliography of international publications to back its claims. Unless the reader is prepared to put in a fair amount of independent research, it could appear quite convincing.

I had also visited the museum at Kars, and had seen the section labelled 'The Genocide' which was devoted to explaining these events in terms of the Armenians being the perpetrators. But this propaganda had indeed seemed ludicrous, and the so-called evidence so transparent that only the most gullible could be taken in by it. It was only when I realized that Turkish school children are exposed to such ideas as part of their education, that it too seemed deeply sinister.

The whole subject made me sad for many reasons, not least because I liked the Turks, and felt that their government's need to dissimulate in this fashion demeaned them. After all, what country has ever possessed a completely blameless history? And unless the events of the past, painful though they might be, are faced up to, how can understanding begin, and lessons be learnt?

11

Approaching Mount Ararat

THE rain, which of late had been such a feature of life, fell abundantly upon Kars during the time I was there; and although the skies cleared just in time for me to leave, the town drains were either nonexistent or grossly defective, and, in consequence, the streets were several inches deep in liquid mud, with piles of decaying waterlogged rubbish slowly subsiding into the general ooze, making cycling both perilous and messy. It was always like that, a French tour leader told me. 'Kars' he said, 'is a terrible place, to which no one would come, but for Ani.' But I couldn't wholly agree with this view. Having wandered around the back streets the night before between showers, I had some indelible images to offset the mud and the more depressing aspects of Kars. There had been a stout woman in a long red dress and white headscarf and apron driving her cow slowly over an old grey hump-backed Ottoman bridge. The dark brooding citadel on its wall of rock towered above the scene, with the rugged mountains behind, and the enormous cutwaters of the bridge dividing the rushing brown flood of the river below. In the narrow alleyways huge amorphous piles of masonry, their purpose long lost in antiquity, lent an air of grandeur to the

158

jumble of low dwellings and tiny vegetable plots, where hanks of uncarded wool, newly dyed in greens, blues and reds, were hung to dry on the grey stone walls.

Near the bridge was an ancient, once grand hammam, to which two villainous-looking types beckoned me with a 'Psst, psst', and then escorted me through a succession of high-domed empty rooms, all a strange mixture of squalor and luxury. The fine stone walls were decaying and stained and oozed moisture, and the floors were engrained with ancient dirt; but there were marble basins filled with ice-blue water and marble slabs to lie upon. We came to a halt in a very hot room full of steam where one of the men began to mime a massage so graphically sensuous that I said a very firm and hasty '*Yok!*' before he could get carried away. He countered with a great show of offended innocence, but even so it wasn't easy to get out of the place. Whether it was my body or simply my custom they were after I wasn't sure, but they did at least make me feel welcome, which was in marked contrast to my hotel.

One night in the Hotel Yilmaz was more than enough. It was a reasonably comfortable hotel for these parts, but the service was terrible and, I thought, calculatedly and untypically rude. The Frenchman said the problem was that the whole purpose of life in Kars had been to watch the Russian border, and with this necessity so suddenly removed the inhabitants were completely disorientated. But I still thought it was more a case of misogyny and general male chauvinism. The manager clearly hated women, or else his religion wouldn't allow him to look at, or speak to one directly. He would fix his glance some way above and to the right of me, and address his remarks into space. The pampered boy he kept by his side would then repeat the gist of the exchange with an air of lofty condescension. It was intensely irritating or rather funny, depending upon my mood. But I couldn't think why the manager was in such a job, nor could I find his attitude consistent with the way he pored over the soft porn pages in his daily paper.

Once clear of the horrible mud of Kars, the great gassy plains closed around me like a sea, until I began to climb up out of them over the Pasli Pass. Just before the summit three aggressive-looking shepherd youths came tearing across the rough ground towards me, shouting and brandishing sticks, ferocious dogs slavering at their heels. I was going quite slowly at the time, my thoughts on the well-earned rest I would enjoy at the top. One startled look, however, and I was up out of the saddle and stamping on the pedals, and only just in time. A heavy cudgel came whistling past my ear, missing me by inches; had it hit me it would have felled me like the proverbial ox. I saw my jacket fall from the rear carrier as they gave chase, but I was not tempted to go back for it. It achieved the same effect as tossing a Circassian slave off the back of a speeding sledge as the wolves closed in, delaying pursuit long enough to make a getaway. Once I was over the summit they had no further chance.

The Pasli Pass marks the end of the North-Eastern Anatolian Plateau, and the beginning of quite a different weather zone. I was not to see another drop of rain for the rest of my journey, and wouldn't miss the sacrificed jacket, not that I realized this at the time. But in any case, I was so thankful to have escaped unscathed that a lost coat seemed small loss, and fortunately there had been nothing in the pockets.

I sped down through a landscape of rugged, eroded brown hills, quickly forgetting the shock of the attack in the pleasure of the descent. There were small green oases dotted about here and there. In some of them men were cutting grass with the same two-handed scythes that I remember being used in the Outer Hebrides. The slow turn and swing of the mens' bodies as they wield this implement is one of the most graceful and evocative movements in husbandry. Seeing it now gave me a sudden sharp pang of nostalgia for a gentler world. But it was only a momentary twinge, for everything else here was as different as could be. The smaller meadows were furnished with neat rows of beehives, hundreds of them, each with a little white tent at their centre. Eastern Anatolia has always been a famous area for bee keeping; the Ten Thousand feasted on honey on their way through the region. Reading the account of this in Xenophon, I wondered if 'the natives' had deliberately doctored the honey in order to poison the Greeks, or whether it had fermented somehow, because its effect upon them was little short of disastrous:

> . . . there were great numbers of beehives in these parts, and all the soldiers who ate the honey went off their heads and suffered vomiting and diarrhoea, and were unable to stand upright. Those who had only eaten a little behaved as though they were drunk, and those who had eaten a lot were like mad people. Some actually died . . .

I had been a trifle wary about Turkish honey in the light of this passage, but the marvellous fragrance of it permeating the dining room of the Yilmaz overcame my reluctance, and I tried some and found it as good as it smelt. After that I ate it as often as I could, and it never seemed to have any effect, either for good or ill, on my troubled stomach.

All the way down the two-and-a-half-thousand-foot descent beside a sparkling little river there were tiny green meadows, each with rows and rows of beehives and its little round white tent for the bee keeper. I did not think that such quantities of bees could find sufficient pollen in this area of bare brown rock, and imagined they flew vast distances over the great flower-strewn grassy plains I had traversed.

By the time I was down to the valley floor, the whereabouts of food for myself was the immediate concern. I had forgotten to stock up my emergency food supplies in Kars, and had passed no tea house or village in fifty

162

miles. With sustenance of any sort so very scarce, even the congealed, flyblown chickpeas in a meat sauce, which was all there was on offer in the sordid little eating hovel I came to seemed better than nothing. There was a slightly less depressed-looking place a half mile further on, doubtless the reason that I had been the sole diner in the first one — another of the ironies of travel. In this land of vast distances I had to seize the first opportunity to refuel: cyclists cannot run on air, and I had a further forty miles to pedal to Tuzluca, the nearest place where I would be likely to find a bed and further refreshment.

The ground gradually fell to the three thousand foot mark during the afternoon, and it grew appreciably hotter. The scenery was splendid all the way, for I was in the valley of the Aras, the ancient Araxes that runs in a canyon whose northern wall forms the edge of the plateau I had just left. My road had taken me in a huge loop to the west, and was now running back eastward again towards the Russian border. But although I was enchanted by the lonely splendour of the land, the increasing heat and a strong headwind more than balanced the benefit of the slight downhill run, and slowly but surely sapped my energy until I was almost past appreciating anything. Tea would have raised my enthusiasm considerably, but I didn't dare stop to brew some because of having to get to Tuzluca before nightfall. The incident with the shepherds had reminded me of the need to exercise due caution in this area.

By the time I began on the long upward incline

towards the town I was definitely struggling. Ninety miles is really much too far to ride a laden bicycle in one day, and I always try to limit the day's run to no more than sixty. But as camping alone in these parts was out, unless under someone's protection, I had little choice but to press on.

Walking up the final steep slope into the outskirts of Tuzluca, I began to be harassed by the local children. A fat boy on a bicycle began it. I think he just wanted a race to show off his prowess, but I was too far gone to oblige. Some of his cronies began to follow me, boys and girls shrieking with laughter and lobbing stones. One little girl kept creeping up and splashing me with the water she was carrying. As soon as the slope flattened out a little I got on again and outdistanced them. But then bigger and more intimidating boys threw larger stones with a bit more force and accuracy, and seeing a sign indicating there was a police station down a side turning, I followed it to seek protection.

Quite a number of policemen were sitting under a shady pergola, enjoying the late afternoon in their pretty garden. After showing my letters and the newspaper article I was offered a seat, and refreshment — a glass of tea and several litres of cold water from a hosepipe with which the garden was being watered — which worked wonders for my view of life. One of the policemen had learnt a little French at school, and as he found very few opportunities to use his skill, he was thrilled to practise it with me, he confided. Unlike the insular British, Turks

164

Princes Islands on the Sea of Marmara.

Mount Ararat.

All photographs were taken by the author.

The Sumela Monastery, Trebizond.

The Church of St Gregory the Illuminator in the ghost town of Ani.

The Mosque of Selim the Grim, Dogubayazit, with the remains of a Byzantine citadel beyond.

A courtyard in the Ishak Pasha Palace.

The Great Rock of Van capped with its citadel.
The ruins of the city of Van are to the right.

Church of the Holy Cross, Akhtamar Island.

Hosap Castle and the bridge over the Güzelsu.

A Kurdish nomad camp.

Flocks being watered on Nemrut Dagi.

Selçuk *türbe*
beside Lake Van.

Kurdish boys in traditional
dress in the courtyard of the
Great Mosque, Diyarbakir.

In the village of Hasan Keyf.

Remains of the Byzantine bridge over the Tigris. The ruins of the ancient city of Cepha are on the cliffs above.

Harran.

are always glad of the chance to air any few words they have acquired of another language, and suffer no inhibitions at all about any lack of grammar. They also have an innate curiosity about foreigners and any verbal exchange with one, no matter how slight, raises their status with their friends. Here, as usual, the store of words was quickly exhausted, and we were soon resorting to my Turkish dictionary and phrase book.

No interest at all had been shown in my complaints about the stone throwing. Had it not been such an obvious and calculated ignoring, I might have thought that they hadn't understood me. Instead, I was convinced that it was because they did not want to admit, even tacitly, that such a thing could happen to a traveller in their town; especially not to a writer featured in one of their own newspapers. Criticism of anything Turkish means a loss of face, which Turks seem to find particularly hard to bear, and which, perhaps, is the root cause of what makes them deny justice to the poor Armenians. When I left the police station, however, I was escorted to the town's lodging house by at least a dozen policemen, which not only preserved me from further pot shots, but also made quite a difference to my reception at the hotel. Although no more than a flea-pit, and right on the main street, with a constable to oversee the results, efforts were ostentatiously put in motion to bring a room up to scratch for me. I selected one at the rear for quietness, and this was swept out and the sheets were changed for others — no cleaner than those they replaced, but the thought was there. A low-wattage light bulb was found for the empty dangling socket, a washroom was unlocked and perfunctorily hosed out and the missing tap replaced so that I could take a welcome and much-needed shower, and finally, Roberts, complete with luggage, was hauled up the two flights of stairs and placed in my room. I attempted to tip the general factotum who had carried out all these tasks on my behalf, but he refused, telling me, with the aid of my phrase book, that it was an honour to serve a writer!

Washed, and dressed in my clean set of clothes, I rode off to explore Tuzluca on an unladen mettlesome Roberts which could have shown a clean pair of heels to any fat tormenting boy on a small-wheeled bike. But now the town was quite a different place. Perhaps it was enough to have been seen hobnobbing with the constabulary, or else word of my enhanced status had been passed around the juvenile Mafia, for I had no more trouble in Tuzluca. Instead, I was met only with smiles, offers of tea, and with gifts of fruit from quite delightful children in gardens and orchards at the back of the town. Beyond the orchards were low cliffs containing salt caves for which the town was noted, but they were already locked up for the night.

Nor was I eager to stay and view these caves the following morning, for this was the day I would reach Agri Dagi, Mount Ararat. Had the weather been less hazy, the mountain would have been in sight since the previous afternoon, together with Alagoz Dagi, another outlier of the majestic mountain wall that divides North-Eastern Anatolia from the Transcaucasus. The two great peaks, Ararat at around seventeen thousand feet, and Alagoz at fourteen thousand, are fully sixty miles apart, but so high do they tower above the surrounding landscape that both can be seen from afar as part of one vast panorama. But not in these hazy conditions. And now I was so close to it lesser peaks obscured the view. I set off early to make the ascent of the final mountain pass that separated me from Ararat, hoping to get the bulk of the climb over before the sun was high.

The further east I travelled the more decrepit were the aged worn-out trucks, and on this long steep climb they were experiencing great difficulties. Moving hardly faster than I, they took an age to pass, spewing out nauseous black clouds of exhaust fumes as they went. Even so, I was glad of their presence, for as I began to pass a series of small Kurdish villages, the lorries afforded some protection from the hordes of small children who seemed intent on waging a one-sided war on lone bicyclists. The villages were no more than collections of rough stone huts on either side of the road, but they were quite extensive, and on the steep ascent it took me a good while to get through some of them. Never before, not even on the roads of southern Egypt, had I met such implacably hostile children as these young Kurds. I came to dread the high-pitched shriek that announced I had been spotted, followed by rattling stones as two or three tough ragged boys came swooping across the hillside on a course to intercept me. To stop and attempt friendliness was useless, it only allowed time for more of them to gather. I tried smiles, greetings, sweets even, but they would simply snatch whatever I offered, and menace me for more. In any case, I didn't gain the impression that it was necessarily largesse they were after. It seemed rather that they were mirroring some deep-seated attitude of their elders. No adult tried to stop them attacking me, even in the centre of villages. In fairness I must say that there were no men about on this occasion, only women, and they turned their backs as their offspring hurled stones at me.

In one place where the road described a series of huge bends across the slope, a complete village was enclosed in one snake-like coil of it. I passed a pretty little girl, no more than five years old, at the lower end of this village. She hadn't been aware of my approach, but reacted immediately. Turning on her heel, she ran with enviable speed straight up between the stone huts, snatching a stone as she went, and this she flung at me with all her puny might as I came round the upper bend. It had nothing to do with me personally, I told myself as the sadness of the situation struck me. I felt I had to find out the cause of all this unchildlike hostility; but for the moment the priority was survival.

Concentrating as I was on avoidance tactics, Ararat caught me by surprise, the upper slopes appearing suddenly as I rounded a rocky outcrop. It seemed close enough to touch, and yet insubstantial and unreal in the hazy

168

light. It towered up into the clouds, a great silvery wall, more dream than solid mountain. No sooner had I stopped to contemplate this wonder than I was hailed by a lorry driver who a little further down the road had spent ten long minutes getting clear of me while I had gasped and panted for air in his choking wake. He had stopped at the first possible place and waited in order to offer me a lift. He was most surprised when I refused. The very last thing I wanted now that Noah's mountain, the catalyst for this long journey, was finally in view, was to be hurried past, or disturbed in my first acquaintance with it. Nonetheless, I appreciated his offer; a little Turkish kindness coming after the sticks and stones of the Kurds warmed my heart, and his offer to refill my water bottles was a godsend. With the temperature well up in the eighties, and the gradients one in six all the way, I found I needed to stop and drink after every few hundred feet of ascent, children permitting.

Once over the summit of the pass, the road swept down and away to the right and Ararat stood revealed in its entirety, from base to summit snows, an enormous mass in the centre of surrounding flat plains. It is higher than Mont Blanc, but gazing at Ararat for the first time I didn't feel that shiver down the spine that I get from the classic Alpine peaks or from the Himalayas. There was no sense of menace about Ararat: no avalanche slopes poised to sweep away the unwary, no soaring ridges or sheer rock faces to challenge and inspire that frisson of fear that is a part of the love affair with great mountains. Ararat might well have its share of dangers, but it appeared entirely serene and approachable. Once I had got used to the majestic bulk of it, I did not even find it particularly beautiful. In the flat unclear light, it looked a rather shapeless mass, like a vast steamed pudding that had not been turned out cleanly from its basin, and had then been topped with a dollop of white sauce.

Eventually, vast as Ararat was, I had ridden past its western flank, and could no longer see it except in the cycle mirror, where, more remote and diminished in size, it took on a more ethereal aspect. In the fast fading light I headed on up a long straight incline towards Dogubayazit, a town on the historic Silk Road, and the jumping off point for those bent on climbing Noah's mountain and searching for the Ark.

12

On Noah's Mountain

I COULD see immediately that I was going to enjoy Dogubayazit. It seethed with the sort of excitement that felt right for a town straddling one of the most ancient trade routes in the world. Dogubayazit gives no hint of its long pedigree, but rather appears to have been thrown up overnight, like some dry dusty Wild West town. It is an image totally in keeping with its present-day role of catering for the vast crowds of Iranians who cross the border, just twenty-two miles further east, in search of the consumer goods unavailable in their own country. Every building is a shop, a restaurant or an hotel, and the streets are one extended market place full of women in *chadars*, swooping from stall to stall like flocks of black crows, the air about them clamourous with high-pitched bargaining. Western clothing, Asian clothing, shampoo in gallon bottles, washing machines and toasters, videos and cameras; everything imaginable was on sale, including alcohol!

In spite of Turkey being nominally secular, a double standard towards the demon drink had dogged me wherever I had travelled so far. Getting any sort of alcohol, even Turkish-brewed beer, was difficult, except in the better restaurants and the costlier hotels, where raki especially could flow like water. Only by scouring back streets could an occasional off-licence be found, again stocked mainly with the fiery aniseed-tasting raki. Artvin with its one window actually displaying foreign drink had been a rare exception. But here in Dogubayazit there were stores stocked with nothing but cans and bottles bearing familiar Western brand names, and the Iranians were taking crate loads back to a country where alcohol was expressly banned under strict Koranic law.

Dogubayazit even possessed that almost forgotten luxury, a bar which served cold beer, the first I had seen since Istanbul. I was escorted to one of them by a young man named Hüseyin, who worked in the travel shop where I had gone to enquire about climbing Ararat. The bar was a fly-blown crumbling little room tucked away at the top of some death-defying stairs, and empty of customers but for us. The way the two boys in charge rested their elbows on the rough counter, the easier to stare at us and follow our conversation, made me suppose that women seldom graced the premises, and I was rather sorry that we were not discussing something more titillating than how to obtain official permission to climb Noah's mountain.

Somewhat frayed by the stone-throwing and the indifferent lodgings of the past few days I had been determined to find what comfort I could in Dogubayazit. Accordingly, as soon as I arrived I had made my way to the best hotel in town, the Isfahan, to negotiate for a room. Everyone in the hotel, from manager to the most junior scullion, had joined in the bargaining, giving me a most favourable picture of the egalitarian values of Kurds. I didn't have to haggle very hard. The combination of Roberts and my newspaper cutting quite charmed the management, and for a modest sum I was given a clean comfortable room with a balcony from which I could contemplate the southern and most famous face of Ararat, together with its far more shapely neighbour, Little Ararat. Roberts was installed near the desk in the large lobby where the television stood, and where it could duly be admired by the other guests, while being protected by the staff.

That the whole town was Kurdish was the first thing I had discovered. The second was that all the Iranian shoppers were also Kurdish. I was having extreme difficulties distinguishing Kurds from Turks. To me Turkish Kurds looked no different from other Turks, though they appeared quite different to these Iranian Kurds. It was all most confusing. 'How can one tell?' I was to ask despairingly from that time onwards. The answer was that I probably couldn't. While Kurdish villagers tended to be distinctive, chiefly because of their poverty, Kurds dressed in Western fashion and living in towns looked much like anyone else in Turkey. Even Turks didn't necessarily know at a glance. For centuries Turkey had insisted that Kurds had no separate identity, that they were 'Mountain Turks' and as long as Kurds didn't want to speak their own language, practise their own culture, or exercise any degree of autonomy,

Turkey would be more than happy to continue so regarding them.

The very idea of a separate identity for the Kurds is anathema to Turkey, and as recently as 1979 a Turkish ex-minister was sentenced to two years in prison for admitting in a speech that there were both Kurds and Turks inhabiting Turkey. Unlike the other minority groups — the Christian Greeks, Georgians and Armenians — Kurds are Muslims, therefore, in Turkish reckoning, there should be no problem of assimilation, for in spite of Turkey's secular status, it is also without doubt one hundred per cent Muslim. To the Turkish mind assimilation has no unfortunate connotations. Disfiguring half the hillsides in Eastern Turkey, in bold white letters several feet high, is carved a saying of Atatürk, the gist of which is, 'How glorious to be able to say I am a Turk', and I do not doubt that most Turks are mystified that anyone who had the chance would not gladly be included among their number. The Kurds, of course, have entirely different thoughts on this subject.

The borders of Kurdistan always tended to be fluid, but in the sixteenth century Kurds were moved into former Armenian homelands in one of those wholesale shifts of populations that have been a frequent occurence in this part of the world since ancient times. The idea of this particular move was that a Muslim race would provide a more reliable buffer to the Christian lands beyond the Caucasus. Certainly when the Armenians were being massacred, both in the 1890s and again in 1915, the Kurds co-operated willingly with the Turks, and urged on by their *imams*, joined in the killing with enthusiasm, gaining religious merit from the despatching of infidels.

Being spread over four countries — Iran, Iraq, the former Soviet Union and Turkey — has not helped Kurdish autonomy, even their language has developed such wide variations that often Kurds from one country cannot communicate with Kurds from another without employing a separate tongue altogether. Because the mountainous borders, particularly those between Iran and Turkey, were not finally fixed until 1913, the Kurds were able to some extent to play one country off against another. But attempts by the Ottomans to consolidate their control over the independent-minded Kurds caused major uprisings from the mid-nineteenth century onwards, and after the caliphate was abolished in 1924, it was the turn of the Kurds to be 'pacified'. It is generally reckoned that a quarter of a million of them were killed and another million or more deported to other parts of Turkey. At the same time all Kurdish associations, publications and schools were closed. None of this lessened Kurdish resistance to the 'turkizing' process, however, and the present situation is as volatile as it has ever been, possibly more so. The Turkish government's heavy-handed response to the upsurge of unrest throughout the past decade has been the imposition of curfews, the prohibition of the use of Kurdish language, further forcible resettlement and curtailment of freedom of movement, all of which has resulted in increased support for the guerilla activities of the PKK. Had Xenophon still been around, he could have predicted just such an outcome, for in the whole of their long march from Persia, the Ten Thousand found no territory where 'the natives' were as implacably hostile as in Kurdistan.

Had I not read up on the Kurdish situation before leaving Britain, it would not have mattered. Within an hour I would have been filled in on all these salient facts; Dogubayazit was full of people eager to educate me, and to enlist my support for their cause. I had absolutely no need of the letter in Kurdish which I carried explaining that I was writing a book about my travels, and was eager to hear people's views. I was going to hear them anyway, whether I wanted to or not. Like most minority groups suffering under a repressive regime, people were eager to buttonhole any Westerner in order to spell out their grievances, though nowhere have I found a people quite as eager to do this as the Kurds. In cafés, in the hotel lobby, across shop counters, often with no preamble at all I was told their stories. Some were terrible, like the accounts of imprisonment in the notorious Diyarbakir prison, where a regimen of a semi-starvation, torture and frequent beatings by the military guards ensured less than a fifty per cent chance of survival. I talked to a Kurd who had survived five years in this prison, one of the gentlest and most impressive of men. He had been a writer, which was why he was imprisoned, and the only reason he was released was because a British group from Amnesty International investigated his case, and actually came to visit Diyarbakir Prison. He was freed on condition that he never wrote again, and he claimed that he was now under constant surveillance, and was running a risk even in talking to me.

But what most Kurds wanted to tell me about was the daily accumulation of smaller wrongs, the actions that, like water dripping on a stone, slowly but surely erode cultural identity — the arrests in the streets for speaking Kurdish; arbitrary house searches and the confiscation of anything remotely subversive, such as music tapes by a popular Kurdish singer; coming at the bottom of the pecking order for jobs; having inferior schools or none; living without hope of any change for the better.

Against this background I could begin to understand the hostility I had met with riding through Kurdish villages. Those around Dogubayazit were inhabited by people who had been forcibly resettled, many of them formerly nomadic. None of their children attend school, partly because their parents do not want them to be taught in Turkish, but also because the PKK is against it. The same embargo does not apply to Kurds living in towns; they can even learn English, which enables them to tell travellers their grievances. The PKK guerilla army living in hiding in the hills needs to rely on the complete support and loyalty of all the Kurdish villagers for food supplies and general liaison, and believes that Turkish village schools would be used for indoctrination of the young. Denied any sort of education, any hope for the future, it is a bleak outlook for these children and young people, and their feelings of frustration and hopelessness must be acute. As I had sensed at the time, it was not really in the hope of handouts, or even because they thought I was Turkish, that the children had attacked me. It was because I represented the privileges and the freedoms that were denied to them. The enemy was anyone and everyone who was not Kurdish, who was not sharing their hardships. They threw sticks and stones because it was the one way they could give vent to their anger, all of which was rather hard luck on a slow-moving traveller.

The eight Germans kidnapped on Nemrut Dagi by the PKK were still being held by them at this time, and the question of the safety of any tourist in Eastern Turkey loomed large. Every Kurd I talked to about the incident thought abducting Westerners was a perfectly justifiable way of drawing attention to the Kurdish problem, and nothing I said about it being counter-productive changed this attitude. They justified their views by saying that whereas tourists were welcome to come to Kurdish lands, they should first seek permission from the Kurds themselves. I pointed out that there were as yet no Kurdish embassies or consulates where such visas could be issued. To which they replied, 'Quite so, that is the whole point.'

The Kurds are a prolific race. Older men often

178

have the four wives allowed them by the Koran, so families can be enormous. They had long ago grown out of the area marked in my historical atlas as Kurdistan, and were numerically the greater proportion of much of Eastern Turkey. As a result they were demanding autonomy over a region of vast proportions, taking in about a third of the land mass of present-day Turkey. This meant I would be travelling in what Kurds reckoned to be Kurdistan for the remainder of my journey, and every town would have a predominately Kurdish population. I could only hope that in the event of my being kidnapped, the two-line letter I had been given by the Kurdish Cultural Office in London would be reckoned as good as an official visa. Actually this letter did have an affect upon those I showed it to, because with the Kurdish language proscribed, Kurds considered I was risking arrest by carrying it, and thought I was both very brave and had embraced their cause.

But the truth was that the more I heard, the less I was on anyone's side, and embraced no cause other than that elusive concept, justice. While being unequivocally against oppression in any form, whether it be cultural genocide or the kidnapping of tourists, the Kurdish problem seemed to me as intractable as that of Northern Ireland. If my sympathy was more with the Kurds, it was because it was impossible not to pity them in their present intolerable situation. But as to who should control what parts of Turkey, I could not begin to form an opinion.

Most of the guests in my hotel were Iranian Kurds and quite different to the Turkish ones. All the women were muffled up to the eyes in voluminous black *chadars,* and when the veils of the older women were loosened sufficiently for them to eat, I could see that their lower lips and chins were covered with blue tattooing. Men and boys wore ordinary Western clothing and sported a tough, no-nonsense look, especially the little boys with their shaven or close-cropped heads. In great contrast, little girls were mostly got up like Christmas tree fairies in white frilly party dresses, huge ribbons in their hair and lots of flashy jewellery round their necks and wrists. I wondered if this was some sort of compensation for them having to go into purdah and be dressed like black crows the moment they became adolescent. The fathers doted on their daughters in their pretty finery and were constantly cuddling and petting them, much to the annoyance of the poor over-burdened and unadorned mothers. In consequence little girls appeared to receive far more of the liberally-dispensed slaps and pinches than the boys. Each family group seemed to have at least five very young children, with no more than the bare nine months dividing them, and discipline tended to be a very arbitrary and physical affair.

All day, and all evening until late, these families shopped, resting only for protracted meals in crowded restaurants. I was having lunch in an empty dining room one day when it filled up within seconds, all one hundred odd seats, with a horde of little Iranian Kurds accompanied by their elders. From that moment the noise level was maintained at a constant forte, with wails, shrieks and shouts for the waiters' attention. The attitude of the owner and the waiters to their customers was a curious mixture of pride and annoyance. 'Our Iranian Kurds,' they announced to me with pride. Presumably they also said 'Our English customer' to the Kurds, because everyone smiled and nodded in my direction. Then the waiters set about smacking the heads of the smaller Kurds who were running riot round the tables, and forcibly settling bottoms on chairs, while mothers rushed around rearranging them again into their correct family groups. Even the arrival of food didn't lessen the noise; if something wasn't right or an order was slow in coming, adult or child set up a bellowing until the matter was dealt with or, in the case of a child, until it was cuffed into silence or louder wails. On the whole, fascinating though these gatherings were, I found it easier to eat at different times.

At around 10 p.m. the weary shoppers drifted back to the hotel, the smallest children draped like damp rags across their parents' shoulders, and with three or four other small souls whining and fractious at their heels. But instead of making for their rooms and the blessed relief of bed, the parents collapsed in front of the television in the lobby, propping up the infants in chairs so that they could gaze too. With the children in a state of total rebellion, and keeling over with exhaustion where they sat, slaps flew thicker than ever and sobs and wails drowned out all other noise. Only at midnight when the shops' metal shutters finally thundered down upon the day's trade did the horde come tramping and trumpeting up the stairs.

My balcony at the Isfahan provided a welcome haven to which I could sometimes escape both from contentious issues and fractious children, and contemplate the serene bulk of Ararat, with a restorative sun-downer to hand. Replenishing my stock of whisky had also provided light relief, for I did this before I had sufficiently observed the local customs. No one, and certainly no woman, ever entered a liquor store in Dogubayazit. The method, I discovered later, was to drive up and hover at the kerb with the engine running and the car's blinds down. A youth would dash out from the shop to take the order, all very *sotto voce*, and afterwards the driver would cruise around the block until, at a discrete signal, he pulled in briefly to have anonymous-looking boxes hastily thrust into the boot. Since such goods are contraband in Iran, there could conceivably have been Iranian agents lurking to note the details of the smugglers. But as I had no such worries, and do not suffer complicated heart searchings about drinking alcohol, I had thought nothing of strolling openly into a shop, and asking what brands of whisky were stocked. The owner was so shocked at my boldness, I thought at first he was having a mild heart attack. When he recovered sufficiently to talk, he denied all knowledge of such a commodity, and when, puzzled, I pointed to the bottles in the windows, he showed me that they were in fact all dummies. I was not totally convinced by this, however, so in order to get rid of me he sent his youth off at the run to some hidden warehouse, and when he returned I was handed a tightly wrapped bottle in a plastic bag. The look on the shopkeeper's face convinced me that I had better just pay what he asked, and discover what I had bought later. It turned out to be a well-known brand of whisky, certainly not my favourite, but perfectly acceptable, and cheaper than it would have been in England.

When I tired of the view of Ararat from my balcony, I could turn in the other direction to where bare ochre cliffs provide the dramatic jagged backdrop to the town. These were the defensive bulwarks for the fertile plains around Ararat, and it was here in the many traces of fortresses, the earliest of which dates back to Urartian times, around 1000 BC, that Dogubayazit's long history was written. Through the centuries Byzantines, Selçuks and others had added to them. The Ottoman sultan, Selim the Grim, had garrisoned his troops here when fighting the Persians, and possibly it was to celebrate his decisive victory at the battle of Çaldiran in 1514 that he built the fine little mosque that still stands intact near the ruined citadel. The latest and the most famous of these strongholds, the eighteenth-century fortified palace of Ishak Pasha, was one of the chief delights of Dogubayazit, so magnificent in its day that it was said to rival the Topkapi Palace of the Sultan in Istanbul.

It is an exceptionally steep climb to the Ishak Pasha Palace, and I realized how fit I had become when I managed to ride the whole way on an unladen Roberts. I had taken it only in order to freewheel back down the three miles afterwards, but having been sneered at by an army officer who volunteered the information that an ascent by bicycle was impossible, I felt obliged to prove him wrong. I had started off early in the morning before the fierce heat fastened its grip on the day, and had met the Turkish army out for its morning run. Every town in these border areas had a large army barracks. All the soldiers, for obvious reasons, were Turkish; Kurdish conscripts who hadn't fled to the hills to join the PKK were sent to serve in Western Turkey. The hundreds of young national service men, identically shaven-headed and bared to the waist, were wearing heavy army boots and long thick trousers, and having just run a good way up the cliff were drenched in sweat. They were running down again in tight formation when they passed me, bearing flags and banners, and chanting slogans as they came. The thunder of several hundred pairs of heavy boots on the tarmac, the loud chanting, and the overpowering smell of all those massed bodies was extraordinarily intimidating. Remembering Xenophon's description of the Ten Thousand singing the battle paean as they charged uphill towards the enemy, I realized that warfare does not change all that much. It was one of the Turkish officers running alongside his men, exhorting them to shout still louder,

184

who tossed me the sour remark that made me tackle the hill.

The Ishak Pasha Palace was worth any amount of effort. It had been built towards the end of the eighteenth century by a dynasty of feudal lords as their eyrie from which to control the lucrative trade of the Silk Road. Whether these feudal chiefs, who at that time ruled Eastern Anatolia and the Transcaucasus in virtual independence of their Ottoman overlords, were Armenian, Georgian, Kurdish, or even an amalgamation of all three is a matter of conjecture. Authorities are divided on the question. Their origins are certainly not revealed by the marvellously eclectic palace, half-fortress, half-pleasure dome, for it borrowed freely from Selçuk, Armenian, Georgian, Ottoman and Persian styles, and in the process achieved something totally original and very pleasing. With the fabulous wealth amassed from their system of tolls from the caravans, no expense was spared. It even boasted central heating, running water and a sewage system, rare in these parts even now!

With its trappings gone (the gold-plated doors from the main courtyard entrance were carted off to the Hermitage Museum in St Petersburg in 1917), and in a state of semi-ruin, it still retained an air of luxury and elegance. To find any substantial building in such uncompromising surroundings seemed remarkable, but a palace of 366 richly appointed rooms in the middle of that waste of bare fantastic cliffs and jumbled rock seemed little short of miraculous. Of the whole complex, the mosque was the loveliest

185

place with its cool marble interior diffusely lit and filled with softly cooing doves.

In a sense it was doves, or rather the lack of one, that stretched out my sojourn in Dogubayazit. Like Noah, I was waiting for a sign. Not, in my case, for an olive branch to tell me it was safe to descend from the mountain, but for permission to climb it. Although the whole mountain was officially a military area, there was no difficulty about getting a permit to be escorted to the summit, but it took time, six weeks or so, which of course in my case was too long. My friend, Hüseyin, was attempting to short-circuit the process by applying directly to his cronies among the local soldiery. Sitting on my balcony in the early morning, with Ararat like a vast pale suggestion of a wall, the summit trailing silvery clouds, was to feel challenged. It beckoned, as all great mountains do, and I wanted to climb it for its own sake, simply because it was there. In the late afternoon, when for an hour or so the haze lifted slightly, and Ararat, together with the perfect cone of Little Ararat, achieved substance and stood out from the flat surrounding plains, I was not so inspired. For then it always seemed rather a lump of a mountain, and knowing that there would be no chance in this hazy season of seeing the vast extended view that Bryce described, I felt I wouldn't be completely heartbroken if permission was refused.

Just when I had achieved this degree of philosophical detachment about the enterprise, Hüseyin arrived to tell me that a compromise had been reached with the military. I would

186

be allowed to go up to the halfway point the following day with a group of French and German climbers.

There were one or two Kurdish villages on the lower slopes of the mountain, with friendly Kurdish villagers tending gardens and orchards. They are well used to tourists, for Seventh Day Adventists frequently visit Ararat in large numbers to await the Second Coming, and search the slopes for pieces of the Ark while they wait. More recently, American astronauts and others have also taken to searching for the Ark, and it seems there is now a race on to be the first to discover it. An Armenian monk set out in the fourth century AD to the same end, but having reached nearly to the top he fell asleep and dreamed that an angel told him it was not seemly to go seeking proof of such a seminal event in the re-creation. By way of consolation a piece of wood from the Ark was left beside him to find when he awoke. The Armenians had, quite rightly, abandoned the search after this, contenting themselves with building a monastery on the mountain to contain their relic, both of which were subsequently destroyed in an earthquake.

Having myself now ascended Ararat to the halfway point, where the mountain, at no stage particularly appealing, finally degenerates into unpleasant, ankle-twisting boulder fields, with no good walking anywhere, I could only admire the good sense of the Armenians. Had I been allowed, I would certainly have continued towards the summit, but was not

187

really disappointed to be denied the chance. No one need climb even to this point on Ararat in order to see how it assumed its place in the Noah legend. Towering up out of the great flat plains as it does, where else could the Ark have come to rest? What is far more fascinating is the legend itself, for a flood story lies at the heart of most cultures and belief systems. The pyramids of the Ancient Egyptians, for example, were symbols of the sacred hill rising above the primeval waters of chaos. Somewhere in man's collective memory lies the remembrance of some cataclysmic event. That he survived it is the root of his belief in a beneficent deity, and in his own destiny towards unity with whatever he conceives that deity to be. In that sense, on Ararat, I could feel I was standing at the beginning of the long journey of mankind. Like Bryce, and even without the marvellous panoramic view he enjoyed, it seemed natural to imagine the sons of Noah spreading out north, south, east and west from this spot. Reading Whitman's 'Passage to India' on my balcony as, for the last time, I watched the daily drama of the sun gilding Ararat's summit snows, I felt once more that the poet had caught the mood of this cradle of mankind:

Down from the Gardens of Asia descending, radiating,
. . . their numerous progeny after them,
Wandering, yearning, curious, with restless explorations . . .

13

South to Lake Van

THE short way to Van, as the road was known, hugged the Iranian border. It had only recently been opened to civilian traffic, and was notorious for the fierceness of the villages along the way. Knowing this, my friends in Dogubayazit warned me against riding along it, but rather than telling me directly, they implied the state of affairs by hints, and by recommending that I take a *dolmus*, at least to the summit of the pass between the towns. Lulled into a false sense of security by the amiability of the Kurds of Dogubayazit, I didn't get the gist of what they were trying to tell me, and set off happily on Roberts, eager after my few days rest to be cycling through mountainous terrain once more.

The harassment started the moment I left the Iranian Highway and headed south on the narrow road towards the saddle of Tendürek Dagi. Two thuggish youths unleashed a snarling hound, and deliberately set it on me. The Dazer was in my hand in an instant, and as soon as I pressed the button the creature stopped and backed off, unsure of what to do next. The youths looked even more nonplussed. They replaced the rope around its neck, muttered some malediction in Kurdish and made off.

189

I was so angered by this cowardly attack that when the first stone, thrown by younger boys, came clattering on to the road, I was off Roberts and ready to give chase. Before I could do anything so rash, however, two men appeared, both seeming as angry at what had happened as I was, and one of them pursued the boys, throwing stones at them when he wasn't able to get them to stop. The man remaining with me kept giving appreciative chuckles at his companion's shouted invective. 'These people are not men, they are dogs,' said the would-be avenger in English when he returned, but whether he was a Turk or a Kurd, I could not tell.

That was the only occasion during the long morning when anyone came to my aid. In one village two huge intimidating brutes were set on me simultaneously. Again the Dog Dazer was successful in making them back off, but not before I thought my last moments had come. Everywhere boys, girls, women and sometimes even men hurled their assortment of sticks and stones. The constant fear of attack interfered with the rhythm of my pedalling, making the taxing climb to the pass harder than it need have been, and giving me little opportunity to take in the landscape. All I registered for certain was that it was harvest time, and that there were small fields of grain between rocky hillocks, beyond which rose bare hills and mountains. Grass was the primary crop, and the fields were full of people cutting, raking and gathering the enormous quantities of it needed to support the flocks of sheep and goats, the cattle and horses that I could see everywhere. In the villages the haystacks outnumbered the houses. It seemed to be an economy based entirely on animal husbandry. Ancient rickety lorries piled perilously high with hay, the load often tilting dramatically to one side, passed me all morning while I pressed on, finding it harder and harder not to hate the tormentors who made the ascent such purgatory.

Once past the summit I had no more worries for a while. I simply gave Roberts its head, and would-be aggressors scattered before my path. Although I had emerged from the morning's encounters feeling distinctly frazzled, I was still, amazingly, unbruised. If Turkey ever joins the world cricket league, I believe we will have nothing to fear, not if their side has its share of Kurds anyway, for they are rotten at throwing things.

A sudden shout broke into my reveries, and I saw a young man leap out of a mini-van and wave frantically at me. Suspecting further foul play, it took me a while to recognize Murat, a young man I had met in the tourist office in far-away Trebizond. After the displays of belligerence it was a great pleasure to be hugged and have my hand pumped vigorously up and down and be made much of, though in truth, our acquaintance had been very brief. I had gone into the tourist office one day to ask where there was a pleasant outdoor café for a beer, since all the places I found in Trebizond served only soft drinks and tea. The plump lady in charge had regarded me haughtily through dense drifts of cigarette smoke and informed me that 'In Turkey nice ladies don't drink beer.' At this, Murat, who hung around there looking for custom, decided to redeem the honour of his home town, and had escorted me to a seedy pick-up bar down by the harbour where the beer flowed cool and plentiful.

Like many Turks, Murat worked extremely hard for a bare existence. He spoke an eccentric smattering of several languages, and was trying to build up a travel business, specializing in escorting small groups of tourists on lightning tours of Eastern Anatolia by mini-van. Trade was clearly looking up, for Murat looked terrible. 'Not sleeping ten days,' he told me proudly. Apparently he had done two five-day trips in quick succession, driving as much as fourteen hours at a stretch and maintaining his battered vehicle at night, when his passengers snatched a few hours sleep. It didn't sound much fun. 'No,' he demurred. 'They liking very much! *Çok Gezel!* Only wanting swimming, and beer like you, then all OK, very happy.' He urged me to hurry after them to join up at a restaurant by a famous waterfall, where he was taking his clients for the statutory day's swim.

I pressed on, interested to learn what Murat's passengers had made of an Eastern Turkey glimpsed briefly through the windows of a speeding van. But there was one further pass between me and the Muradhiye waterfalls, and I did not reach it until several hours later, when Murat and his whirlwind tour group were already on their next fourteen-hour stage.

The landscape had grown emptier and more gently pastoral since crossing the second pass. A river coming down from the heights flowed alongside the road, running at times through narrow canyons where bold boys rode the miniature rapids, face down on home-made reed rafts (a far better pastime for them, I thought, than baiting travellers). In other places the river slowed, meandering in wide, lazy ox-bows through meadows where the grass seemed suddenly very green and velvety, like Irish turf. The quality of the day had changed entirely now that no one was throwing stones at me any more. The horrible knot in the pit of my stomach that had been tightening all morning began to unwind. I could once again appreciate what I was seeing, and feel a sense of harmony with my surroundings, so that soon I was singing joyfully, if not tunefully. And in this happy mood I came to the place where the river took its abrupt plunge over a broad cliff face, cascading in a curtain to a pool about forty feet below. Beyond was the wooden hut of the restaurant, with its rickety terrace overlooking the scene, and there was a swaying plank bridge across the gorge to reach it.

Murat had told the manager of the restaurant, Abdullah, to expect me, and I was given a cheery welcome. Within minutes Roberts had been put away in a storeroom, and I was sitting before a welcome late lunch of rice and aubergines stewed with tomatoes and onions and dressed with yoghurt. In the pool below boys were playing among the eddying currents and ducking in and out of the cascades like sleek otters. I was looking forward to swimming there too. The day was now my own, with no more hills to climb, and no more stones and savage dogs. It had been arranged that I was going to camp that night in the flower-strewn meadow alongside the falls, for the site was patrolled by a night-watchman, and therefore relatively safe.

It happened to be my birthday, and when I mentioned this fact to Abdullah, he immediately proposed a party. I was asleep in my tent when I was summoned to appear for it, worn out by fighting the swirling waters of the pool, and by making camp with the help of Abdullah's five lively children, who used a carpet store on the site as their summer home.

The restaurant was really no more than a sort of wooden scout hut, with bare floors, battered deal tables with stained cloths, and rickety chairs. A few torn posters flapped from the walls, and several missing window panes were covered with cardboard. But somehow a sense of occasion was in the air, engendered as much by Abdullah's air of happy expectation as by anything tangible. I'd given them *carte blanche* over dinner and was served with what Abdullah proudly announced to be a special birthday kebab. I can't say that it tasted any different from what seemed like the many hundreds of kebabs I'd already consumed in Turkey; there isn't much variation possible with plain grilled chunks of lamb. But as the cook was hovering expectantly, I had to pronounce it superb. With it Abdullah recommended I try a bottle of a dark red wine called Hasnet Geceleri. Fortunately both he and the cook helped me to drink this, for it was a rather melancholy wine, which would probably have depressed me had I tackled it alone. The second bottle did not seem quite so gloomy (Turkish wine is notoriously inconsistent). Cook chose the emptying of it as the moment to bring in his *pièce de resistance*, a sort of three-tiered pretend birthday cake created from fruit, wine glasses, and toothpicks, and topped with a hollowed out melon, carved into a face like a Halloween lantern. Metal caps from raki bottles, half-filled with oil and with wicks floating in them took the place of candles. It was rather hideous really, but most ingenious, and must have taken several hours to construct. I was so touched by the kindness, especially coming after the day's hostilities, that it was all I could do not to shed a few tears. Instead I ordered another bottle to celebrate it, but as our numbers had mysteriously grown by this time, further bottles were needed to fill everyone's glass.

After this the party began to gather pace. Plump Abdullah was clasped around the waist by the spindly night-watchman who must have been at least eighty years old, and they essayed a decorous little dance together, a few steps right and another few left, handkerchiefs fluttering delicately between finger and thumb of the free hand. Others joined in until a line stretched across the hut, and I was the only one left sitting and clapping out the rhythm. There was no music, only what they made themselves by clapping and singing. It was a little like Greek dancing, but slower. The footwork was very complicated, however, and few could approach the expertise of the old night-watchman. Eventually his double shuffle and hop wrong-footed Abdullah who tripped, and the whole row went down like ninepins, and lay there helpless with laughter. The night-watchman danced alone after that, a beatific smile on his face, while the air in the hut grew blue with cigarette smoke as the others sat around watching him. More men were arriving all the time, and more bottles were uncorked, and went the rounds. Sad though it seemed to leave such a convivial party, I thought I had better call for my bill while I still had the chance of remaining solvent, for the wine was flowing down some throats as though it was water. Having settled up, and it was in fact a very modest amount considering the quantities of drink that had been put away, I was shown one final courtesy. The aged night-watchman, who between dances had downed at least twice as much wine as anyone else, escorted me gravely and courteously across the meadow to my tent, lighting my way symbolically with a non-functioning torch.

There was no need of torches; the heavens were clear and crowded with stars, the milky way like a broad stream that had ever further depths the more I stared up at it. I thought I would not mind how many birthdays I spent like this, in a place where there was the sound of water falling over rocks, and where

196

no light pollution from cities hid the glory of the night sky. It had been a momentous day, a day of great contrasts, beginning with breakfast beside Noah's mountain; moving from friendly farewells, through miserable animosity, to light-hearted junketing, and finally ending in what Walt Whitman described so aptly as 'the teeming spiritual darkness'. Alone in that darkness, in so ancient and significant a part of the world the idea of 'some inscrutable purpose', some 'hidden prophetic intention' seemed very real. My last thought as I lay there cocooned in my sleeping bag, aware of the faint sighing of the wind behind the thunder of the falls was how right the ancient Israelites had been in thinking that men were intended to be 'dwellers in tents'.

It was a very good awakening too in the crisp dry dawn, with not a drop of dew on the grass to chill bare feet. I can imagine no lovelier start to any day than swimming under the curtain of those falls just as the sun was rising above the eastern hills, mirrored in each separate drop of water. Abdullah and his family were still asleep when I left, indeed I think the whole countryside was asleep, for I saw no one about as I negotiated the long descent to the plains of Van on a deteriorating road full of deep potholes. I had to take great care to avoid these holes for fear of damaging a wheel. Most minor repairs to a bicycle I can manage well enough, but I doubt my ability to replace a broken spoke or straighten a buckled rim: When I was finally able to lift my eyes for a moment from the road

Lake Van was in full view, such an amazing sight I had to stop altogether and just gaze at it.

The surface of the lake resembled nothing so much as one of those Victorian brooches made from butterfly wings covered with crystal, in which the deep iridescent blue changes to sapphire and to turquoise, and to a profusion of opalescent shades in between. It is a vast expanse of water, more than six times the size of Lake Geneva, and an early explorer stumbling upon it might well have mistaken it for the ocean. Another huge ghostly mountain, Süphan Dagi, very little lower than Ararat, mirrored its summit snows in the surface near the northern shore.

There was a stand of pine trees near the water's edge, and I stopped under their shade to brew tea and enjoy the scene more fully. A car carrying an Iranian family of mother dressed in the usual black *chadar*, father and two teenage children, the girl not yet in purdah but well bundled up in long skirts and headscarf, also stopped under the pines. Very quickly they had a fire going and had prepared a breakfast of scrambled eggs rolled up in chapattis, to which they kindly invited me. I needed no urging for I was, as usual, very hungry; it had been several hours since my own scrappy breakfast of coffee and dried apricots. They ate raw onions with the eggs which went quite well, and afterwards we shared my remaining dried apricots. The youngsters knew a little English in the form of stock questions such as 'Are you married?', 'Do you have little ones?',

'Are you American?'. It didn't add up to a conversation, since they couldn't understand my replies. But the mother using no language other than her hands and expressive face described a horrible accident that they had witnessed earlier that morning on the way from Dogubayazit. A coach had run out of road on a bend and rolled down the mountainside, killing all fifty-two Kurds on board. When I heard the account again in Van, in words this time, it was the same in every respect. The only thing that was added was the observation that such events were not uncommon in these parts because Iranians, Kurdish or otherwise, were wild drivers, habitually drunk on speed, and given to driving through the night in old badly-maintained vehicles — a sentiment I thought could be applied to many drivers in Eastern Turkey.

Although no more than fifty-five miles, it proved a surprisingly hard ride down to Van. The road rose and fell a good deal, including a climb over a six-thousand-foot spur of one of the great peaks that ringed the lake. A hot persistent wind impeded my progress and sent dust devils swirling over the dry earth. Only from a distance was the marvellous blue of the lake in view, and then only for brief periods, for the road ran well inland most of the way.

By noon I had still some twenty miles to cover, and coming to an isolated café, I stopped for lunch. It was a pull-in for truck drivers, and was no more than a little garden for dining, with a terrifyingly grimy shed which was the kitchen. Once again I chose kebabs because being freshly charred they were safer than stews that might have been standing around for hours, or even days.

Being noon it was prayer time, and each driver who arrived immediately washed at a muddy little stream in the garden, a few feet away from my table. It was all very matter of fact, but thorough. Hands and arms were rubbed and rinsed to just above the elbows; shoes were removed to clean feet and legs as far as the knees (no one had socks, and the backs of their shoes were trodden down, the easier to get them off and on); mouths were thoroughly rinsed; and finally they turned away to discreetly wash more intimate parts. A board was taken from its place under a tree and laid on the ground, and one by one, standing on this they performed their genuflections, kneeling and touching forehead to ground, standing briefly between movements in silent reflection. As always, I found the simple ritual far more impressive, carried out like this unselfconsciously in public, and in such unsanctified surroundings, than when it was performed in unison in a mosque. And I thought that perhaps if Christianity went in for this sort of public prayer, or celebrated its more elaborate and moving rituals in public, it might be better able to compete with Islam, which is currently the world's fastest-growing faith.

The nearer I came to Van, the greener grew the grass in the smooth fields that sloped down towards the lake shimmering in the distance. This fertile area around Lake Van was once the centre of the Urartian culture, a people that scholarship knew almost nothing about until the last century, when archaeologists uncovered many of their cities and fortresses, read their cuneiform inscriptions and realized how important they had been. They are mentioned a few times in the Bible; in Genesis the word 'Ararat' is a corruption of 'Urartu', which in the Latin version becomes Armenia. The Urartians first enter history in the ninth century BC, when they appear in the annals of the Assyrian King Shalmaneser III. Assyria weakened by continual wars and internal unrest was unable to halt the Urartians rapid rise to prominence, and by 800 BC, under their great King Menua, Urartu was the largest and most powerful state in Western Asia. Menua, as the inscriptions on his uncovered structures attest, built temples, cities, palaces, fortresses, and constructed hundreds of miles of aqueducts, canals and irrigation systems for 'his gardens, his orchards and his vineyards', all within the area where legend cites the Garden of Eden.

It is not clear where the Urartians came from. They seem to be rather less bellicose than the Assyrians, but probably this was not the case, for whichever race of people came to power in this, the Biblical centre of the world, they got there only by ousting someone else. And though this was also true of just about every place reached by the sons of Noah, the ousting and the bashing seems to have been more extreme here, and to have gone on for longer. Nor is there much indication of it having stopped even now.

Under Menua's son, Argistis I, Urartu continued to flourish until its borders stretched from the Caucasus to the Mediterranean. It was a brief flowering, however, for during the reign of Argistis's son, Sarduris II, 764 – 35 BC, the Assyrians, under Tiglath Pileser III, once again took the ascendancy and wasted the lands of the Urartians, along with most of the other lands of the Middle East. In the Assyrian annals for the year 735 BC appears the account of this Urartian campaign:

I shut up Sarduris of Urartu in Turushpa (the great rock of Van) his principal city. I made a great slaughter in front of his gates, and opposite the town I set up an image of my royalty.

Which was the sort of things kings commonly boasted about at that time. Assyrian tablets carved in low relief, which the British Museum has in quantity, shows the Assyrians doing frightful things to captives, as well as burning cities, looting, carrying off populations into slavery, slaughtering lions just released from cages; carrying on, in fact, much as modern states still do. But double standards applied hardly at all in those days; conquest and might were all that mattered, and no one attempted to conceal naked aggression under any other guise. The Assyrians were proud of their exploits, and decorated their palaces with these pictorial records of them, covered all over with cuneiform writing to further expatiate on their prowess.

For the next hundred years the Urartians struggled to maintain their lands against the incursions of the Assyrians, the continual warfare weakening both countries, and leaving them open to attack by new conquerors. The Medes seized their moment, defeated the Assyrian Empire at Nineveh in 612 BC, and took Urartu a little later. The last surviving Urartian works date to around 590 BC when all the evidence points to them having been destroyed by fire and sword.

Sometime in the fourth century BC the Armenians succeeded to the Urartian lands, and from the beginning, Van became one of their most prominent cities. It remained so throughout the classical and Byzantine periods, until AD 1021, when the last King of Van, Sennacherib-John, ceded his kingdom to the Byzantines. Fifty years later the Byzantines lost it to the Selçuk Turks. Van, however, retained its importance into the present century, and its population continued to be principally Armenian until the First World War. During that war, when the massacres and deportations of the Armenians were at their height, Van was one of the places where the Armenians made a stand, and during the fighting the many-layered city continuously inhabited for three thousand years was totally destroyed, and the entire population was killed or fled.

As I rode into Van I had only a distant glimpse of the great rock of Van, on whose summit the original settlement was founded, for the ancient city of Van on the plains below was never rebuilt after its destruction. Modern Van is two miles inland, a dull sober town, with drab modern buildings and straight dusty streets. There are a few comfortable hotels, a great many cheap restaurants, all clinically lit with neon tubes, and an inordinate number of carpet shops desperate for custom. Van had once been on the main route to Iran, for the east-west railway came through, with a ferry service across the lake to connect the two railheads. But now that people prefer to travel by car or coach, the old Silk Road under its new guise of the Iranian Highway has given Dogubayazit the benefit of Van's Asian trade. This had not mattered over much to Van as long as there were Western tourists, but the combination of the war in Iraq, the PKK kidnappings, and the war in Yugoslavia that blocked the overland route from Europe, had scared away most potential visitors. The place seemed to be in a state of arrested affluence: the unsurfaced dusty roads were edged with high marble or terrazzo pavements, constantly being washed in a vain attempt to keep them clean; shop windows of modern aluminium construction displayed expensive consumer goods like jewellery, clothing and carpets; hotels were better appointed than I had grown accustomed to, and had lifts that worked. They were also empty as I discovered to my advantage, for I could more or less name my own terms. Whether this interrupted prosperity affected the political climate, or whether it was the large numbers of spies, government agents and plain clothes policemen who were rumoured

204

to be lurking there I could not tell. But for whatever reason, Van was the only town in the east where I met no militant Kurds, nor anyone eager to give me accounts of Turkish perfidy. It was also the only town in the east where shopkeepers and hoteliers expressed the wish that the PKK would stop making trouble for the profitable tourist trade. After all the turbulent currents of opinion which had eddied about me over the past few weeks, this respite from politics seemed almost as remarkable as the wonders I had come there to see.

14

Cats and Kings

VAN I discovered had more charm than its dull streets at first led me to suppose. It also had two intriguing claims to fame, a rash of heavy black tricycles and a unique breed of cats. The inhabitants of Van hated the one and loved the other, sentiments I quickly came to share. Much as I would have expected to feel solidarity with any form of unmotorized transport, so rare a phenomenon in comfort-oriented Turkey, I could not take to the tricyclists of Van. They were a curiously repulsive lot, rather like the worst of London's bicycle messengers, riding as though every man's hand was against them, snarling and grimacing and generally giving the impression that they hated the world in general and the person they were charging at in particular. Their machines had two wheels at the front with a capacious basket between, and loaded with several hundred-weight sacks of produce they made efficient and formidable battering rams. It was not unusual to see a couple of fat live sheep squashed into them too, side by side, their feet tied together, and their heads either up and indignantly bleating, or hanging dejectedly over the edge as though already anticipating death. Propelling such loads up even the slightest of inclines must have been hard work, and at such times they constituted no threat, but on the flat they could be pedalled at quite a lick, and downhill they were lethal juggernauts, their brakes totally inadequate unless supplemented with a foot against the tyre. There was no mistaking the tricyclists' loathing of the superior Roberts, and had not discretion made me give them a very wide berth, they would clearly have delighted in mowing us both down.

Van cats on the other hand are delightful, though sadly their numbers are declining as the tricycles multiply, a circumstance that leads one to suspect a sinister connection. The cats possess the singular distinction of having one bright blue eye while the other is a gorgeous golden-green, though such a bald statement of fact does little to explain their extraordinary appeal. Van cats have none of the haughtiness of Persians or the plangent insistence of Siamese, and in shape they are much like any small fluffy moggy. Their coats are pure white, but otherwise unremarkable. It is only when they look you full in the face, and you find your own vision beginning to swim a little, that you begin to appreciate their strange beauty. By destroying their symmetry the wildly disparate eyes give Van cats a fascination not unlike that of some late picasso portraits. Coupled with this weird split-hemisphere countenance is a most charming disposition, affectionate, playful and fearless. They are said to be intrepid swimmers too, and although I never met anyone who had seen them doing so, the thought of them playing like small white otters in the marvellous blue waters of Lake Van considerably enhanced my concept of the Garden of Eden.

Van is also a great centre for the colourful carpets known as kilims. There seems little that can be done with sheep other than to eat them or turn their coats into carpets, and as vast flocks of sheep are the main feature of Eastern Anatolia, kilims are made in huge numbers, many of them by hand in the villages. Carpet shops are the places to make the acquaintance of Van cats, for the wily owners usually keep a couple to lure in the customers. My special favourite was in the charge of a young man called Osman whose shop was close to the hotel. Osman studied engineering in Erzerum during the winter and worked all through the summer to pay for his course, which was how most Kurdish students managed. He was also learning English so my visits were welcomed as opportunities for practise, especially in the current dearth of tourists.

If ever I tired of Van cats I could visit the brown hens that scratched in the rank grass among the rows of Urartian stele in the museum garden. These free-ranging hens had the run of the place, with a raucous glossy cockerel to marshal them from his vantage point on the crowning turban of a fine Ottoman tombstone. The only spot forbidden them lay behind a tall Urartian block carved with a goddess bearing a pomegranate and a trident. This shady corner spread with a fluorescent modern rug was reserved for the curator to take his nap in the heat of the day. I visited the museum most days, sometimes to enjoy the homely atmosphere of the garden, so peaceful after the running battles with Van's tricyclists. But mainly I came to look at the museum's collection of Urartian jewellery, finding the beautiful amber and glass beads, the golden breastplates and the bronze belts particularly fascinating. Together with the few pots, and the cylindrical seals with their tiny pictographs, they were also very helpful in trying to build some mental image of the long vanished race of Urartu.

Yet another attraction of Van was the tempting pastry shops, their windows filled with huge round metal trays of honey-soaked flaky squares stuffed with almonds or pistachios. I was so thinned down by all the hill climbing and the continuing Turkey trots that I felt I could stuff away calories with impunity. But so rich and over-sweet to my unaccustomed palate were these pastries that I could never manage as much as I had eyes for, and had to be satisfied with half portions, while all around me local people tucked into second and third helpings.

I also found an excellent restaurant where I began to see how much more interesting Turkish food could be than simple kebabs and stewed aubergines. The trick was to eat only *metzes*, and not worry about a main course. At this particular restaurant, which catered for the occasional foreign tour group, I counted fifty separate *metzes*, from taramasalata to pickled mushrooms, and including three different types of puréed aubergine, many sorts of beans variously prepared, potatoes in yoghurt and mint, olives, fish, and cold stuffed peppers. It was organized buffet-style, so that one could sample a little of everything. Guests ate in a dusty garden, less brutally lit than most of the indoor restaurants, under trees that were beginning to shed their leaves, so that there was often an additional flavour in the *metzes*. Above the trees the moon and stars appeared and disappeared behind bronze clouds, adding a touch of grandeur to the scene.

All Turkish gardens must have some sort of water feature, even if it is only an iron pipe dribbling a continuous trickle on to the ground, and this one was no exception. The tables were grouped round a large ugly concrete fountain painted duck egg blue, into which water gushed from a broken spout solely, it seemed, for the purpose of keeping the excellent beer cool. It was necessary to be seated up-wind of it to avoid an unwanted shower. The whole place was typical I thought of the special charm of Turkey: the beautiful hand-in-hand with the banal, the sublime with the ridiculous. The restaurant also boasted a plush interior with neon chandeliers, velvet curtains and the odd touch of gilt. This was where the wealthy locals dined, entertained by a well-rounded male singer and a three piece all-male backing group. He performed through the usual booming amplification, and, matching gestures to sentiments, poured out passionate and heart-breaking love songs to a clientele that was, as usual, exclusively male. The diners all sat facing the stage, watching attentively as they consumed their kebabs and poured down glass after glass of raki. Even though I had by now grown used to the absence of women in public places in Eastern Turkey (only very occasionally were they to be seen after dark, and certainly never dining out or playing tric trac), this scene of gloomy all-male revelry did strike me as somewhat farcical.

Van was as noisy as most towns in Turkey, with the men playing tric trac or watching outdoor television in cafés beneath hotel windows until late, and with the usual surfeit of canned muezzins' calls competing to awaken one before dawn, so that three or four hours continuous sleep was the most that could be expected. But the many compensations far outweighed these disadvantages. The only thing that initially I found insupportable was the lighting in my hotel bedroom. It seemed ironic that while all the restaurants, shops and hotel foyers were furnished with harsh glaring neon strips, my room was equipped with just two tiny twenty-five watt bulbs, further dimmed by being painted green! In other rooms in the hotel, I discovered, the lighting could also be red or even blue; someone told me that it was all to do with Turkish men's sexual fantasies. It was lost on me, however, and not until I finally took matters into my own hands and raided the landings and lavatories for brighter, uncoloured bulbs was it possible to write up my notes, or to find my way to the bathroom without falling over the furniture. After sorting out the lighting I thought I would not mind how long I lingered in Van.

The great rock of Van was the real reason for staying on. One visit was not enough for so extraordinary and significant a monument, nor did I find it possible to appreciate its visible record of three thousand years of history in a single encounter. It was difficult to believe that something so magnificently sited and perfect for its purpose was fortuitous and not man-made; that it was simply a great chunk of mountain left isolated at the lake's edge as a result of some primeval volcanic spasm. All of the towering peaks that ring the lake are extinct volcanoes, as is Ararat itself. In its last eruption, one of these mountains, Nemrut Dagi, blocked up the outflow of the lake, creating its present vast dimensions.

The rock of Van commanded magnificent views of this strange and wonderful landscape. So high was its summit from the ground that the dull thuds of a woman beating washing with a long wooden paddle in a stream immediately below only reached me when her arm was raised again for the next stroke. But there was far more to the rock than an elevated view. Many of the ancient walls and towers of the citadel remained, the earliest dating back to ninth-century Urartu, and the most recent to late Ottoman. Just about every Western Asiatic power there has ever been, Assyrian, Persian, Medean, Babylonian, all had passed through and left their mark. Inscriptions from the first period were said to be sited in the catacombs of the Urartian kings, and I hunted around for these on several occasions before I found them, for the top of the rock is surprisingly large and convoluted, and there are many details to distract the attention. Eventually I teamed up with a small Dutch tour group I met in my hotel, and we systematically quartered the site until we came to some worn and ancient stairs hewn in the rock in the north-west corner. The inscriptions were etched in the rock face above the stairs, yards and yards of the wedge-shaped cuneiform, so clear and sharp-edged as to make it difficult to believe they had withstood the weathering of Eastern Anatolia's harsh winters for two and a half thousand years. There was a locked gate at the head of the staircase, and in order to see the catacombs we had first to go in search of a curator with the key, and negotiate a price for his services.

Crowded into a square rock-hewn chamber in pitchy darkness, because the curator's torch was found not to be working, a sharp overpowering smell of sweat suddenly assailed our nostrils, and in the light of a struck match we discovered that two young Kurdish men had pushed in after us. Whether they were government spies, informers, or plain-clothes policemen, there was no way of telling. Whenever I met up with a group of Western tourists, which only happened around Van, plain-clothes policemen always appeared at some point to prevent our being kidnapped by the PKK. It was only forty miles across the lake to where the Germans had been abducted, and the authorities were keen to avoid a repetition of such adverse tourist publicity. On the other hand this malodorous pair might equally well have been a couple of inquisitive locals taking the opportunity of the catacombs being opened; one simply never knew.

Brief spurts of light from a couple of hand-held matches had to suffice for an impression of further regular chambers hollowed out of the reddish-brown living rock, each one opening out of others, and furnished with niches for funeral urns. There was an overwhelming sense of the passage of time, and of the immense labour of cutting out the rock, but nothing at all to bridge the yawning gulf separating the late twentieth century from a culture so long departed as to seem unimaginable. The guide brought us to where there was a shaft, which he claimed was a chimney for the furnace where the Urartians cremated their dead, but no one wanted to linger there in the dark with the rank smell of the uninvited guests. Emerging into the light was like a benediction; it felt suddenly very good to be alive, and perhaps only now, sharpened by the contrast with the tombs, could one truly appreciate the beauty of the scene, and the intense blue of the lake, with the green fields running down to its edge.

On the south side the great rock was sheer for almost its entire half-mile length, though even here there were faintly etched impressions of flights of steps leading to ancient altar platforms, where once the elements of fire and wind, sky and water had been worshipped. Immediately below this southern cliff was the huge flat area that for three thousand years had been the lower city of Van, and is now an awesome testimony to the ferocity of the fighting between the Turks and the Armenians and Russians during the First World War. Too brief a time has elapsed for the destruction to have been transformed into neat sanitized history. It remains a scene of the utmost desolation, like the centres of many bombed cities of Europe after the Second World War; a place of craters and grass-grown rubble heaps, with here and there a fragment of a vaulted crypt breaking surface like rib cages in a charnel house. Europe's cities have been rebuilt, but only the passage of many centuries will effectively disguise Van's scars. The minaret of the Great Mosque of the Emir Yusuf built around AD 1400 and two sixteenth-century Ottoman tombs that had miraculously escaped the general destruction stood isolated among the acres of wreckage, like funerary chapels brooding over a vast cemetery. If they were symbolic of anything, they seemed to imply that finally this was the only harmony that could be achieved between Islamic Turkey and the much-persecuted Christian Armenians.

I picked my way through the sad mounds one day in order to see the famous inscription that Xerxes had ordered to be carved on the rock around the year 482 BC. Western history gives little praise to Xerxes, writing him up as an eastern despot. He was certainly a keen self-publicist, and his inscription is by far the most imposing in Van, being carved large on a prominent section of the sheer rock face. It is about eighty feet above the ground and about thirty feet below the top of the rock, so that the craftsmen must have done their work suspended

215

on ropes or cradles with a terrifying drop beneath them. When I returned to London I looked up a translation of the inscription, and found that it had really been intended to honour Darius, Xerxes' father, who had conquered Van. But one would have had difficulty working this out from the text. It mentions Darius just twice in passing, and concentrates almost entirely upon the glory of Xerxes. It is long, rambling and somewhat repetitive, but the gist of it runs:

A great God is Ahuramazda, the greatest of the gods, who created this earth, who created the heaven, who created man, who created happiness for man, who made Xerxes king, the one King of many kings, the King of kings . . . I am Xerxes the great King, King in this great earth far and wide . . . Me may Ahuramazda, with the gods, preserve, and my kingdom, and what has been done by me.

After leaving his mark on Van, Xerxes had swept on through Anatolia to build his mile-long bridge of boats across the Hellespont, and add Greece to his lists of conquests. And because, with Xerxes, the Greeks and Thermopylae, I had entered a time scale I could relate to, with events and people which have become a part of the fabric of Western history and culture, I felt the greatest thrill at seeing this particular inscription. I had a more illuminating glimpse into the more nebulous Urartian civilization when I crossed the mountains south-east of Van, to visit the site of Çavustepe. On a low slender ridge

216

overlooking the road and the site of Urartian canal was what has been unearthed of the palace of King Sadur II, built around the year 750 BC. One of the most helpful aspects was the book the guide showed me of a French archaeologist's reconstruction of the palace, a grand place of tall tapering buildings, not unlike those of Assyria or Babylon. Turkey is frequently frustrating in the total absence of any kind of information at historical sites, even though there is always someone to collect an entrance fee. Nor is there any way of knowing if the guide imparting copious details is not making it all up, as I found to be the case on several occasions when I knew something of the subject. Perhaps these drawings were equally fanciful, but they seemed to make sense of the excavated remains. Substantial portions of wall were still standing, cyclopian walls of enormous irregular blocks of stone, beautifully though irregularly cut and fitted to one another like a jigsaw. In contrast there were highly polished basalt slabs at the entrance to a temple, and finely inscribed cuneiform tablets beside them recording the history of the place. The excavated foundations showed well-proportioned rooms built around courtyards containing water cisterns. There was also what was claimed to be the royal loo, and this homely and essential provision, although now no more than a hole in the ground (like many modern Asiatic loos), was a help in imagining real-life Urartians looking out on the same plains and hills that I could see, as well as upon their canals and their aqueducts, their gardens, vineyards and orchards so long obliterated by warfare and by the destructive passage of time.

Another day I went by bus to visit Hakkari, deep in the heart of ancient Kurdistan, where the borders of Turkey, Iraq and Iran meet in wild mountainous country. There was some doubt as to whether I would be allowed to bicycle there in the current unrest, and in any case it would mean a long hard ride of around one hundred and thirty miles, only to have to return over the same route. As a compromise I changed buses on the way so as to spend a few hours in the village of Güzelsu. Güzelsu means sweet water and presumably refers to the Hosap river which is spanned here by a very pretty triple-arched bridge built in 1500 by Zeynel Bey, a local Kurdish war-lord cum robber baron. The fairy tale Hosap Castle perched on a great needle of rock high above the village was what I had come to see. In its heyday it was a notorious stronghold from which the lawless war-lords preyed on all who dared to pass through these mountains, and many hapless traveller had mouldered away in its grim dungeons. Its teeth had been drawn a long while since, however, and now there was little left of the interior, in fact it was rather like a hollow tooth with only the splendid outer shell left virtually intact. The best view of it was from the road where it still appeared dauntingly impregnable. When I climbed up to its battlements I found the eroded walls of a much larger Urartian stronghold confronting me across the valley.

In order to photograph bridge and castle

together I had to climb down to the river where the 'Sweet Water' was rather marred by the accumulation of centuries of smelly rubbish heaps. I had just managed to negotiate these and get myself in position when a tractor drove on to the bridge, and stopped in the middle. The driver saw that I was wanting to take a photograph and made a helpless shrug with his shoulders to let me know he had broken down. The usual huddle of men sitting around watching immediately got up and pushed the tractor off the bridge! When I climbed up to the road again, I was invited into the motor mechanic's shed for a glass of tea. Kurds as well as Turks have a commendable pride in the places they inhabit, even though it doesn't extend to conservation, and they love people to show appreciation of their towns and villages by taking photographs. The men enjoy having their own photographs taken too, but this is not so helpful, because they strike stiff unnatural poses, or else rush into the foreground of some study of a mosque or such like, and ruin the composition.

The drive up to Hakkari was extraordinary. Although we were never higher than nine thousand feet, the way led through narrow precipitous valleys, more continuously rugged for their height than any mountains I've seen. Ravines led off the main valleys into ever deeper fastnesses. Green rivers, contrasting with the stark rock, ran down through them. These would become rushing torrents as soon as the rains came, making the region even more difficult to traverse. What dwellings there were could seldom be seen from the road, but were tucked into the folds of the ground. The whole land had a secret closed-in look. Xenophon's description of the difficulties of the Ten Thousand fighting their way through these canyons was easy to relate to the scenery. Nothing had essentially changed from his account of their march. I was looking at the very vantage points the Greeks had fought so hard to secure; often they had ousted the defenders from one summit only to find they had climbed another equally high, and having again routed them from that too, had seen them occupying yet a third. It was also easy to imagine the frustrations and dangers of commanding the rear division in these long narrow valleys, as Xenophon had done, the van getting ever further ahead as they rushed on to secure the pass before the enemy got to it first, and all the time the Greeks at the rear coming under attack by spear and arrow from the cliffs above.

These mountains were always a haven for bandits or guerilla fighters, and were now home to what was reckoned to be many thousands of young armed PKK activists, scattered in small mobile training camps, which doubtless was why the bus was stopped so often by the military, and why unsmiling armed soldiers came down the aisle to scrutinize everyone's papers. Even my passport was checked and rechecked, though I wouldn't have thought I could be mistaken for a young Kurdish insurgent.

Hakkari marked the limit of normal travel in this direction, a raw hilltop town with little to commend a night's stop there, even though, with all the stops, it had taken some six hours to reach it. The road, such as it is, continues south through similar rugged mountains, bending around to the west to run close to the Iraqi border. All of it is the haunt of the PKK, who cross and recross the borders of both Iraq and Syria with an ease impossible for anyone else, including conventional government troops.

I sat in the small tea gardens in the centre of Hakkari waiting for my bus back to Van. Fierce-looking men with hooked noses, huge black moustaches and dark flashing eyes, wearing the traditional voluminous trousers and rough turbans, sat drinking tea and avidly watching cartoons on the outdoor television. A few were in western garb, and I thought these might well be government agents for they were not interested in the cartoons, but watched the viewers over the top of their newspapers. The few women who shuffled past the garden seemed aged and bent under their enveloping shawls, their eyes fixed on the ground at their feet. At the very summit of the town just beyond the tea garden sat Atatürk in bronze on a mettlesome charger, and above him was a banner with the over-familiar sentiment 'HOW WONDERFUL TO BE ABLE TO SAY I AM A TURK' Writ large. I wondered idly how the Scots, the Welsh or the Irish would react to banners with 'HOW WONDERFUL TO BE ABLE TO SAY I AM AN ENGLISHMAN' adorning their main squares and carved into mountain sides?

The superficial air of normality in Hakkari

felt ominous. The authorities had the place under tight security, even though there were few obvious signs of it. The clearest indication of this was that no one at all tried to talk to me, which was so unusual as to make me nervous. At the same time I had the distinct feeling I was being watched. I could feel the hairs rising on the back of my neck, and had to stop myself from continually glancing over my shoulder. Not a single small boy appeared to ask for a pen, or stood around on one leg plucking up the courage to deliver his two or three words of English or German. It seemed a very sad place, and it was a relief to finally board the bus and ride back down through those marvellous wild canyons to the plains of Van, and drink tea with my friend Osman in the carpet shop, his purring white cat in my lap, its mismatched eyes closed in contentment.

15

Round About Eden

STUMBLING upon the site of the Garden of Eden doesn't seem such a wildly improbable notion in the area of Van. Perhaps the daily contact with works of great antiquity encourages a different appreciation of time and reality; or it may simply be the unique quality of this mountain-ringed lake at the centre of the earth. Whatever the reason, as I rode around the southern margins of Lake Van and approached the island of Akhtamar, the idea seemed rather more than a vague possibility. It was certainly an ideal setting, a small offshore island lapped in the infinity of blues and greens of lake, sky and ethereal cloud-capped mountains. The light was marvellous, giving everything great depth and clarity, and the air appeared charged with pinpoints of gold that danced over the rippled surface of the water.

Akhtamar lies about two miles from shore. At its western end is a prominent hill on which once stood the royal palace where Gagik I of Vaspurakan was crowned King in AD 908, amidst scenes of great pomp and splendour, as described by the chronicler Thomas Artusini:

Mounted on a horse with gilt trappings, he shone like the sun amid the stars; large

223

companies of soldiers, armed from head to foot stood to the right and the left; the weapons clashed, the trumpets resounded, the horns blared, the flutes shrilled, the lyres gave forth melodious sounds, psalteries and banners preceded and followed him, and the soldiers of the royal army let out a mighty shout which shook the earth. With such pomp was he installed.

Not a single trace of the palace remains, but on the level eastern end of the island stands the incomparable Church of the Holy Cross, which Gagik built a few years after his coronation. From where I stood on the shore it looked as though the thousand and more years had not touched it.

The boat that took visitors across to the island was very full because the Dutch group with whom I'd explored the citadel of Van had turned up, along with the French people I'd met climbing Ararat; and just as we were about to cast off from the jetty a van pulled up, and a dozen plain-clothes policemen and one girl who might have been a plainclothes policewoman spilled out of it and hurried across to join us. So much for Eden! I feared that we would all be falling over one another trying to take photographs of the church, but I need not have worried. After a perfunctory glance around, most people headed for the other side of the island where there was good swimming. The plain-clothes policemen didn't even bother with the cursory look, but changed straight away into their bathing trunks, and took it in turns to swim, while their colleagues assumed manly poses and stood guard over the Western girls sunbathing in bikinis. My friend Osman from the carpet shop in Van had told me that the police were supposed to keep a low profile and not let tourists know why they were there in case it made them nervous. As a result, most of the women and girls didn't realize they were being protected, and cast angry glances at the men standing between them and the sun, and muttered about harassment by oversexed Turks.

Swimming in the lake felt strange because the water is highly alkaline as a result of the natural chemicals that have accumulated and become concentrated in it since its outflow was blocked. It was almost as buoyant as the sea, and as cleansing as a warm bath. The only drawback was that I couldn't stay in for very long because it made all the small cuts and abrasions that bicyclists tend to acquire sting like mad.

It seemed a good idea to delay exploring the church until the others had left the island, because when I had first looked in I surprised one of the policemen locked in a tight embrace in the chancel with the girl, who might or might not have been a plain-clothes policewoman. Later I came upon them scratching their initials on the wall of the western porch, and was so incensed by this act of vandalism, that I had to go away quickly before I could voice the protest that sprang to my lips.

I walked around the island while I waited,

225

reflecting on the strange compulsion that drives people to leave their mark upon the monuments they visit. It is a practice that has been going on since earliest times; the Greeks and Romans certainly did it, and doubtless Persians, Assyrians and Babylonians too. The Victorians shamelessly left their signatures wherever their increasingly wide-ranging travels took them, and they were not above helping themselves to 'souvenirs' from the monuments either. I expect the Urartians had also carved their marks on all those miles and miles of walls and fortifications around Van; though we cannot be sure about the Urartians, because of time and weather having eroded the surfaces of most of their walls, together with any of the unofficial marks they might have made on them. If any idle Urartian scribbles were discovered archaeologists and historians would be thrilled, as they are when any early graffiti comes to light; which just goes to show how the vandalism of one age is treasured by a later one.

I suppose everyone who scratches their name in a place of significance does so with some idea of immortality. Being in the presence of something extraordinary, which has stood there for centuries, seems to inspire even the least thoughtful of people to consider, if only for a moment, the briefness of the human span, and to think, 'This will still be here when I am gone'. The oak tree carved with lovers' hearts, enlarging with the tree's growth, is carrying the same thought, except that here it is the love that is being immortalized. At its most urgent, the need to leave a record of one's passing can be seen on the walls of Dachau, or in the bleak dungeons of Carlisle Castle, where hundreds of Scottish Highlanders awaited execution for their part in the '45 Rebellion. Similar sad epitaphs continue to be scratched on the walls of prison cells the world over, pointing to a universal need to believe that individual human life has a significance beyond its immediate span. In some cases, particularly with hostages or political prisoners, it also points to the individual's burning need for the world to know what has happened to him.

I wondered just where the 'How wonderful to be a Turk' message carved deeply into the turf of Turkish hillsides fitted into this scenario. I supposed it carried the sincerely held sentiment of the people who put it there, just as Xerxes probably believed all he wrote about being King of kings.

The essential difference between a great work of art like the Church of the Holy Cross and the graffiti that so copiously disfigured it seems to me to be one of perspective. Both might arise out of the same desire to transcend the limitations of time and space, but where graffiti is, at best, purely a personal statement, the mark of a great work of art is its ability to communicate its ideas to all men. It certainly doesn't help if it is covered in scribbles.

Such a work was the reason for my coming to Akhtamar. Of all the architectural wonders of Eastern Turkey, this church was what I had most looked forward to seeing, my interest in it going

227

back to a time some years before, when I was staying in the Armenian quarter of Jerusalem. One of the monks there, Bishop Cyril, had a passion for medieval Armenian architecture, and he spent much of his time, when not intoning the liturgy at Holy Sepulchre, in making models of his nation's most famous churches. Holy Cross at Akhtamar was considered to be the apogee of all medieval Armenian churches, and Bishop Cyril, who was growing forgetful, had several times expounded its finer points to me. When I left he gave me a poster of a detail of one of its carvings, which now hung in my study.

Standing before the actual building at last, it seemed both very familiar and yet totally new and exciting. It is rather smaller than most Armenian churches, and built of superbly crafted pink sandstone blocks, with the typical central dome raised on a high drum. Its most unusual and delightful feature is the exterior sculpture, liberally adorning every façade. Directly under the roof of the dome, is a frieze of animals: lions, hares, foxes, dogs and gazelles chasing each other, nose to tail, at full stretch. A similar frieze of wonderfully lifelike animals runs the length of the eaves of the main roof on all four sides. A metre below this is a second frieze, this time of fabulous beasts, birds and human-like figures entwined in a continuous burgeoning vine. This is a much more stylized work, with something reminiscent of Celtic art in its flowing unbroken lines, but also something spontaneous and Brueghel-like in the characterization, and in the details of the faces. Near the base of the walls is a band of pine cones and flowers, and in the space between these two lower friezes are large Biblical scenes carved in the round. There was the Jonah I knew from my poster, looking decidedly apprehensive as he is cast into the awaiting jaws of a very cheerful whale, who seems just on the point of giving a reassuring wink. On another wall a sturdy young David prepares to slay Goliath. High on the west façade Gagik presents the church to Christ. And on part of the north wall, as though echoing my fancy about this being a possible site of the Garden of Eden, are Adam and Eve. The artist has made them the least attractive of all the figures, heavy limbed and with pendulous stomachs; coarse, primitive types, curiously like Rembrandt was to depict them in a later century. They have clearly already eaten the apple; their days of innocence are lost forever, and they are caught in the act of reaching out for the fruit of the Tree of Life.

Then the Lord God said 'Behold the man has become like one of us knowing good and evil, and now, lest he put forth his hand and take also of the Tree of Life and live forever:' Therefore the Lord God sent him forth from the Garden of Eden, and at the east of Eden he placed the cherubim, and a flaming sword which turned every way, to guard the Tree of Life.

I already had some idea of the quality of the carving before I came, but I couldn't have imagined the marvellous effect of the light playing on the multi-faceted planes of the walls, which added tremendously to the already great liveliness of the sculpture. The architecture and the carving were all of a piece, a unified whole, a combination of consummate skill and a deep tenderness of execution. Whoever had been responsible for the work I felt he had not only observed the natural world closely, but had also loved it.

That such a marvel had managed to survive largely undamaged for a thousand years and more seemed miraculous, though I suppose that up to seventy years ago, when all the local Armenians were either expelled or killed, it had still been used as a place of worship. The addition of an ill-conceived nineteenth-century bell tower unhappily appended to the west front, confirmed this; it was the one part which no one would miss if it fell down. I suppose being on an island saved this church from the Turkish heavy guns which levelled other Armenian churches. Numerous bullet holes pepper the carvings, but rifle shots could wreak little serious damage on the structure; neglect was a far more serious enemy.

Its value as a tourist attraction is its best chance of surviving into the next century Together with other great Christian churches in Turkey, the official status of museum protects it from Muslim iconoclasts who would consider it a religious duty to deface any representation of man, bird or beast in a place of worship. But as has been the case with so many priceless treasures in Turkey, for want of a little maintenance Holy Cross may well not be standing in another decade. Already the interior is a crumbling shell, the murals almost entirely obliterated, and rubbish and rubble beginning to build up against the walls. A keystone carved with a running hare has recently fallen from the frieze in the eaves beneath the dome, and the roof tiles are just beginning to go.

Perhaps it was the thought that it might not be there at all in a short while that made my delight in it all the sharper. But for whatever reason just being on Akhtamar was to experience again that sense of supreme happiness that had been such a feature of this journey. I would have spent the night there if this had not been officially forbidden. But in some ways I was glad not to. I'd walked around most of the island, enjoying the stupendous and varied views of the towering mountains all around, and the gem of the church itself which looked so perfect from even a short distance away. I wanted to retain my first sharp impressions and not blunt them with over-familiarity.

I camped instead on the lakeside opposite, at a ramshackle little restaurant built to take advantage of the tourist trade. The French were bivouacking there too, and Jules, who was their guide, and who had been coming to these parts for several years, echoed my fears about Akhtamar. The deterioration he had observed in all the Armenian churches had been very rapid, and was due, he thought, to the severity of the winters in the east, coupled with the fact

231

that nothing at all was being done in the way of preservation. He felt that the Turks would be only too happy to see the last of them in ruins, for they kept alive the whole question of the Armenian massacres, and remained an embarrassment to Turkey while they stood.

'Akhtamar Res/Camping' was run by two Kurdish brothers with the help of a number of young men, whom I gather were all distantly related, and could therefore be overworked and underpaid. Trousers rolled up to their knees, a cigarette permanently drooping from the corner of their mouths, one eye screwed up against the smoke, these young retainers wielded their hosepipes, buckets, mops and brooms only when chivvied into activity by roars from their elders. But they were all friendly souls, particularly the brother who went by the ominous name of Gengiz. He took over from the police in protecting tourists and their belongings. With a show of reluctance I was allowed to pitch my tent on the 'campings', a narrow ledge cut in the hillside for that purpose, and barely wide enough even for my minute and aptly named Tadpole. But Roberts, who was much admired, had to remain hidden away inside the rickety main building where it had spent the day while I was on the island. 'Bad peoples come in night, steal; safer sleep with me. You too, sleep with me inside,' said Gengiz, but although I was sure he had nothing amorous in mind, I declined, being happier on the hillside with my view of Akhtamar and the privacy of my own domed roof. Later he cooked me a special Kurdish meal, bringing it sizzling to the table in an iron dish. It was a greasy, fiery concoction of meat, onions and peppers, which I felt I had to eat, so as not to give offence. Later I was to regret this decision, and even at the time my much abused insides gave warning groans.

The peace and beauty of that night defies description. A midnight-blue sky frosted with stars totally transformed the rough site, imbuing it with magic. Soft pools of yellow light shone from the terrace, making haloes about the heads of the few diners. Faint strains of music came and went. Crickets chirruped. Across the lake the moon laid a silver swathe towards Akhtamar, and I fell asleep with the thought that Eden was here and now, and all around me.

At some very early hour in the morning I became aware that I was struggling to remain asleep against an implacable force that was determined to wake me. I was vaguely conscious of a noise like the droning of thousands of oversized bees. When I surfaced more fully I thought perhaps the bees were wearing boots. Then my intestines took over, and fully awake, I struggled out of my sleeping bag to make a dash for the lavatories. The island lay in its peerless lake looking like a Chinese painting under the pale dawn sky, but between the lakeside and my ledge, a further transformation had taken place. Three coaches, their roofs piled high with bales and bundles, were parked by the side of the road, and the ground swarmed with Iranian Kurds, men, women and children, all chattering on a continuous high-pitched wailing note, and scurrying to and fro, more like ants than bees. I'd time for no more than a general impression of a scene of litter and chaos, as I staggered, as fast as pain would allow, to the ramshackle buildings that housed the loos.

The only modern aspect of these latrine huts was that each of the two doors bore an international sign for male or female. I stumbled into the appropriate one only to find my way to the hole in the ground barred by a mixed crowd of villainous-looking men and veiled women. They were all milling about competing for a glimpse of themselves in the sliver of mirror on the wall above the washbasin. There was no time to argue, especially not in Iranian, of which I know not a single word. My need was desperate and I did the only thing I could think of in the circumstances. I grabbed the men by the shoulders and pushed them outside, one after the other. I had the advantage of surprise, which must have helped, but even at the time I was astounded that it should prove so easy, and that I could clear the hut so swiftly.

When I emerged some time later, it was to even greater pandemonium. The brothers were trying to organize their young helpers into a force to repel the Iranian invaders, and the French were standing around in amazement, as though not believing what they were seeing. '*Comme des chickens*,' Jules muttered to me, shaking his head in disbelief. '*Toute la nuit come des chickens*, cluck, cluck cluck.' Actually he was right; the noise was far more like a poultry yard than the battalion of earthbound bees in boots which I'd visualized. Either way it was not a pleasant awakening. No barbarian horde could have caused more havoc in so short a space of time; and the wonderful scenery only emphasized the squalid chaos. Reams of blown plastic and paper, soiled rags, excrement, broken bread and peelings were all over the road and throughout the garden, even the bushes bore a crop of foreign matter. The Iranians had already washed out babies' napkins, pots and pans, clothes and bodies in the lake, and had carried out their bodily functions along the shore, so it was not clear why they needed to invade the restaurant, except to get at the fresh water. This was a finite supply, and quickly exhausted, so that lavatories, showers and the kitchen were now effectively out of action. Yet still the Iranians tried to push in under the outstretched arms of the brothers and their employees. Gengiz was intoning, for some reason in English, 'No more Iranians. No more water. No more Iranians', over and over, but with no real conviction. Stout matrons in their black *chadars* kept brushing him aside as if he were no more than a gnat in their path. I could see now why their men had proved so docile when I'd pushed them out of the loo, clearly no one dared gainsay an Iranian matron.

The impasse was finally ended by the old cook who had been quietly brewing tea in his kitchen shack (doubtless from some hoarded store of water). He carried a tray of little tulip glasses out to the littered road, where the drivers of the three battered buses and a few bowed elders stood, backs turned in aloof detachment from the general hullabaloo. As soon as these tokens of hospitality and friendship had been drunk, the two hundred or so passengers were summoned into the vehicles, which, visibly sagging under their loads, continued on around the lake towards the Iranian border.

The cook carried out a second tray of tea to a secluded table at the back of the garden, and shepherded the French, Gengiz and myself towards it. And there we sat, shaken but recovering, mulling over the incident, while the boys got to work with their mops and brooms. I could now well believe Gengiz's claim about employing one boy just to keep the lavatories clean. Apparently these caravans of buses, returning from shopping sprees in Turkey, possibly as far afield as Ankara, frequently halted outside. They usually pulled in around midnight, after which the roads in these parts are deemed unsafe. The passengers, fresh from a few hours sleep on the bus, all pile out, light their cooking fires and catch up on their chores, and their social life, chattering like starlings the while. They pay nothing, ruin what tourist trade there is, and leave the whole area looking as though a fleet of municipal dust carts have just shed their loads. No wonder Gengiz was close to tears as he explained his predicament. There was, he said, nothing he could do about it. Ancient laws of hospitality, as well as solidarity with fellow Kurds prevented any complaint to the authorities. Not that complaining would do them much good anyway — the authorities already had their hands full trying to cope with the current spate of Kurdish terrorism. Eden post the Fall was certainly not without its share of problems.

16

A Tricky Ride to Tatvan

I HAD anticipated a memorable ride to Tatvan through the rugged countryside that bordered the southern margins of Lake Van, and so it proved, though not in the way I was expecting. As I toiled up towards the head of a steep pass, I became aware of a figure in greyish-white clothing squatting among the rocks on the hillside with a rifle trained down on me. That I did not give way to panic was no doubt greatly helped by the fact that most of my energy was absorbed in tackling the gradient. With the adrenalin already flowing freely, and my heart beating at a brisk pace, the degree of shock was probably a good deal less than it might have been. Since I was moving so slowly, however, there was ample time for the tension to build. The only thing to do, I felt, was to keep pedalling and hope that the person holding the gun would decide I was not a legitimate target. I tried to keep my gaze any place other than where he was, as though unaware of his presence; I think I reasoned it would be harder for him to fire at an unsuspecting victim. But as I drew level, I couldn't resist a brief glance towards the spot, and suddenly, as though my eyes were zoom lenses, I found my frame of vision filled by a foreshortened rifle barrel, a dark face grinning sardonically above it, and a hand closing around a trigger. Perhaps the smile was a perverted attempt at a friendly gesture, but by this time my sense of humour was somewhat strained, and I didn't feel like grinning back. From the moment the road had left the lakeside to climb up into the encroaching mountains I had come under attack of one sort or another. At the time the possibility of being shot seemed just another form of harassment.

I had realized I was passing through an area of greater unrest then usual, even for these parts, because trucks crammed with heavily-armed soldiers were dashing to and fro, and the villages, which occurred every three or four miles, were ominously silent and empty, except for occasional groups of armed civilians. My passing was noted, however; in every settlement young boys braved whatever was keeping everyone else out of sight, and rushed to hurl their missiles at me. Once or twice, where the village was on a steep hillside and I was reduced to walking, perhaps realizing I was a woman, an adult emerged and tried to call the boys off. But they were not amenable to persuasion, and it always ended up with the adult hurling stones at them in sheer frustration. Child psychology, I decided, had not yet reached these parts!

At no time did anyone even try to rescue me from the dogs. I was convinced they had been sent out deliberately to intimidate anyone who was travelling through; a defiant gesture aimed at the military presence perhaps, for the dogs attacked anything that moved, including vehicles. The Dog Dazer stayed permanently in my hand, and if I prayed, it was that its battery would hold out under the heavy demands I was making on it.

What I thought at the time was my Waterloo occurred in a place called Balaban where I was suddenly surrounded by four of these huge brutes armed with their menacing spiked collars. I had become adept at seeing off two at a time by now. As long as I could concentrate a steady beam for three or four seconds in each dog's direction, it was enough, they would back right off, and seldom come back for a second attack. But four of them, and four, moreover, who knew how to work together, were quite another matter. They came at me one from each side and two from the rear, and they held their positions, dropping back only for a moment as the sound hit them briefly. The road was going uphill so I could not maintain enough speed to control Roberts with one hand while aiming the Dazer at each leaping dog in turn. I would have had more chance had I been on my feet, but I couldn't dismount without giving the dogs the opportunity to rush in. It was probably highly amusing for the spectators, like a parody of a Wild West film, with me 'shooting' wildly over my shoulder at each dog in turn, wobbling all over the road on the lurching Roberts as I did so. At one point I became convinced that the Dazer was no longer working properly, for the dogs were just shaking their heads a little before coming back for more. They leapt again and

240

again, each time their teeth just failing to close on me — partly, I think, because the panniers got in their way, and partly because I was swaying about so much. I was also yelling as lustily as I could to try and summon help. But although all this was happening in the middle of a village street, and I could see people watching the show from doorways and windows, no one did a thing. I don't know how long the attack continued before my yells and the repeated blasts from the Dazer wore the dogs down, probably no more than a few minutes, but at the time it seemed to go on for an eternity, and I had given up hope of it ever ending. My legs felt like jelly by the time it was over. It was without doubt the most frightening incident of the entire journey; a sniper's bullet seemed almost tame in comparison.

Another jolly game was played on the steep slopes that took the road up to a point two thousand feet higher than it had started. It was an area of rugged magnificence, where the mountains stretched unbroken to the burning plains of Mesopotamia, far to the south. Decrepit Iranian lorries, their cabs emblazoned with pious Islamic mottoes such as, *Allah Korusun* (God protect me), and *Maasallah* (Wonder of God), their bets hedged by the addition of large painted eyes to avert evil, crept down the slopes on suspect brakes, even more slowly than I was winding up them. Possibly to relieve the monotony of this creeping descent the drivers, grinning with the same malicious smirk the sniper had worn, deliberately veered

241

their trucks across the road on a collision course with me, mostly where there was a sheer drop on my side. The first time this happened I was so incensed, I didn't even consider what I was doing, but immediately turned Roberts into the line of attack and quickened my pace — a furious mottoless mouse taking on an Islamic juggernaut — but it worked! The unexpectedness of my response seemed to terrify the driver, and he immediately returned to his side of the road. After that, I reacted in the same way every time a truck tilted at me, and mostly I won, but sometimes they did, hanging on to the collision course until I had to turn away or be crushed beneath their wheels. Honours, I reckoned grimly, were definitely better than evens, which childish though it might seem at this remove, cheered me immensely at the time.

To complete this saga of persecution, a short way before reaching the comparative safety of Tatvan, I was crashed into heavily from behind by a rare local cyclist. He was one of a party of five riding heavy Chinese bikes. They had all been crowding in around me, giggling and generally making nuisances of themselves, until I had applied my brakes, rather too sharply, in order to let them get ahead. In the ensuing collision I managed to keep Roberts upright, but a rear pannier was torn off and sent flying. The culprit, who had come off his bike and torn his trousers, appeared beside himself with terror, and fell on his knees before me, wringing his hands in what I took to be abject apology. He had no English, but I guessed he was frightened that I would complain to the authorities. His panic seemed so genuine that it totally dispelled my anger, and I hastened to reassure him that both Roberts and I were unhurt. This was not the case with his cycle however, which had twisted its steering, bent the down tube, and displaced several components. I got out my tools, and by the time we had restored it to something approaching roadworthiness, all six of us were on amicable terms, and we hurtled down the steep hill into Tatvan together. Actually, they were so competitive that it was safer to let them take the lead, which had the double advantage of preventing further collision, and of clearing the path of importunate stone-throwing boys.

Tatvan is built on the shores of the south-eastern corner of Lake Van, with the bulk of Nemrut Dagi towering up behind it, a setting entirely wasted on such a run-down dump of a place, which looks inwards, away from the sparkling blue water and the hills, towards the piles of rubbish festering in its broken streets. The overwrought atmosphere that was immediately apparent was in keeping with its reputation for kidnappings and nightly shoot-ups by the PKK. I wouldn't have stayed there even one night had there not been two places of great interest in the vicinity that I very much wanted to see.

I found a room for half the original asking price in the run-down hotel, built in more settled times to serve the wealthier passengers of the now moribund railway service. It reminded me of some of the crumbling British-built resthouses

243

in which I'd stayed in India and the Sudan. There was a similar air of faded gentility combined with very few creature comforts; drains tended to be blocked and overflowing, doorknobs came off in one's hand, and it did not do to drop things, for in bending down to retrieve them you became aware of the ancient dust and detritus lying in heaps beneath the bed.

On the strength of my Kurdish letter I was adopted by a young man called Mehmet who ran the hotel. The owner, a clone of the unpleasant manager of the Hotel Yilmaz in Kars, sat in the dusty garden piously refusing to meet the eye of any female guest, while poring avidly over the pages of semi-nude females in his newspaper. Mehmet studied chemistry, and spoke excellent English, which was why he was employed there for the summer, working a seven-day week, twelve hours a day for a miserable pittance. He was positively sick with longing to leave his turbulent roots and live in the West. 'Anywhere in the West I would go, for here is worse than nothing. But I will die dreaming,' he told me sadly, as we sat eating ice-cream in the only café open in the comatose town that evening. We were the sole customers, and although it was only nine p.m. the owner was anxious for us to leave. Contrary to Turkish custom, people in Tatvan stayed home after dark, because of PKK activity. Few nights passed without some shooting incident, and the previous night there had been a particularly heavy raid on a bank, which was the reason for all the military activity

I had encountered on the way.

Mehmet was cynical about Britain's and America's role in the Kurdish problem. He thought both countries worked hand-in-glove with the Turkish authorities to destroy the PKK, and claimed that in the last few days American planes stationed on Iraq's border had bombed Kurdish villages, on the pretence that they were PKK terrorist camps. Since this allied force was supposed to be there expressly to watch over Sadam Hussein's treatment of the Iraqi Kurds, the likelihood of them getting involved in such an operation seemed extremely remote. Everywhere in Eastern Turkey, however, Kurds believed it to be true, and I was to hear the accusation repeated many times before I left the country. It was advanced as ample justification for the kidnapping of Westerners. The eight or nine German tourists who had been abducted while camping on Nemrut Dagi had just been released unharmed, but several others had already taken their place, and while I was in Tatvan PKK guerillas stopped a bus near a town fifty miles away and abducted five Americans and Australians whom I had met briefly at dinner the previous evening. After this the Turks placed an embargo on the reporting of all such incidents, on the grounds that it was playing into the hands of the PKK who were doing it only to keep the Kurdish problem to the forefront of international attention.

The many conversations I had with Mehmet over the next few days gave me a deeper appreciation of the frustrations of intelligent young Kurds, frustrations which must apply, in some degree, to the youth of minority populations the world over. His longing to live in the West, to enjoy a better standard of living and to embrace a different set of social values, alienated him from his own culture, which in turn made him hate the West for causing him such inner turmoil. Moreover, because he believed the West to be a goal forever beyond his reach, he felt rejected by it, and to ease the pain of this, it was necessary to find ways of hating and despising it, so that it became less desirable. Rumours such as America and Britain becoming involved in Turkey's fight with the PKK were seized on avidly and believed in unquestioningly. Whichever way he turned he didn't look like winning.

He had already turned his back on his parents' lifestyle, particularly on multiple marriages. His father had been wealthy, but with the four wives permitted him by the Koran, each of whom had borne between twelve and twenty children, there was little for Mehmet who came near the end of a line of some fifty brothers and sisters. His mother had struggled to get him educated, but he wondered now if the effort had been worth it. His self-taught English made him realize how little competence his teachers possessed in that subject, and, not unnaturally, he suspected that other subjects were similarly ill-taught. But even if he obtained his degree it would make little difference to his future in Turkey. There were few jobs for Kurds, he told me, and almost none in the professions. His brother had qualified as an engineer a couple of years before and was still seeking an opening.

If this was the life for a reasonably privileged and educated young Kurd, how much more hopeless for the greater number who didn't even receive the benefit of primary schooling? In such a climate I found the desire to emigrate as understandable as the desire for an autonomous homeland. Nor did it seem strange that when young Kurds reached the age for compulsory military service, many chose to take to the hills and join the PKK instead.

Nemrut Dagi, my main reason for visiting Tatvan, is one of two famous mountains of that name in eastern Anatolia. The other, which is further west, has on its summit a pantheon of giant stone deities which the megalomaniac king, Antiochus I Epiphanes (God made manifest), set there two thousand years ago as a sort of family gallery. The Tatvan Nemrut on the other hand is a natural wonder, an extinct volcano whose last eruption sealed off Lake Van. When the top of the mountain was literally blown off, an extraordinary crater was left. The western end became a vast lake with a diameter of about two miles, one of the largest crater lakes in the world, and which, at almost 8,000 feet above sea level made an impressive feature, even on my small-scale map. Visits to Nemrut were currently severely restricted because of the kidnapping of the Germans. Overnight camping there was strictly forbidden, and passports had to be left with the military to make sure all foreigners were off the mountain before nightfall.

I was also obliged to drive up there on a vile axle-bending track with the old rogue who had the monopoly on the tourist taxi trade. It was he who had supplied the kidnapped Germans with daily food at their camp beside the crater lake. After he had taken me on a tour of the spot where this alarming incident had taken place, and given me a blow-by-blow recital of how the kidnappers had gone about it, shooting out the tyres of the Germans' cars, blindfolding them, and so forth, I wasn't surprised to hear that the military had taken him in for questioning and given him a hard time.

Long contact with tourists had made him assume a rather tedious conversational style in the hope of provoking reaction: 'Every month I make new baby. I want eighty kids. I love the kids.' But he had his reasonable side for all that, and he settled down for a few hours to share a melon with some of his nomad cronies beside a squalid little lake, warmed by hot springs and littered with the usual plastic and paper rubbish, leaving me free to explore on my own. I went off to swim in the great crater lake, and, possibly because it was now well into September, I did not find the water as glacial as some travellers have reported it (though anyone who has regularly swum in the seas off north-western Scotland seldom finds anywhere else particularly chilly). It was a marvellous place, where I too would have been very happy to set up camp and stay for a while and see what the fishing was like. I knew there were fish because two men from the nearby nomads' camp came

248

and dangled their lines from the rocks where I had left my clothes — either I had chosen the very best spot in all that vast lake, or Turkish curiosity was operating as usual. Apart from these two and any hidden PKK guerillas debating whether one lone female was worth kidnapping, I had the place to myself. Across the water the northern rim of the crater reared up in a great two-thousand-foot sun-baked rock wall, up which I would have been tempted to find an easy route had my driver not just then come in search of me.

The eastern end of the crater was equally memorable, a wasteland of lava beds that had cooled into a dark tortured landscape of jagged peaks and troughs. From the crater rim Lake Van was, if possible, more deeply and sublimely blue than ever, spreading as far as the eye could see into the hazy distance, with here and there the snowy summit of some other vast peak glimmering above it.

Another day I took a *dolmus* northwards round the lake to the famous Selçuk cemetery at Ahlat. There had once been a major Urartian town on the site, and later, an Armenian one. This fell to the Arabs in the eighth century and was subsequently held by just about everyone who passed this way, Byzantines, Selçuks, Ayubids, Kharizmids, Kurds, a second wave of Selçuks, Mongols, Akkoyunlus, Karakoyunlus, and finally the Ottomans, under whom the place declined.

There were a dozen or so large and elegant *türbe*, or mausolea, many of them in perfect condition; Turks seldom seem to vandalize Islamic structures. All were from pre-Ottoman times, and were of great beauty and variety. The earliest was built in 1273 for a Selçuk emir, and the latest, 1492, for a Karakoyunlu princess. These *türbe* are freestanding structures, rather like scaled down mosques, or, when the roofs are conical, something like miniature Armenian churches without the exedrae. Sometimes they are two-storied and the small coffin-sized tomb is on the lower floor. There are usually windows or fretted lattice-work embrasures, and a door or two. The workmanship is a marvel and the detail exquisite, for they were meant to be great works of art, and have none of the gloomy dankness so often associated in the West with the word tomb.

But lovely as I found these small masterpieces, what made Ahlat unforgettable was the extraordinary Selçuk cemetery that spreads unbroken over acres and acres of gently undulating ground, the most romantic burial ground I have ever seen. Forgetting that a great city had once also stood here, my first reaction was amazement that there could be so many illustrious dead in so remote a place. Hundreds of thousands of tall slender shafts of grey granite, each taller than a man, rise uncluttered, straight out of the green turf. Each stone is virtually identical in outline, differing only in height and thickness, and in the details of its fine flowing Arabic calligraphy and floral motifs. Lichens, wind and weather and the passage of eight centuries has further eroded the individual nature of the monuments. There are no straight rows any longer and each stone leans in a slightly different direction to its neighbours. Time has changed them into a stone forest growing beside a peerless blue lake.

When I left the cemetery I thought I would continue the half mile to the modern village of Ahlat and find some lunch, before returning to Tatvan. A tractor passed, and seeing me walking the driver immediately stopped so that I could step up behind and balance perilously on the towing bar. Turkish tractor drivers are amongst the kindest people in the world, and invariably stop for pedestrians. It was a hot day and a cold beer seemed very desirable. As usual, there were no restaurants serving anything other than sickly cola or equally sickly orange, so I asked in a shop where I could buy a beer . . . and unleashed a tirade: Ahlat had nothing so vile, so degenerate, so altogether beyond the pale as beer! I left with a flea in my ear, but had no sooner reached the pavement, than another man, who had followed me out of the shop, offered to escort me to where beer was not only readily available but cold to boot. I accepted and was led to a perfectly respectable little bar in a side street. I invited my guide to join me, but he declined courteously, adding that as a Muslim he didn't drink alcohol.

My last morning in Tatvan I went fishing, simply because at around six a.m. I was sitting on some lumps of concrete enjoying the dawn breaking over the lake when a smart little launch pulled in and I was invited aboard. The boat

251

had been designed for private cruising, and the present owner had acquired it with the idea of offering trips around the bay to tourists, but since foreigners were proving so scarce he was trying his hand at fishing instead. I had eaten some of his catch at my hotel on the previous evening, small dab-like fish which are, I believe, the only species able to tolerate the high alkali concentration of the lake. Unlike the usual run of lake fish they had rather soft bones and not too many of them, and were a most welcome change from kebabs. A small army of boys and youths, aged between ten and twenty, already occupied most of the space in the luxurious little cabin. Under their combined assaults the boat was already losing its smartness, and a thick brown patina was spreading everywhere from the continuous pall of tobacco smoke. Even the youngest of the boys had the statutory symbol of manhood glowing in the corner of his mouth, with the eye above it permanently screwed up against the smart of the smoke. I stayed on deck for I couldn't have survived in there for more than a minute. As far as I could see, the boys were paid in an unending supply of a noxious local brand.

They were all having a wonderful time, and there was fierce competition for the privilege of tossing overboard the half-dozen badly torn nets, and for the painful task of pulling them in by hand, when the remaining areas of mesh were so thick with small shining flat fish, that the coils of the net bit deeply into the hauler's hands and forearms. The work of picking the fish out of the nets required everyone, for never have I seen fish get themselves quite so entangled; what they didn't have in the way of bones they seemed to make up for in the quantity and sharpness of their fins. From the time it took some boys to free even one tiny fish, it could have seemed like a terrible task, but for the rapt expressions on their faces.

Most of the boys were friends of Mehmet, and the day before some of them had been in the hotel's garden when Mehmet's elder brother had paid a visit. He was a young man of about twenty-six whose handsome face was twisted by dislike and suspicion. He had taken the opportunity to pour out a tirade against the West in general and Britain in particular. 'For', he informed me, 'all Westerners have quite the wrong idea about history; mostly it is just lies to cover up the facts.' The truth was that Kurdistan had once occupied all the land which is now called Iran, Russia, Syria, Iraq, and Turkey. It was the West who had divided it up over the centuries, just as it was Britain who was now supplying the chemical weapons to destroy the Kurds once and for all. Turkey and Iraq were working together to eliminate the Kurds, and America and Britain were only maintaining their planes on the border to assist in the destruction. It was the sort of mishmash which results from taking a grain of truth and blowing it up into monstrous distortions. But in the mouth of an intelligent, good-looking young fanatic, of an age to influence the boys and youths who were listening avidly, it was poisonous stuff, and it left a nasty taste in my mouth.

I was glad therefore to be able to take my farewell of Lake Van in a way I would prefer to remember it. Boys fishing created a sort of primal image, if not of the Garden of Eden, at least of a Huckleberry Finn type of innocence. I found it salutary to remember that this too could exist in a world of mindless xenophobia and organized terrorism.

17

On the Walls of Diyarbakir

CLIMBING out of the great bowl of
Lake Van marked yet another distinct
and dramatic change in the journey.
The mountains are a watershed signalling the
end of the Eastern Anatolian Plateau and the
beginning of the long descent to the Arab
borderlands. From their vast snow-crowned
slopes innumerable streams flow south to feed
the great River Tigris. It was a hard ride to the
top of the escarpment, with a headwind adding
to the effort, and nothing in the rough scenery
to make up for the splendours I was leaving.
Forgetting the aggression I had encountered
around its shores, I felt such a wave of nostalgia
for the blue expanse of Lake Van that I was
almost on the point of turning round and going
back. But the road finally levelled out and quite
suddenly I was over the top and turning down
into the Güzel Dere, the Beautiful Valley.

If I had indeed just left the cradle of
civilization, the place where 'man had first
set foot on the unpeopled earth', I was now
embarked on one of the main routes of his
great dispersal. Down from the high plains of
Ararat and the mountain fastnesses, following
the natural flow of the rivers, had come the
sons of Noah seeking fresh pastures and new

worlds. Already the air felt markedly drier and hotter, and the wind blowing up the valley from the south-west brought with it a faint peppery smell, exotic and exciting, the scent of the deserts of Syria; I was heading down towards the area of Abraham's early wanderings. No sooner had I thought of Abraham, than sweeping round a corner I came to a fine thirteenth-century Selçuk caravanserai. Spread about on the thinly-grassed slopes around the crumbling walls were five or six black goat-hair tents of nomads surrounded by their parti-coloured flocks, unchanged it seemed from the days of the Patriarchs.

A little below, in a steep narrow canyon where four streams come together to form the Bitlis Suyu, a tributary of the Tigris, was the bristling citadel that stands guard over the valley and the ancient Kurdish town of Bitlis. The medieval city filled the slopes of the narrow valley, and with no room to expand further, it has preserved its character, together with its cobbled streets and its awesome middens crowned with elegant cocks crowing out their challenge above the competing uproar. Spanning the river was an old humpbacked bridge where I stopped to buy bread and fruit, and I sat there on the parapet eating my lunch and enjoying the scenes, while far below goats browsed beside the river's edge on further accumulations of Bitlis's ancient rubbish heaps. It all seemed so different to the place I had left only hours before, that I felt I was in an entirely new country.

All afternoon I descended the Güzel Dere, thinking how aptly named it was with its jade-green river strangely studded with little towers of rock where it flowed through narrow canyons, its villages perched high in the folds of steep hills, its stands of dark pine trees, and the bright green, close-cropped clearings where nomads gathered with their sheep, their cattle and their horses. As I descended and the mountains receded it grew hotter and hotter, and the pepper-scented wind, continuing to blow strongly out of the burning plains of Mesopotamia, was like the blast of an oven in my face. Flocks hung their heads under the shade of enormous acacia trees, while the shepherd boys swam in the green water, and I wished very much that I could join them.

Even so, it was far hotter off the bicycle without the air flowing past, as I discovered when I stopped at Veysel Karani, a rough little hamlet where the heat and the flies descended like a blanket. This was the point where my route turned west, and as I had already ridden the sixty miles that I consider a reasonable day's journey, I thought I would either look for a bus to take me the remaining hundred miles to Diyarbakir, my next objective, or find a stopping-place for the night. I was out of luck on both counts; there were no buses, and only an unsavoury flea-pit of a 'hotel'. Another small town was marked on my map about twenty miles further on, and I hoped that this would provide some sort of accommodation should I not succeed in finding a suitable place to camp on the way.

The road crossed several pretty streams

flowing south to join the complicated course of the Tigris, and beside all of them were fine places to pitch a tent. But a sudden rash of stone-throwing juveniles made me realize that camping anywhere in the area was out of the question. Horrid shrieks rent the air as posse after posse of nimble-footed boys leapt down the hillsides to intercept me, snatching up stones as they went. Only once was I tempted to stop, and that was when some menacing youths had managed to get ahead of me, and I was sure that, rotten shots as they were, they couldn't fail to hit me at point-blank range. I told them sternly, by word and gesture, that unless they dropped their half bricks that instant, I was going straight off to an army post I could see on a hillside to complain about them. This was pure bluff, and it surprised me that it worked, since most of these boys were bigger than I, and could easily have overpowered me. But they were clearly intimidated by my performance and, as on previous occasions when I had countered aggression with the threat of involving the police or the army, it achieved the desired result. A part of me was conscious of the ridiculousness of the scene even as it was happening, and I felt I needed only a brolly to complete the picture of indignant Victorian maiden aunt.

Nonetheless, with the continual alarms and bombardments, I was feeling distinctly frayed and out of temper by the time I reached the unpromising little cluster of hovels that crowned a low hillside surrounded by extensive fields of tobacco. A petrol station and restaurant stood beside the road, and I went there to take stock of the situation. The owner was sitting at his desk counting money, and enquired in broken English how I was enjoying Turkey. I found myself telling him exactly what I thought just then about his country and its hassles, miming the stone throwing when he failed to understand. He seemed shocked to the core by my recital, and I suppose if you are a Kurd, and travel everywhere by car, you wouldn't necessarily know about the sort of things that can happen to a rare non-Kurd, and one rash enough to pass through by bicycle.

A man who had seen off several louts harassing me as I'd ridden across the last bridge came into the restaurant at this point and corroborated my story, though as it was all in Kurdish I gleaned this only by looks and gestures. Soon there was a gathering of several men, all tut-tutting and pressing gifts of tea, soft drinks, cakes, kebabs and fruit upon me, and assuring me of their vigilant protection and a safe place to sleep on the roof. I would have been perfectly happy to trust them and to spread my sleeping bag under the stars, but the brother of the owner had been sent for, and he arrived speaking excellent English, and took me off to spend the night with his wife and himself in a house across the road.

Osman and Vara were newly-weds, she in her early twenties, he a few years older. They were wealthy by local standards, owning a large acreage of the enormous plains of tobacco, recently established with the help

259

of a government irrigation scheme. They also owned their own house, a raw, ugly little place of exposed concrete and unfaced breeze blocks built above workshops on a patch of rough land.

After climbing the perilous outside staircase from the rubbish-strewn ground, shoes were removed and we stepped into a bright clean interior full of new plastic furniture and garish fluffy nylon rugs, with Vara's crocheted mats and doyleys covering every possible shiny surface. There was electricity and the usual refrigerator, television and neon lighting, but water was fetched by bucket from some distance away.

Vara was very attractive, and Osman was patently delighted with her. He pulled her forward several times as we sat drinking coffee, in order to display her charms more fully, saying, 'She is beautiful, no, this woman of mine? I do not choose for her to go covered,' he continued, meaning that she was unveiled. 'I want her open, so.' Another time, pulling her roughly forward and laying his hand on her stomach, he said proudly, 'Maybe seven months there is a baby here.' Vara seemed as embarrassed as I was by all this, but she made a show of laughing it off.

Osman had been an archaeology student in Diyarbakir but had abandoned his course for agriculture. He said he couldn't stand the hassle of constant arrests which Kurdish students were subjected to. Diyarbakir as I knew, was the centre of Kurdish resistance, the city considered by them to be the capital of Kurdistan. Secret police were everywhere, Osman told me, bribing, blackmailing, working on people's weaknesses to betray their brothers. Children as young as fourteen had been tortured in the notorious Diyarbakir prison. Anything could be a pretext for being hauled off to a police station for questioning. All the hardships I'd been told about by Mehmet and other Kurds were endorsed by Osman. While economic conditions were hard for many in Turkey, for Kurds they were always worse. Many had no schooling, no medicine, no jobs and no housing. Worst of all they had no say in government.

I showed him my map and asked him to indicate what lands he thought should be included in an autonomous Kurdistan. Like every other Kurd of whom I had asked this question, he indicated an area that stretched as far west as Gaziantep and included a little over a third of the entire country. It was, said Osman, the area that had been promised to them by Atatürk.

The only way forward for Kurds now, he was convinced, was through the PKK, which had begun eight years before as a student movement based on Marxist ideals. He was sure that the PKK had the support of the entire Kurdish population, and that young people were flocking to them in ever increasing numbers. The picture he painted was of the hills filled with high-minded young men and women sacrificing themselves for the greater good of Kurdistan. It made me think of the idealistic early Russian films of Eisenstein. But although I didn't necessarily doubt the truth of anything he was telling me, somehow, of all the Kurds who had talked to me about the current struggles, Osman was the only one for whom I failed to feel sympathy. Perhaps this was because his affluence, compared with the way most Kurds lived, didn't square with what he called his Marxist principles. Or maybe it was his answer when I asked him why he was not in the PKK since he admired it so much, and he said he couldn't because he was married and had other responsibilities. But most of all I think it was because of his treatment of a pretty twelve-year-old girl, Kari, a poor neighbour's daughter, who had adopted the couple and who spent all her time in the flat copying Vara in everything, including wearing her make-up. She sat gazing up adoringly at Osman most of the time, as though practising for her future role, and he handled her in the same physically proprietorial way he treated Vara. 'I like this one, she is very pretty,' he said, turning her round into the light. 'But maybe one more year, and her father say to close it,' and he mimed the veil of purdah being drawn over the child's face. And for me, in that one dismissive gesture he managed to concentrate all the unbearable arrogance of the eastern male. Whatever freedom was being fought for here, I did not feel that the women would benefit greatly.

I was given the bridal chamber, for like most people in these parts, Osman and Vara preferred to pass the hot nights in the open, which in their case was on a mattress on their tiny balcony. The bedroom was at the back of the house and

I slept well, wrapped coolly in my sheet sleeping bag and away, for once, from the noise of traffic. There had been shooting in the night, Osman told me the next day, and he had come in to see if I was alright, but I had heard nothing.

I awoke early to a view of endless flat fields filled with tall tobacco plants stretching unbroken far to the south where low flat-topped hills broke the skyline. Dotted about the edges of the fields were small booths built of boughs with the withered leaves still on them. In front of each little hut was an enormous metal cot on tall legs, exactly like a baby's cot except in size, in which families of six, seven, or more slept together high off the ground, cool, and safe from rats and snakes. A foetid green ribbon of water lay between Osman's house and the booths, and several people were washing their faces in this and cleaning out cooking pots.

The previous night a promise had been extracted from me that I would stay on to meet Vara's extended family who had been told of my visit by telephone, and who wanted to meet me and to cook me a special Kurdish meal. Once I had eaten their *dolmasi*, they promised, I would not wish to leave.

Vara and I walked though the fields to pass the time until her relations arrived, and the family of the adoring Kari, who lived in one of the booths, came with us. As soon as she saw us approach Kari disappeared inside the dark little hut where all the family goods were tied in bundles suspended from the roof. She came out liberally made up with rouge and lipstick, looking like a little doll, and everyone laughed at her, at which the poor child blushed even through the brash colour. There were eight other children (seven more had died in infancy) and Kari came somewhere in the middle. Seeing her together with her family, it was impossible not to realize how dissatisfied she was with her lot, and how passionately she longed to be like Vara. Her mother, who was little more than forty, looked ancient. I thought she was about to give birth to another child, but it was simply that her stomach muscles had never had the chance to recover from the constant child-bearing.

Kurdish women, like their menfolk, are physically demonstrative with their own sex, and there was a good deal of affectionate touching and stroking, and everyone linked arms or held hands as we walked through the fields. Away from Osman, Vara was a different person, intelligent and amusing, and the walk through the fields was in many ways the best part of the visit. Only young Kari held herself aloof from the camaraderie, jealous at having to share Vara. We were broiling in the fierce sun, even at nine in the morning, but the tobacco plants were high above the smaller children's heads, so for them it was like walking in a forest. In between the rows of tobacco were water melons, cucumbers, sunflowers and indian corn, so that while the cash crop was being grown there was also enough food for daily needs; some indication of how very fertile this once barren plain had become. We ate some of the crisp young cucumbers as we walked, and the children floated sunflower heads down the narrow irrigation channels.

The flat-topped hills had their counterpart in hidden flat-bottomed gulleys that appeared suddenly without warning, and into which it would be all to easy for a stranger to plunge to his death in the dark. It was to one of these cool shaded ravines, the original dwelling places of the people of these once-arid plains, that the walk had led. A great pool lay in the bottom a hundred feet below, and the women threw stones into it to show how deep it was. There were substantial caves in the vertical walls, which had been inhabited until recent times. Only cattle roamed the canyons now, feeding on the luxuriant vegetation, for the area had been entirely changed by the new irrigation scheme. I wasn't sure that I wouldn't have preferred life in these luxuriant shaded gulleys to the featureless hot plains above.

Back at the house relatives of all ages descended *en masse*, some twenty-five in all, and the formal ceremony of greetings took the best part of half an hour. In my case they consisted of the briefest of handshakes with the men, kisses from the younger women, and a very lengthy message delivered earnestly to me by each older female, while my hands were tenderly clasped in both of theirs. Although I could not understand a word of it, it made me feel most tremendously welcome, almost like royalty. After this, all the women and girls settled in circles on the kitchen floor, chopping, peeling, boiling and frying all the ingredients that go into the making of *dolmasi*, or stuffed peppers, the whole while keeping up an animated chattering like starlings in a tree at dusk. To my mind *dolmasi* are not one of the world's great gastronomic treats, certainly not worth the extraordinary amount of effort that goes into making them, but perhaps the lengthy preparations are their chief attraction, since they give the women such ample opportunity for socializing.

The men were fewer in number, and stayed firmly away from the kitchen, spending their time playing with the small boys. This play was decidedly rough, a mixture of slaps, pinches and tickling, designed to provoke a reaction and make the child fight back. I began to see why Kurdish boys were so aggressive. These little lads escaped to the kitchen as often as they could where they were petted back into good humour by the women.

After four hours concentrated preparation the feast was ready, and two separate places were prepared for eating it, the men at the table and the women around a cloth on the floor. It was proposed to seat me with the men, but I preferred the company of the women, even though I don't find it easy to eat at floor level. I did my best to show a proper appreciation for all the work by eating a lot, but what I most enjoyed was the happy easy atmosphere of mutual liking, and all the lighthearted teasing, of which it was perfectly easy to get the gist.

Suddenly all this changed. Vara's mother, a women of my own age, had rather taken me under her wing. She had spent a long time talking loudly and slowly to me in Kurdish, convinced I would understand if only she repeated things often enough. Now she leant over and reached into the neck of my shirt, attracted perhaps by a flash of gold, and drew out the small cross I wear. She let go of it at once and said something in a shocked voice, which Osman translated as meaning she had never expected to sit down to eat with a Christian! I asked, 'Why not, when I am happy to eat with Muslims?', at which a general impassioned conversation broke out over my head. I couldn't understand a word, and Osman was too busy arguing to translate.

Then a tiny shrivelled old woman, Vara's great-grandmother, started speaking, and everyone else fell silent. After a while Osman began telling me what she was saying. Apparently the incident had awoken memories of the massacre of the Armenians which she had witnessed as a little girl in her village some way to the south. She spoke of the *imams* going through the streets urging the Kurds to 'Kill the Christians, kill the infidels'. Three little Armenian boys had sought refuge from the slaughter in her parents' house she said, and the women had tried to protect them. 'Not these, not these,' she remembered her mother pleading. But, she said, the men had dragged them out just the same, and the streets had been full of screaming and burning. Her words uncannily echoed what I had read on the subject: 'They went into the houses of the Armenians and killed the women and the children; the men were already dead.'

It was a strange ending to a feast, and

everyone was a bit subdued. But while it had been difficult and embarrassing, I was nonetheless glad to have been the inadvertent cause of unlocking this old woman's memories. It was good to know that there are still living witnesses prepared to speak of those awful events which the Turkish authorities deny ever happened, and it was also very good to hear that there had been ordinary Muslims who had demurred in the general heat of 'religious' killings. Osman's remark at the end of the recounting also gave me food for thought. The difference between nationalism and religion is so often blurred, but I have never heard it so clearly expressed as on this occasion. 'The Armenians are our brothers in the fight against the Turks; we don't think of them as Christians.'

Because of the feast, I did not arrive at Diyarbakir until well after dark, and it was not until the following morning that I could begin to appreciate the sombre magnificence of this most ancient of all southern Anatolia's cities. Inhabited since the Bronze Age, the city was known in classical times as Amida, and later as Amid the Black because of its extensive black basalt walls which the Romans built after they annexed it in AD 297. These walls were strengthened in the sixth century by Justinian, and successfully withstood the emerging might of the Arabs until AD 39, when they took it and gave it to the Beni Bakr clan, from whom it derives its present name, the Place of Bakr. All its subsequent conquerors, Kurds, Turcomans, Persians, and finally the Ottomans under Selim the Grim, added to the city's defences and kept them in good repair, so that today, even though they are beginning to collapse and are dangerous to the unwary (as I was soon to discover), the walls of Diyarbakir, with their defence towers, their inscriptions and carvings, are still almost complete, and an amazing and inspiring sight.

The mosques of Diyarbakir are splendid too. There are more than a dozen of them spanning a period of five hundred years from AD 1091, when the very first of the Selçuk Great Mosques of Anatolia was built here. Tremendous variety has been achieved in the design of the mosques, particularly in the minarets, no two of which are alike. The Ulu Çami, the Great Mosque, is the most impressive and the most used, as though it has remained the true heart of the city. It is entered, like many mosques in Turkey, straight from the clamour of a busy fruit and vegetable market. A solid double portal, oddly decorated for a place of prayer with the figures of two lions attacking a bull, leads into a huge rectangular courtyard. It is said to be modelled on the Great Mosque of Damascus, and is similarly full of re-used classical material, particularly Corinthian columns. Men and boys in traditional baggy black trousers and waistcoats gave the place an air of another century, as did the children coming in and out of the Koranic classes held inside the prayer hall, their Korans in embroidered bags carried on their chests.

It was towards midday when I thought I would make a circuit of the walls of Diyarbakir. I had read somewhere that this was a worthwhile thing

269

to do, and having seen local people walking up there it seemed perfectly feasible. Getting up was no problem, although they must be all of thirty feet high, possibly more; but I found some broken steps which could be negotiated without much trouble. Once on top it was fascinating. The defences themselves were formidable, even in their ruinous state. There was a tower of some sort every few yards, seventy-four I believe in the three-mile circuit, and many of these were more like small-scale castles, jutting out from the walls to provide crossfire against an invading force. Although the floors had fallen from most of them, they could be circumnavigated without too much difficulty. Down below, the town and its doings was wonderfully open to inspection.

The suburbs of Diyarbakir have spread far beyond the walls, and only in one place was there a clear view outside the city. This was towards the south where the Tigris flowed broad and green through fields and orchards towards an arid plain. Although I had been following the tributaries of this great river for days, to see it actually before me, and to recall in such a setting the almost legendary part it had played in the history of civilization, was another significant moment of the journey.

For a couple of hours I made my way along the top of the walls stopping to inspect whatever caught my interest. One place I didn't linger was where hundreds of sheepskins from freshly slaughtered animals were being pegged out to cure in the hot sun, for the stench was terrible. I became entirely caught up in the life of

Diyarbakir, the markets, the streets of metal workers, the daily life of washing, cooking and tending children in the tiny courtyards. I failed entirely to register the fact that after a short while I had stopped passing other people, for the stretch of the wall in general use was a mere hundred yards or so, providing a short cut across a section of the city.

Fascinating though the exploration continued to prove, however, there came a time when the burning sun began to make itself felt. Stupidly I had neglected to bring a hat or a drink with me, and I began to feel a little faint and thought that it was high time I came down. It was then I realized that I was quite alone up there, and had passed no one for a very long time. It suddenly seemed a terribly long way back to where I had climbed up, and I thought of the many tricky places I had negotiated on the crumbling walls. I could not remember having passed any obvious way down, and thought it better on the whole to continue. Another half hour passed, and all the time I was alert for any stairs that did not end abruptly half-way down. I began to worry a little. It was really very hot now, and I had been several hours with nothing to drink in a climate where dehydration is rapid, especially when exposed to the full heat of the sun in the middle of the day.

The very next set of steps I came to I decided I must explore more carefully. There was only an inch or two of the treads left and slippery grass grew from cracks in them, but I felt my way cautiously down their remains until they

271

petered out altogether at a corner about twenty feet from the ground. There were people below sitting in open-air cafés by the wall. Some looked up, and I called down to them to ask if there was a way to descend. Some said, '*Evet*' (yes), and some '*Yok*', and I clung there at full stretch, the tips of my fingers clinging to a crack in the burning rock, not knowing which to believe. There was no way I could both hang on and look around the corner. It was a question of either committing myself irrevocably to reaching a foot round and hoping there was something to support it, or retreating immediately, because I was becoming quite faint again from the heat, and my finger tips were scorching on the burning stone. A few moments longer and I would probably have been past making any decision, and might well have fallen. But like an angel of mercy, a young waiter, still wearing his apron, climbed up to where I was, and helped me to ascend again. He clearly knew the intricacies of the wall, and I was quite happy to relinquish all decisions to him. He led me back a hundred yards or so to a ruined tower, where we made an airy traverse before coming to a series of reasonable holds that led down to the ground. Like a true story-book hero, he vanished before I could reward him.

It was wandering through the oldest quarter of Diyarbakir, an area of high and narrow winding alleyways, built of the same black basalt as the walls, that I became aware of the taut atmosphere of the city. The semi-modern main streets were no more than a façade, behind which was an atmosphere of brooding tension, not unlike that of certain parts of Belfast. I hadn't seen this area from the walls because it was right in the centre, and well away from them. Architecturally it was the most interesting district in Diyarbakir with its fine decorated stonework and carved windows; in its heyday it had probably been the quarter of the rich merchants. Now it housed the poor and appeared to be the hub of resistance and discontent. An armed policeman stood guard on every corner, and wild barefooted children lurked in doorways, ready to leap out on any passer-by. Silent alleyways bisected narrow thoroughfares where there were small shops and people sitting on their doorsteps. I murmured a greeting to everyone I passed, and sometimes I was answered, and sometimes a stone clattered down the cobbles after me. Even in the silent shuttered alley I felt eyes boring into the back of my head.

In one of the thoroughfares an old man tapped me on the shoulder, and putting one finger across another in the sign of the cross, beckoned me to follow him. Other men standing in the doorways of shops jeered nastily, but he took no notice, and I continued to follow him, because I felt sure he was leading me to one of the ancient churches which I knew existed in Diyarbakir, and which I had hoped to find.

We passed through a maze of narrow dim alleyways, until we came to an unremarkable wooden door in a long high wall, and unlocking this my guide led me into a sunny garden, the light coming so suddenly and unexpectedly after the gloom of the streets that for a moment I was blinded. A few tiny hovels, hung about with bright strings of drying peppers, edged the open ground, while in front of me was an enormous and unmistakable Armenian church. So high are the walls, and so narrow and crowded together are the alleyways of this ancient quarter of Diyarbakir that a stranger would never have guessed that so vast a building could be hidden there. The church door was locked with a huge padlock, and what looked like official Turkish proclamations were scrawled on it. All the windows had boards nailed across them and the bell had been removed from its outside belfry. The building appeared to have been officially closed, but peering in through gaps in the barricade I could make out an interior gleaming with colour and hung about with Armenian lamps and icons: it looked like a fully commissioned church. For once I could find no way of communicating with my guide, and after I had tipped him, he wandered off. There was no one to unravel the mystery, nor did I manage to find any of the other churches of Diyarbakir.

The next morning I left, departing by the southern gateway, where a fine historic *han*, where merchants had once rested after their journeys, has been preserved by being turned into a comfortable modern hotel. The gate itself has long vanished, but the steep cobbled ramp leading down to the fields and orchards below is much as it would always have been when laden camel trains swayed up and down it. The ancient highway, well-trodden route of so many invading armies, is now just a muddy littered byway on the western bank of the broad green Tigris. I paused there to look back at what is undoubtedly the most impressive view of Diyarbakir, towering there, dark and seemingly impregnable on its rocky bluff. It was plain to see why it had retained the name of Black Amid for so long. The high black basalt walls which had nearly proved my undoing have lost none of their ancient menace, breached and crumbling though they are. They could serve as a symbol for the notorious prison they shelter, where there seems no end to the cruelty and to the gross abuse of human rights. But they could also stand for the intransigence and the fierce spirit of resistance of the Kurds themselves. Either way, and fascinating though I had found this city, it was a relief to be leaving it and heading south.

18

Along the Banks of the Tigris

TEN miles south of Diyarbakir the River Tigris, known in Turkey as the Dicle, makes a dramatic swing to the east, flowing jade green through lonely fields of cotton and sugar beet on its long convoluted journey to the Persian Gulf. I turned with it on to a minor dirt road, doubling back on my route in order to visit the plateau of Tur Abdin which lies between the deserts and the mountains, along the borderland of Turkey and the north-eastern corner of Syria.

It was an uneventful, totally rural little road, a welcome change from the noise and tensions of Diyarbakir, and I pedalled along it the whole morning without being passed by a single car or truck. It wasn't until I arrived at the outskirts of Bismil that I discovered the reason. '*Yol bozuc*,' shouted a policeman in a brown uniform with a sheriff's star, emerging from a wooden hut by the side of the road to bar my passage. My phrase book, which in his excitement he had snatched from my hand, translated this as 'broken road'. Ways impassable to motorized traffic seldom deter travellers on bicycles like Roberts, and as there were only another twenty-two miles to the town of Batman, where I planned to sleep that night, I was quite

276

happy to take my chance on the 'broken road'. But the policeman was adamant, continuing to block my path with stern cries of '*Yol bozuc!*' I could go no further it seemed. By this time several other uniformed men had gathered and the general consensus was that the only way of reaching Batman, other than by train — and I was very lucky to have arrived on a day when there was a train — was to turn around and approach it from the other direction, a detour of about one hundred and fifty miles. I bowed to the inevitable; at least there would be the compensation of sampling Turkish rail travel. But I didn't discover what major catastrophe had closed the road so effectively.

I went into Bismil to pass the time until the train came. It was a very small Kurdish town, with horses and carts the main form of transport. Strangers were a great rarity, and I was drained for every bit of interest I had to offer in the four hours before the train came. The entire male population it seemed, both senior and junior, turned out to watch me eat lunch at the restaurant, until the street became completely blocked, and the owner suggested I move inside to finish my stewed aubergine, meat and rice. In the meantime a waiter mounted guard over Roberts for as usual, it attracted quite as much attention as I did, with everyone trying to fathom out what all the attachments like gears and water bottles were for. Many of them came to the conclusion that it had some new-fangled sort of motor, and that the water bottles were the fuel tanks.

Months later, after I had returned home and was writing this book, I turned on the television one night to find that the insignificant little country town of Bismil was making headline news. It had gained brief and horrible notoriety as the centre of an area where the Turkish security forces had been making raids on villages, rounding up and summarily executing PKK guerillas and anyone else thought to be aiding or abetting them. Soldiers had pinned down the villagers, shooting at all and sundry, while those to be executed were dragged up a hill with chains around their necks. They were shot within sight of the village and dumped in a hastily dug common grave. This time the usual Turkish secrecy and careful timing had failed. A British delegation had arrived just as the soldiers left one village, and a television crew filmed the distraught relatives tearing at the fresh earth of the mound with their bare hands. There were thirty-eight bodies in that particular grave. Two had been buried alive.

Visiting a place, riding through it slowly on a bicycle, meeting the people, makes a profound difference to how one relates to it subsequently. After the brief report was over I sat there sick and stunned, while faces, scenes and voices from my journey flooded through my mind. Many incidents I had witnessed that at the time had seemed without particular significance, now assumed sinister overtones. I even wondered if a similar operation had been in progress the day I was stopped from travelling the minor road beyond Bismil. In particular I remembered what a Turkish hotel manager in Diyarbakir had said to me over a glass of tea in his smoke-filled office. 'The Kurds are not a problem to Turkey. Turkey is strong. We know where the terrorists are, we know who they are; anytime we choose we can deal with them. No, our problem is with the Americans, the British, the French. They interfere. They stop us doing what is necessary to end this terrorism.' In the light of these latest barbarities I felt he had been grossly over estimating the power of world opinion to curb Turkey's tried and tested methods with troublesome minorities.

At Bismil's one platform station, which looked like a set for an Edwardian film, I was welcomed by the station master, and taken to sit in the cool dimly lit room where the 1920s German signalling equipment and the Morse code machine were housed. Every so often the station master donned his resplendent red peaked hat and went out to remonstrate with the youths and boys who had climbed on to the window sills and were staring in at Roberts and me. Several men were paying afternoon calls on the station master, turning the air blue with their endless cigarettes; it was rather like a gentlemen's club. The centre of attention was a doll-like two year old who was being teased by her fond grandfather with mock slaps and pinches. Eventually she was goaded into hitting him in the eye, much to the delight of all the males present. Most Turkish and Kurdish men appear totally enthralled with small children, male and female alike.

A long-distance lorry driver home on holiday, and claiming to speak Bulgarian, Romanian and Polish, as well as the appalling amalgam of German and English with which we struggled to communicate, translated for anyone who wished to speak to me. The station master wanted to apologize for the antiquated equipment, waving his hand disparagingly over the beautiful mahogany interior, the shiny brass levers and the hundred and one details which were all collectors' pieces. The Turkish government would not spend money on railways, he said, cars were everything now, and the railways were being allowed to fall to pieces. I told him it was much the same in my country, and we agreed that it was a great pity and that trains were a wonderful way to get about, much more friendly than cars.

A very old man, leaning heavily on a stick, made his way slowly into the room. It appeared that extreme age is as highly regarded as extreme infancy in Turkey, for all the men got to their feet to clasp him affectionately round the shoulders and kiss him on either cheek. He was introduced proudly to me as 'old fighting man of ninety-seven years'. At first, he seemed far too vague and frail even to register that I was there. It was all he could do to collapse on to a polished bench and light the cigarette he was given — a grim effort of trying to co-ordinate his sparse breaths with his shaking hands. But after a while, when the thick choking clouds of smoke were billowing around him, he suddenly pointed a finger at me through the murk, and said 'Bang,

bang!' with no small degree of venom. With the lorry driver to translate, he launched into a stream of reminiscences about fighting the British at Gallipoli in the First World War, and nearly dying of starvation until the good Germans had come and given them bread. It was strange to hear the story with the Germans cast in the role of angels of mercy, and the British Tommies as the hordes of Genghis Khan. The memories were clearly distressing the old man, and tears began to course freely down his lined cheeks.

Fortunately at this point, after a string of Morse had come tapping over the wires, and several of the long-handled gleaming signal levers had been pushed and pulled backwards and forwards with a satisfying degree of effort, the station master donned his cap and ushered us all out to await the approaching train. I think it had a diesel engine, but my attention was entirely confined to the guard's van into which I was hoisted, and Roberts after me, not without difficulty, for the step was a good five feet from the ground.

Inside the dusty windowless interior, lighted by leaving the doors open, a picnic was being prepared by the dozen or so train personnel. They removed their smart grey jackets and caps and folded them neatly before organizing a little table out of crates covered with an old mail sack. Little spirit stoves were lit to warm up their rice and vegetables in old army mess tins, and they perched around on boxes tucking in with the enthusiasm of boy scouts on an outing; not one of them was under fifty. They would have been delighted to share their meal with me, and I would have been equally pleased to accept, had I not already eaten. Afterwards one of them sprinkled water over the floor and swept and tidied up most efficiently, tossing the litter out though the open doorway into the great outdoors, which in Turkey, as in so many other countries, is treated as a communal dustbin of infinite capacity.

I was totally unprepared for Batman, a town grown rich overnight on newly discovered oil, and as weird for those parts as its name. There might have been an older village there, but all I saw was a new town in the making — tall featureless modern hotels and office buildings, all laid out in a grid of wide unpeopled concrete streets, with cows browsing the rubbish heaps on the empty lots in between, the whole thing set in countryside that hasn't changed since the days of the Ottoman Empire. It felt as if I had been suddenly translated to another continent altogether, as though the forty-minute journey had been by magic carpet rather than antiquated train.

There was a local TV station run by the man who owned the one plushy hotel that was more or less finished, and I traded an overnight stay as my fee for filling in a slot as a visiting bicycle celebrity. It can't have been easy finding sufficient material in Batman. I'm not sure who got the bargain, for it was no sinecure. The hour-long interview was conducted by the owner's daughter, Pitah, a formidable fourteen year old who appeared to have learnt her technique from the more abrasive Western political interviewers. No sooner had I answered one question than, without any acknowledgement that she had registered my response, she was barking out the next. It was even more exhausting than the filming, when I had to demonstrate my riding skill by hurtling along the streets of Batman crouched over the exhaust pipe of the camera car, trying not to show how terrified I felt.

Later Pitah and her father took me to eat ice-cream in the heavily fenced and guarded camp which housed the oil rigs and the living quarters of the foreign technicians who worked on the drilling installations. It was open to a few privileged local people who wished to make use of the alcohol-free facilities for sport and recreation. The camp covered an extensive area on the top of a hill, and was even more disorientating than the town. Anonymously international in style, it could have been anywhere in the world, and seemed therefore to belong nowhere, like a space capsule.

We toured clean neon-lit roads lined with houses, schools, hospital, shops, gymnasia and sports halls. Pitah and her father were proud of their association with the camp, and wanted me to see it all, even in the dark. We stopped eventually in the recreation area, designed, Pitah informed me, by a famous international landscape architect. Some sort of close-cropped greenery resembling a lawn surrounded ornamental ponds, swimming pool, children's playground, hotel and outdoor café.

To my eyes, after four months of wandering through a marvellous and varied landscape, it all looked unnaturally manicured and synthetic, and totally lacking in gaiety. Even the air was manufactured: every so often great clouds of foul-smelling anti-mosquito chemicals were blown over the area, leaving everyone gasping.

All the while Pitah kept up a running commentary in her flat insistent voice that ran on and on like a buzz-saw. She didn't smile either, even when she said things like 'Coke's my drink I guess, I'm really a Coke person'. She was a very serious girl who saw life entirely in terms of the need to succeed: and success meant money. Her father paid a great deal for her to attend the private school on the oil campus, she told me, and therefore she had to do well, she had to be top at everything. When she left school she would become a computer analyst, for that was the best-paid job.

So unreal was the whole Batman experience, including my room with its luxurious bathroom, that I began to doubt the town's existence the moment I rode out of it the next morning. Only after I had been stopped three times by police who had already seen the first showing of the television interview and wanted my autograph, was I convinced I hadn't dreamt the whole thing. One permanent reminder, however, was the fact that my bicycle now had a badly bent carrier. This was the result of being so intimidated by my unusually plush surroundings that I had not insisted on locking Roberts when the desk clerk told me grandly that it wasn't necessary, as it would be his responsibility. Clearly someone, probably the desk clerk himself, had taken it for a spin with someone else sitting on the rack, Turkish fashion, a function for which it was not designed.

Within a few miles I came once more to the banks of the Tigris. Sheer cliffs of golden sandstone hemmed in the southern bank, and clumps of tall pine trees grew at their feet, wonderfully dark and vibrant against the bare rock. The river, now a marvellous emerald colour, together with the blue sky, the fields of tenderest green that lay between the river and the road, and the golden cliffs beyond created a scene of such splendour that I had to get off and walk for a while in order to take it all in.

Close to the village of Hasan Keyf I began to notice ruins of an ancient city on the cliff tops. A fine early Ottoman blue-tiled *türbe* was stranded in a green field, together with slabs of worked stone from an ancient abandoned cemetery showing through the grass. The village was on the further bank, where there was a break in the cliffs through which the road came down to a bridge. It was from this modern metal structure that I had my first sight of the astounding remains of the sixth-century Byzantine bridge, a little further upstream where the river was at its broadest and most shallow, and where vast flocks of parti-coloured sheep were being watered. Only the piers of the bridge remained, four enormous brick structures, one on either bank and two centre stream. In its day the bridge had been considered one of the wonders of Anatolia, and even now the vast stumps inspire a sense of awe, not merely because of their size and the scale of the achievement they represent, but because even in ruin they possess an intrinsic beauty that does justice to the superb position and the splendour of the surrounding landscape. It was one of the most impressive Byzantine monuments I had seen.

I supposed the 'Keyf' of Hasan Keyf to be a corruption of the city's original name, Cepha, an important stronghold on the borders between the Byzantine Empire and Persia. From the ruins of the bridge it was clear that tremendous resources had been lavished upon the place, but even so, it remained within the Christian world for only about 300 years. Since AD 640 it had been ruled by a succession of Muslim rulers, but had maintained its importance as a frontier post until Ottoman times, when it had shrunk to its present position of a very small village crouched in a shallow gorge at the foot of the lovely sandstone shells of its past glory.

Once across on the southern side, I could see a venerable Selçuk mosque tucked into a side valley. Above it a road wound up to a beautiful fortified gateway, continuing upwards in a series of zigzags, through layer after layer of the ruined golden city. Although I was expecting to find some signs of ancient Cepha here, I was totally unprepared for the extent and the beauty of what remained, and hardly knew where to begin.

The first thing was to arrange with the authorities about somewhere to pitch my tent, since there was no kind of accommodation in the village. Feeling virtuous about doing the sensible thing I went, as instructed, to the army post which was in its usual prominent position. The young captain to whom I was eventually brought had clearly not heard of the instructions impressed upon me, and certainly didn't consider finding safe places for foreign females to camp to be part of his brief. Looking past me as though I was a bad smell under his nose, he called an Arab youth in from the street, and gave him instructions to escort me to the village chief at the town hall. The chief had no English, but after reading my letters of introduction, he told the youth, Mehmet Ali, that I could stay there. His office had a sofa, there was a lavatory and washroom next door, and as it was Friday, he would not need to be there as he spent the afternoon in prayer. I would be safe in Hasan Keyf's town hall. At least that was what Mehmet Ali claimed he said. Later this turned out quite differently. Satisfied that I had done all that was necessary for safety and propriety I locked Roberts, parked it out of the burning sun in the safety of the town hall, and went off to find some lunch before beginning my explorations.

Mehmet Ali came with me, refusing to be shaken off, even with a generous tip for his troubles. He followed me into the restaurant, ordered food and calmly expected me to settle the bill for us both. I didn't mind the money, which was minimal, but I resented his cool assumption of my largesse, and his air of familiarity. When I started off towards the

287

citadel, he followed. I thought the fierce heat and my unflagging enthusiasm for ruins would wear him down, but it didn't. He found patches of shade to wait in, while I poked about the various layers of the city, continuing upwards with me, level after level, until I began to think that perhaps the captain had instructed him to keep an eye on me. He knew nothing at all about the place so he was of no use as a guide. For several hours I explored the high extensive site, thinking there was no arch or vaulting known to man that was not represented there, so many different cultures had built one on top of the other, re-using material, incorporating old plans into new ideas. It would probably prove impossible to unravel it all entirely.

The city was on one of several separate heights which had narrow winding canyons in between them. So close together were they that it would have been perfectly possible to shoot arrows or throw spears from one summit to another, making it a difficult place to defend unless all of them were held, something Xenophon's men had found on their march through terrain some way to the east of this place. On one cliff I could see the marks of Urartian steps cut into the rock and what looked like very ancient altars, so it seemed certain that occupation of the site went back at least to the Bronze Age and probably a good deal earlier. It was galling to have no good written guide to unravel the many mysteries of the place, although this had the dubious advantage of allowing me to imagine whatever I chose. Actually history itself is so full of wild improbability and romance that imagination can seldom better it.

There were a few families living in cellars and vaults among the ruins, together with their goats and donkeys, and a bizarre touch was the electricity cables that connected these troglodyte dwellings to the town's recently installed supply. Turkey with its superabundance of water has built many massive dams in recent years, particularly on the Tigris and the Euphrates, and now has more electricity than it knows what to do with, so that even these nomads were encouraged to use it. This new wealth of power and the irrigation facilities that go with it have not been obtained without cost to countries further south, like Iraq, Syria, Israel and Jordan, lands which since the dawn of time have been dependent upon the water of the great rivers that rise in the mountains of Turkey. Formal talks between Turkey and these other countries were soon to begin in order to try to find a way of controlling the flow of water which would be acceptable to all parties. But already I had heard many Turks saying, 'It is our water; why should we give it away? We should exchange it for oil.' And it has been darkly prophesied that the next war in the Middle East will not be over oil, but water.

From one of the troglodyte dwellings among the ruins a boy of about twelve emerged. He had the strangest square-shaped head, with almost right-angled corners to it. We had come to steal his things, he accused us, and then immediately changed tack, demanding a pen, or anything else

I might like to give him as a placatory gift. 'Kurdish dirty people,' said Mehmet, ignoring him. Unlike Mehmet, the boy soon gave up.

It was while I was on the summit, looking down on the green spread of the Tigris and the great flocks of sheep and goats being led across the wide sandy margins, that Mehmet Ali crept up behind me and clasped me round the middle in an amorous embrace. Without pausing to consider possible consequences, I swung round and struck him a resounding slap on the side of his head, only to be immediately appalled by the echo of it reverberating around the cliff walls. Fortunately he responded by apologizing, but then tried to save face by claiming he had only been trying to make sure I didn't fall! The incident must have finally convinced him that I was not going to succumb to his masculine charms, however, for very soon he wandered off, and I had the place to myself at last.

Back at the town hall it transpired that the mayor's offer of accommodation ceased at 5 p.m., when the place was locked up for the night. I was welcome to pitch my tent in the tiny public garden outside, which was very pretty with beds of bright flowers, but which was bordered by several cafés and open to all and sundry, including Mehmet Ali. There were any number of men already waiting to enjoy the spectacle of the foreign woman making camp.

From the cliff top, just before Mehmet Ali's arm had slid round my waist, I'd noticed that the beautiful old tiled *türbe* on the banks of the Tigris just outside Hasan Keyf had an advertisement for beer alongside it, and chairs and tables set under the trees of a large orchard. It seemed a lot more private than Hasan Keyf's public garden and I decided I would ride there and investigate it.

It was an excellent decision. The place was run by an amusing old Turkish rogue of about seventy, another Mehmet, but seemingly a good deal more dependable. He had lived in Australia for several decades, he told me (no one would have guessed this from his knowledge of the language), and after several years of running a restaurant in Sydney, had retired, and was living on a monthly disability allowance from the Australian government. He showed me his residence permit in case I doubted him, telling me he was back in Turkey only for a long visit. 'I not come for family, mind you,' he said. 'Family stink. Little boys, girls, very nice; but him grow up no good. I go Australia to get away from family. My son, him a bum. I no tell him where I go. Finish.' And in the same breath he asked, 'So what you want, a beer?'

The rough shady orchard with the Tigris at its foot and the beautiful blue-tiled decaying *türbe* at the entrance was the nearest I ever came to the Turkish garden of romantic legend. Mehmet rented it for a peppercorn rent from the government, and it came equipped with fridge, a primitive cooking place, tables and chairs and a regulation blue-painted concrete pool — currently empty of water — all of which took up only a small corner. There was plenty of room for any number of tents. The only snag

291

was the absence of any sanitation except for some latrine pits at the far end, near the river, which Mehmet said I had better not get too near in case I was sick. He reckoned the rent he paid for the place was cheaper than a hotel room, and that it was ideal for a summer's dalliance with his 'girlfriend', Ayla, a dumpy little matron of about my age, with a waist up somewhere near her armpits, and a look in her slanting eyes which I interpreted as meaning she knew what outrageous things he was saying about her even if she couldn't understand the words.

Mehmet and Ayla spent their nights in one of the giant cots I'd seen further north, and he was quite happy for me to pitch my tent under the trees. All he insisted upon was my staying within the circle of electric light bulbs that were strung across the trees in the top half of the orchard in true profligate Turkish fashion. 'Plenty bad guys here. You safe OK with me, so long I see you.' I did as he instructed, but when I went to bed I unscrewed the bulbs which would have shone into the tent and obscured the brilliant stars: it was difficult to take danger seriously in that magical place. In any case, I doubted that Mehmet with his age and weight and general stiffness of joints would have the speed to come to my rescue, even if he and Ayla had not by that time downed the best part of a couple of bottles of raki between them.

We sat for hours, I with my beer, they with their raki, splitting sunflower kernels and talking a little as the heat of the day slowly mellowed and swallows began to swoop low under the trees after the evening rise of insects. The fading light slowly bled the colours from the land and the river, and stars began to appear out of the gathering darkness, one by one. It was a period of utter contentment.

There was a brief hiccup to this dreamlike passage of time when the telephone rang, and it turned out to be the army wanting to know where I was, which seemed rather odd after their general lack of interest in my sleeping arrangements. Mehmet said of course it was odd, the whole damn country was odd. But he had to drive into town to square the arrangement and, I gathered, take formal responsibility for my person.

When he returned he seemed a little subdued. 'Too much focking hassle,' he said. 'When I leave this country I never coming back. Government here no damn good. Australia look after you. Australia you no got work, government listen, say "You want work? We give you work. You no want work, we give you cheque." Here they say "You got arm, leg, head, what more you want? Get out of here you shit!" Pardon me.'

But in spite of Mehmet's grumbles and his protestations of disillusionment with his country, he seemed to me to be in his element in this absurdly romantic Turkish garden. Later, lying in my tent listening to him and Ayla making their decidedly inebriated way to their cot, it was lines from Fitzgerald's *Rubaiyat of Omar Khayyam* that for once occupied my thoughts: ' . . . A loaf of bread, a flask of wine, and thou beside me singing in the wilderness . . . ' It was certainly the closest I felt I had come to Paradise since Lake Van.

19

With the Christians of Tur Abdin

SWALLOWS woke me at first light in the Turkish garden, darting and swerving under the fruit trees after the morning flies. I got up at once, for there was a big climb ahead and it seemed sensible to get on with it before the sun grew too fierce. I had the tent struck and packed away in record time for there was not a trace of dew or condensation on it, so dry was the air. Underneath the groundsheet was a tiny frog which had taken cover from some terror of the night, and had somehow managed to survive without me squashing it. After it had recovered from the shock of the sudden exposure it hopped away without showing any signs of being a prince under a wicked enchantment.

Ayla and Mehmet were still in one another's arms, snoring gently on a low contented note, and as I had settled my account the night before, I did not need to wake them. I set off into a magical rosy-pink morning, so fresh and perfect that some sort of thanksgiving seemed imperative, and I broke into an untuneful *Te Deum* as I rode back towards the golden stumps of the Byzantine bridge.

I waved to the soldiers on guard duty outside their barracks, so that they should know that I had survived the night without being killed or kidnapped. At the summit of the steep escarpment I stopped to look down on the Tigris, for it would be my final sight of it on this journey. From here it flowed on eastward towards Cizre and the curious little corner where the borders of Turkey, Iraq and Syria meet, and where Syria and Iraq face each other across a twenty-five mile stretch of the life-giving river.

Once out of the narrow valley of the Tigris, I was on the long ascent across the summit of the plateau of Tur Abdin, a hot dusty climb where the cool water in the bottles grew first tepid, then warm, and finally hot. There was nowhere to stop for refreshment along the way and precious little shade to be found in which to sit and brew tea. The only events were when two separate truck drivers relieved the monotony of the stony wilderness by seeing if they could edge me off the road.

Tur Abdin is today a remote, seldom visited region, but in the Byzantine period it was a great centre of Christian learning and monasticism. It was here, in the sixth century, that one of the great schisms of Christianity occurred when the Bishop of Edessa, Jacobus Baradeus, broke with the patriarchate of Constantinople over his Monophysite doctrine. It happened at a period when the Church was struggling to root out pagan heresies and to establish the tenets of orthodoxy which had been laid down during the great fourth- and fifth-century Councils of Nicea, Ephesus and Chalcedon. One of the most hotly debated subjects of these councils had been the nature of Christ: to what extent he was divine, and to what extent human. Orthodoxy maintained that Christ was human and divine in equal measure; the Monophysites, who included the Armenian and the Coptic Churches, believed that the divine nature predominated. It was an issue that attracted a degree of passion difficult to understand today. So central was it to faith itself, however, that excommunication, persecution, death even, was meted out to those who thought as other Christians preferred them not to think.

For the Jacobite Christians of Tur Abdin the split from the Greek Orthodox Church became permanent as the area was conquered and settled, first by Persians, then Arabs, and finally by the Turks. For fourteen centuries they were isolated in a sea of Islam, forgotten by the rest of the world. They re-emerged into history at the time they were being decimated in the massacres and mass deportations of the late 1920s. I had read that there were still a few thousand Jacobites worshipping there in their ancient churches and in one or two remaining monasteries, celebrating Mass in the original Aramaic, the language of Christ. It was a fascinating story of faith surviving incredible difficulties and I wanted to see this for myself.

Sometime around mid-morning, I passed through the village of Gercüs, and began to feel I might be sickening for something. I don't carry a thermometer, so I can't be sure if I'm running a temperature, especially in weather as hot as it was then. But I had been feeling uncommonly tired since I'd started the climb, and my general zest for life seemed sadly diminished: I hadn't even retaliated when the lorry drivers challenged my right to the road. By the time I reached the top of the plateau my head ached abominably, my chest felt sore, I could barely swallow and my eyes were dry and painful. If nothing worse, I was in the grip of a feverish cold, a strange ailment in such hot conditions, but one a cyclist always risks in mountainous country because of getting so over-heated and soaked in sweat on the upward gradients, and then cooling off very rapidly on the long descents. Tour de France riders pause at the top of a stiff climb to stuff newspapers up the front of their shirts; perhaps I should have been taking similar precautions.

I rallied somewhat on the long descent towards the town of Midyat, where I hoped to find out about the exact location of the monastery of Mar Gabriel. Several ice-cold fizzy drinks and a meal in an unusually cool and pleasant restaurant run by a family of Kurds gave me a new lease of life. I almost forgot my feelings of malaise altogether in the effort to respond to the owners and their friends, two of whom spoke some English and welcomed me with enthusiasm, launching immediately into an account of the present Kurdish troubles, as Kurds had done throughout my journey. I told them where I had been, and showed them my Kurdish letter which produced even greater enthusiasm and an offer of a tour of the town with one of the brothers, Veysi, who owned a taxi. This did not take long as there are few streets in Midyat, none of them particularly beautiful or memorable. Veysi said the town was famous because Christians and Muslims lived together there in peace, and he pointed out a church to me, firmly locked, but certainly ancient in appearance and in reasonable repair. He would have taken me on to the monastery of Mar Gabriel which was, he told me, thirty miles away, but it was not possible to get Roberts into the taxi. At least I now knew the direction I had to take.

The road eastward towards the border at Cizre had the worst surface I had yet encountered in this country of barbarous roads. The tarmac had been entirely ripped up, in order, it seemed, for a new wider road to be built. The work had probably been in hand for several years, or decades even, for weeds had established themselves on some stretches, and it was not the sort of land where things grew easily. It seemed to me that the workmen had the machinery for destroying the existing road but had not yet received any resurfacing equipment, so that rather than waste time hanging about they just went on tearing up further stretches. The way alternated between deep soft dirt and jumbled boulders. Even with an all-terrain bike the going was tough, and the air was permanently thick with clouds of dust that any passing vehicle, even Roberts, raised; I soon began to feel decidedly unwell again. There was nothing to do but battle on, trying to take my mind off it all by recalling snippets from my triumvirate of poets. It was while I was croaking, 'The unpurged images of day recede; the Emperor's drunken soldiery are abed', that I was hailed by the only other living persons I had seen since leaving Midyat, an elderly couple miles from anywhere picking their way though the dust and debris of the dreadful road. 'Allemand?' cried the man with delight. 'Ja' I affirmed, unable to bear the thought of his disappointment if I told him I was British. He went through his small stock of phrases, about where and when he had worked in Germany, one word in three of which I thought I understood. Not that it mattered anyway, all I had to do was listen, nod, and finally mutter, 'auf Wiedersehen', and I left behind me a happy man.

Not until twenty appalling miles were behind me did the roadworks cease and a stretch of crazed tarmac open up (the sheer sybaritic delight of tarmac can only truly be appreciated after such horrors as I had just won through). The euphoria did not last, however, for I had dug deep into my reserves of energy, and the monastery seemed over long in appearing. The road rose and fell interminably, on and on, and it wasn't until I had quite decided that Mar Gabriel did not exist, and that on the very next hill I would give in and lie down until death or rescue found me, that I saw it, the unmistakable representation of the City of God, set on a hilltop, about a mile away across the stony undulating fields.

Young boys speaking English with an Australian accent met me at the gate and took me in search of a monk. Very soon I was being conducted by a tall monk in black Syrian robes to the guest wing, a row of bare little modern

300

cells on a first floor level, with washrooms and lavatories underneath. Each cell was furnished with four metal cots set head to foot, and each had a window looking out across a small shady garden to the massive venerable stones of the end wall of a sixth-century church.

I should have gone straight to bed at this point, preferably having begun a course of antibiotics. The monk however wanted me to come and meet the sisters, and I felt too shy to explain to him that I was feeling ill. In any case, the delight of arriving at last in this wonderful place had given me a new burst of energy and I wanted to explore it all at once.

It was the hour of relaxation, and the nuns were sitting on cushions on the floor of their parlour, about eight of them wearing black robes and tight headdresses. There were also some young children and a young woman in ordinary dress, breast-feeding her baby. The youngest nun, Sister Ayesha, spoke French and explained a little about the place and the rule. The main function of Mar Gabriel, I learnt, was to teach boys the Aramaic language and train them in the ancient Jacobite worship (now in serious decline), to which end twenty or so pupils were boarded at the monastery. The teaching was carried out by the three remaining monks, helped by a few lay-teachers — the young woman was the wife of one of these teachers. The nuns' tasks were to cook, clean, wash, tend the cows and the gardens, and generally to look after the physical welfare of the boys and the monks, a purely Martha role which many women in the great days of Western monasticism had entered the cloisters in order to escape. But apart from the sweet-faced Ayesha who came from Syria, and who had received a little formal education, the nuns were recruited from the small primitive villages round about, where life for women was even harder than in Mar Gabriel and, apart from the opportunities for marriage and child-rearing, even more circumscribed. The future of the Jacobite religion was seen as being largely dependent upon the pupils of Mar Gabriel, and the nuns considered it the greatest honour to serve the boys, explained Ayesha.

Just then a bell tolled and all the sisters smiled and crossed themselves. To hear the sound of a Christian call to worship in this part of the world was a shock, for it is anathema to Muslim ears, a reminder of the presence of infidels. Whether the bell of Mar Gabriel was rung by special dispensation, or whether the ear of Turkish officialdom was conveniently deaf, I didn't discover; I suspected the latter as only three brief clangs sounded before it ceased, and there was something conspiratorial as well as joyous about the smiles the nuns exchanged.

They took me with them to the church, and sat me on a bench while they crouched against the wall at the back. A young deacon in a long robe came through the curtain of the inner sanctuary with a censor, and glided swiftly and silently around the walls, almost dancing as he bowed and swung the censor in an antique ritual before the icons and the sacred hangings.

302

Two young boys assisted the aged priest at the lectern, chanting from an enormous tome; the rest joined in antiphonally, sounding flat and a touch raucous to my Western ears. It was just as I remembered hearing Mass in Jacobite churches in Syria and in the wonderful little Church of St Mark in Jerusalem which is believed to be site of the Last Supper. There was the sense of being transported back hundreds of years to the young church of the early believers, an exciting and moving experience. But at the same time just as in those other Syriac churches I felt totally adrift in the worship. The chanting ran on and on, and I had no idea what stage the liturgy had reached until I was poked in the back by one of the nuns, and realized that I had failed to rise for the Gospel reading.

After the lengthy service the whole congregation processed with candles to the catacombs, and prayed before each of the fifty or so neatly cemented and whitewashed mounds which were the tombs of saints and martyrs going back to the very beginning of Christianity. Some bones had been brought there for interment: the remains of Christians thrown to lions in the arenas, or burnt as human torches during the centuries of Roman persecution. It made history seem suddenly very vivid.

When we emerged from the cloisters the last of the day was draining from the western sky. The nuns hurried off to their large modern kitchen to serve supper, while the boys began to carry out their bedding to spread in the middle courtyard. It was not a large monastery but there

303

were several open courtyards at various levels, with rooms and buildings of different periods opening off them. The oldest part — the original fourth-century basilica and kitchens built by Theodosius, the square sixth-century church where we had just worshipped, and the cloisters — were all on the lowest layer.

The ancient little garden with its well and shady trees, was at the same level, and this was where I made my way, for off it lay the small room in which stood my bed, the only spot in the entire fascinating complex that by then held any interest for me. I felt really ill now; my nose and eyes were streaming, and when I tried to swallow my throat and chest appeared to be lined with sandpaper. It was as much as I could do to fill my water bottles at the well, look out my store of medicines, and swallow some Cephradine before collapsing fully-clothed on a bed and dragging a sheet over me.

I awoke at odd times during the next day and a half, but saw no one. The church bell tolled its twice-daily quota of three brief clangs. Swarms of mosquitoes by night, and insufferable probing flies by day forced me to bury my head beneath the sheet, until the heat became stifling, and I had to emerge and restart the cycle. At times I heard the piping of boys' voices as they came to draw water from the well, and that was rather comforting because I thought if I called they would bring water to me too. But I was also jerked into consciousness on numerous occasions by the metal covers of the well being flung back with a great crash, followed by strange cries, curses and loud prolonged muttering. Later I discovered that these alarming commotions were made by the half-mad old Muslim gate-keeper, kept at the monastery out of charity, and who was, apparently, suffering from some deep-seated trauma that drove him to scrub himself and his clothes at all hours of the day and night. When I was up again I came upon him frequently, sluicing himself down in the guest lavatories. He reminded me of Lady Macbeth trying to wash the imaginary bloodstains of Duncan from her hands.

When I surfaced sufficiently I took further doses of antibiotics, and I must have got it more or less right, because there came a point when I began to feel much better, and got up and washed, and made my way to the nuns' quarters in search of sustenance.

The sisters had assumed I had departed the previous day, and had no idea I had been lying smitten in my cell. I think I probably looked so fit at this time, particularly with my deeply tanned face, that no one would have suspected I was ill unless I had told them. Gentle French-speaking Sister Ayesha was particularly glad to see me, as she feared I might have been offended at being poked in the back in church. Everyone was suddenly very kind: one of the three monks, Brother Cyril, produced various pills guaranteed to cure anything; the sisters pressed me to eat lots of nourishing food; and various people took me on tours of the buildings and the gardens. I began to enjoy my visit very much.

I was also lent a book in English which

explained all sorts of previously obscure things about this Jacobite branch of the church. One thing I hadn't known was that there was no difference between Syriac and Aramaic, both meant the language that had been spoken throughout ancient Mesopotamia, and learnt by the Jews during their exile in Babylon. It was not only the tongue spoken by Jesus and his disciples, but also the language of the first Christian church, established in Antioch, the first Christian See with no less a personage than St Peter as its founding bishop.

In AD 518 the headquarters of the See of Antioch was transferred from monastery to monastery in Mesopotamia, as the upheavals of war and conquest dictated. Dayr Zafaran, a neighbouring monastery which I was also planning to visit, became the seat of power in the thirteenth century, and remained so until 1959, when it was transferred to Damascus. Such monasteries, centres of scholarship and excellence, had not only furthered the spread of the Gospel, but had also preserved the scholarship of the vanishing classical world by translating Greek works of science, philosophy and literature into Syriac. These translations eventually found their way into the emerging world of Islam and were translated into Arabic. A few centuries later, translated again, this time into Latin, they became a corner-stone of the European Renaissance.

Having served such a seminal role both in religion and scholarship, Syriac is now in serious decline, as of course is Latin, Classical Greek,

Welsh, Basque, Gaelic and many other ancient tongues. Nonetheless, the chief reason for the continuation of the monastery of Mar Gabriel is the perpetuation of the language, inseparable, it would appear, from the ancient worship. Whether this means that without Aramaic there would be no Christianity for the Jacobites I could not ascertain, as there was no one at Mar Gabriel at the time with whom I could discuss this.

Culturally the language clearly had enormous importance for Jacobite Christians scattered now all over the world. The Australian boys I had met on arrival illustrated this fact. Their father, a taxi-driver in Sydney, had been born in a village on Tur Abdin and, like the majority of his generation, had escaped the hard life of material deprivation as soon as the opportunity arose. Yet in spite of this, when he had been able to afford the fares, he selected two of his four sons who were of the right age and was in the process of settling them at the monastery where they would remain for the next seven years or so. His reasons for doing this were not simple. They hinged on a remembered quality of life he had found missing in Australia. For him the sense of strong cultural cohesion and identity which he had lost when he emigrated was embodied in Mar Gabriel. By giving his sons this opportunity of being immersed in the language and worship of the Jacobite Church he felt he was giving them something far better than they would find in their adoptive country. At the same time he was helping to perpetuate something he considered infinitely precious (like Samuel being given to the temple, or in more recent times, the younger son being marked for the priesthood). In short, he felt he was paying a debt to the future and to the past. Whether his sons, who had been born in Australia, would come to feel the same way was, I thought, very much in the balance. They were eleven and twelve years old respectively, old enough to have a good idea of what they were giving up by moving from a modern city to an ancient building in remote barren countryside. Already there was trouble. I met the father because he had been sent for after the elder boy had broken his brother's front tooth in a fit of aggression that was essentially alien to the ethos of Mar Gabriel.

It was with Elizabeth, the wife of the principal (currently absent on a business trip), that I gained most insight into what Mar Gabriel represented. She had accompanied her husband when he was doing a course at Oxford University in the early days of their marriage, and after she stopped feeling shy about using the English she had learnt during that time, she was delightful company. Elizabeth had four children. 'It is necessary for Christians to have many children, to replace the ones who leave,' she told me, echoing the sentiment that Kurds had frequently expressed, though Jacobite numbers were indeed declining whereas the Kurds were not. 'But won't these children go too?' I asked. 'Yes, they too will go, but we do not think of this,' she replied, and I realized she had the enviable gift of being able to live in the present. It wasn't that she was unaware of the chill shadow of decline hanging over the whole plateau, but rather she wasn't prepared for this to influence her, or to affect the quality of her life. And after all, the Christians of Tur Abdin have already lived through fourteen centuries of the greatest uncertainty. They have survived against such extraordinary odds, that it would take someone with more temerity than I to predict that they will not somehow outlast the present difficult times.

Buoyed up by Elizabeth's company I did something I would normally consider quite impossible for me. Mar Gabriel, for whom the monastery was named, like the Desert Fathers and many of the Church's other early saints, had sought periods of solitude away from the pilgrims who flocked to him for spiritual guidance. St Cuthbert had made his space in which to commune with God on a remote rocky island in a dangerous sea; Simon Stylites had escaped to the top of a forty-foot pillar; Mar Gabriel's refuge was a tiny windowless cave deep in a hillside, reached through a narrow low underground passage behind the present-day sanctuary. It was this passage, the Way of Mar Gabriel, that was the real focus of a pilgrimage to the monastery.

It was a horrible route in which the body had to be squeezed and folded through a series of alarmingly tight places and finally bent through a narrow opening in the cave floor. For anyone weighing more than nine stone it would hardly be feasible I decided. For someone like me, whose lurking claustrophobia is ever ready to erupt and reduce me to a state of panic it was the stuff of nightmare. An electric bulb or two had been installed which certainly helped; nevertheless, the awful sense of tightness and pressure, the dread of getting stuck, as well as the fear of losing control were all present, even when I also became aware of the sense of holiness there. When finally I reached the temporary haven of Mar Gabriel's tiny cave, filthy and clogged with dust, I wondered if this intimation of holiness was simply euphoria, the result of conquering my fears, and I suppose it was in part. But there was also some other quality over and above that, which had its existence quite apart from me. It was the same atmosphere that I had sensed in the cave at Sumela, the same too that seems to cling to those scraps of rocky islands in the Hebrides and in the North Sea where Celtic monks had lived out their days in pursuit of a closer intimacy with their God.

The last night I spent in Mar Gabriel I escaped from my hot mosquito-ridden room and slept on the roof among the sisters and Elizabeth and her children. Mattresses were spread with ample space around each, and with mosquito nets suspended over them each was transformed into a separate cell. Awake early as I was the following morning, early enough in fact to see the constellation of Orion dragging Sirius up into view, the nuns were well ahead of me, already at work in an enormous walled garden that had been supplying the monastery's needs for the best part of two thousand years. The rich brown earth bearing its crops of fruit and gourds in the middle of a stony wilderness that stretched in all directions also seemed a kind of miracle, especially when I knew that the water table in this dry land is a good thousand feet down.

The black-clad figures were gathering and garnering like patient squirrels. This cool early hour was not work to them, but a pleasant interval before the demands of the day began. They kept coming over to me with gifts, a few small gherkins, a handful of cherry-like nuts, one ripe fig; and it was there I made my final farewells.

20

No Friend of Caesar

PLOUGHING my way back along the ruined road to Midyat made me realize that three days rest and half a course of antibiotics had been insufficient to get me back on form again. By the time I reached the friendly restaurant I was feeling almost as wretched as when I'd first arrived there. Riding in the heat and dust was clearly not very sensible at present, and I decided to look for a bus to take me the remaining forty precipitous miles to the town of Mardin, from where it was only a short way to the monastery of Dayr Zafaran.

My taxi-driver friend, Veysi, came with me to the bus halt, but even with his help the only conveyance we could find going to Mardin was a large *dolmus*. The driver insisted that I paid for half a dozen places, which was patently unfair, as Veysi pointed out, because only three places were available. There seemed little point in arguing, however, and I removed Roberts' front wheel, which allowed me to slide him in along the floor in front of the allotted seats. With the wheel and four panniers stacked up on one seat, this left two places (without any floor-space) for me to sit in sideways. At the last minute a man climbed in alongside, so really Roberts, the luggage and I occupied only two seats; needless to say there was no refund. 'Plenty bad men in Midyat,' muttered Veysi darkly.

Before we left a heated argument was waged between the driver and a young woman sitting in the corner seat behind me. The driver was trying to get more money from her, or failing that, to get her to leave the *dolmus*, and she was protesting vigorously and refusing to budge. She had a baby in her arms, a very still small bundle, and she seemed to be saying that it was ill. Her air of desperation had me reaching for my purse to pay whatever the difference was, but at that point the driver shrugged bad-temperedly and squeezed in behind the steering wheel. All the other passengers were chain-smoking men, and not one of them had spared the woman a look, or said a word on her behalf.

After a short while, the man who had climbed in beside me decided he wanted to sit with his friends in the back, and peremptorily ordered the woman to move into his place. This was extremely difficult for her, so I took the baby while she edged herself in, and even holding the little bundle briefly made me suspect there was something seriously amiss. Seeing my concern (and in that grizzly company the merest nod would have seemed like a heavenly salutation) the poor girl drew back the clean gauze napkin that protected the baby's face from flies, and revealed a pitiful little form with a skull-like head, the features yellow and pinched, almost mummified from dehydration. There was no perceptible breathing. Before I had time to compose my features, the girl read there what I was thinking — that her baby was already dead. It had clearly been hovering on the very edge of life for some time, but she seemed to be hoping against hope that she would get to the hospital at Mardin in time for the doctors to perform a miracle. Perhaps it had taken her days to find the fare, I thought. She took my hand and placed it beneath the baby's wrappings to try and persuade me, and herself, I think, that it was still warm. Then she rearranged the napkin over the still features, and turned away to hide her face. I needed to hide mine too; somehow the irrelevant fact that the baby's garments were so clean and fresh made the young mother's situation seem infinitely more pitiful.

The last range of dramatic hills dropped abruptly to the vast plains of Mesopotamia, grey and shimmering beneath the smoky heat haze. Mardin perches on one of these final hills, and I hoped desperately that we would reach it before the young mother accepted the fact of her baby's death. The *dolmus* was too bleak, too derelict a setting for such an event, with only these hard-faced, uninterested men and one foreign woman who had no words to comfort.

But she already knew. When I dared to look at her again the still bundle was no longer clasped in her arms but lay there loosely on her lap, a tiny Pietà. Her shoulders were slumped, and a tear rolled down either side of her nose, the first tears I had seen anyone shed in this country. I reached for her hand, and she let me hold it until the *dolmus* stopped at the outskirts of Mardin where the hospital was. Then she was out in a flash, bent double over the little corpse, her breath coming in great gasps between screams, as other women began to surround her, coming it seemed from nowhere. The last I saw of her as I reassembled Roberts and wheeled it away, was in a knot of women whose high-pitched spine-chilling ululations showed that the healing rituals of grief had already begun.

The first impression of Mardin perched on its sharp winding ridge was of a tense city, with numbers of armed policemen standing around, and small boys, made jumpy by the atmosphere, inclined to throw stones and be generally aggressive to strangers. An amiable twelve year old named Ishmael homed in on me, however, and I was more than happy to let him earn a little by pushing Roberts up the steep main street. Unfortunately, Ishmael felt so proud of himself in this role that he wasn't able to restrain calling out to acquaintances, who then wanted to help push too, and soon Roberts had almost disappeared beneath a sea of boys, and I had to wade into the rescue as fights and scuffles broke out. Since progress was so difficult I locked my long-suffering companion to the kiosk of a friendly cigarette seller, and leaving Ishmael standing guard over it, went on alone. I climbed a flight of steps to the Isa Bey Medrese, the finest building in Mardin with a particularly beautiful south façade, but derelict now and locked. Further flights of steps took me up through an ancient gateway carved with two fine lions and into Mardin's crowning citadel, built around 1430 when the Akkoyunlu took over the city.

There wasn't much of interest left within the walls of the citadel, but the views south over the plains were stupendous. So flat and featureless, so parched and dry are these vast nebulous expanses that every patch of shade, every blade of grass assumes a heightened significance. These were the ancient lands between the Tigris and the Euphrates, the Biblical lands where the drama of the Patriarchs began, where Abraham, after leaving Ur of the Chaldees, had wandered with his flocks from well to well, encountering his god, Jahweh, in the desert.

Dayr Zafaran, the Saffron Monastery, was set on another dramatic hill, with the remains of older monastic buildings and hermitages scattered on the slopes above. The beautiful stone walls, which account for its name, were rebuilt around AD 700, when it became the ancient patriarchal see of the Syrian Orthodox Church. It lies only about five miles from Mardin, but what with the inclines and the terrible oppressive heat I arrived there bathed in sweat. The door was opened by a man of about thirty dressed in skin-tight jeans, cowboy boots, and a crimson shirt open to the waist to reveal an outsize gold and blue medallion of the Virgin nestling against the black curly hair of his manly chest. Dayr Zafaran receives infinitely more visitors than Mar Gabriel, and I assumed that the patronizing attitude this colourful personage adopted towards Roberts and me probably had to do with the size of tip he expected from one travelling in so lowly a manner. A coach party of Scandinavians were just filing out to their coach and with them he was all deference, bowing to each as they pressed lira notes into his outstretched palm.

But if I found the custodian a touch arrogant, it was nothing to the attitude of the monk holding court in the cool cloistered garden. His imposing corpulent figure clad in black flowing robes was flanked by an entourage of local men, there, it seemed, for no other reason than to pass the time of day, and all drawing deeply on cigarettes as though their lives depended upon it. He acknowledged my arrival by gesturing me towards a seat with the merest twitch of one heavy eyebrow. There were pupils here too learning Aramaic, and one would occasionally come to the monk's elbow and read to him from a book. But there was nothing of the gentle other-worldly atmosphere of Mar Gabriel. I felt I was at a public performance, with pupils, cronies and custodian acting the role of a sycophantic chorus, dancing attendance, laughing to order and competing with each other for favours.

A sinister-looking American, dressed as a poor village Kurd, and playing with Muslim prayer beads dropped into a chair beside me. He had apparently been staying at the monastery for several weeks while he plucked up the energy to move on in the direction in which I had come, and eventually cross into what had until recently been the USSR, where he thought his true roots might be.

My reception went wrong from the beginning. 'I don't speak your English,' said the priest, with a curl of his lips, as though mentioning something obscene, when, after some twenty minutes or so, he deigned to acknowledge my existence. The admiring, smirking entourage nodded as though in agreement, and the swashbuckling custodian repeated the remark in slightly less fluent English, adding, 'What you wanting?' I explained I wanted to stay the night, and had come from Mar Gabriel. I had my documents ready, and handed them over thinking that he would now realize that I was perfectly respectable, whatever prejudices he might have been harbouring against someone arriving by bicycle. For the letters and article in Turkish the monk spared no more than a cursory glance, merely wrinkling his nose disparagingly as he tossed them aside. But when he spotted the two-line Kurdish letter he sat up, forgetting he didn't speak English. 'This is Kurdish,' he said. 'Yes,' I affirmed, puzzled at his air of shocked outrage. Earlier that year when the Iraqi Kurds had been fleeing in thousands through Tur Abdin from the persecutions of Saddam Hussein, the monks of Mar Gabriel told me they had turned the monastery into a centre to help them find relatives and friends in Turkey. But apparently eighty miles away in Dayr Zafaran different criteria applied. 'Kurds murderers, no good, steal, kill,' he said, and he drew his finger in the unmistakable universal gesture across his throat. 'You friend of Kurd?' he demanded, his lip curling again. I realized this

318

was an ultimatum and was eager to placate him, having by this time fallen into the general mood of subservience. 'Some Kurds are good,' I said weakly. 'No Kurd is good,' he roared thumping his hand down on a table. 'You friend of Kurds, go to mosque; you not stop here.' 'But I'm a Christian,' I said, displaying my cross. This seemed to persuade him to give me one more chance. Facing me full on for the first time he delivered his challenge very deliberately with narrowed eyes. 'You like Kurds?' There was only one answer I could possibly have given, even had the string of kindnesses received at Kurdish hands on this journey not flooded through my mind as I cast about for a way out of the dilemma. 'Of course I like some Kurds,' I said finally, and bold now that I'd blown my chances, attempted to add that I tried to like everybody, albeit without much success, and that I would have thought this was the very least any professing Christian could aspire to, particularly one representing the faith in a sea of Islam. 'No Kurd is friend,' shouted the fierce old bigot, cutting me short. 'You get to mosque.' And all the entourage laughed at his wit, whether they had understood what he said or not.

As his flashily attired minion led me out, I was reminded of one of the moments in the trial of Jesus, when Pontius Pilate had wanted to release him, and the trouble makers in the crowd had shouted, 'If you let this man go you are not Caesar's friend.' Unlike Pilate, I had failed to confirm my allegiance to the ruling

319

authority. As a parting shot, the custodian told me they were going to ring the police in Mardin and tell them I had a Kurdish letter.

I can't pretend that being turned away from the one gate where I would expect to find a welcome was not a bad experience. Had I not pedalled off at once I might well have shed tears from a combination of anger, rejection and sheer exhaustion. But it was half-past three, and the heat was terrible; any sort of effort made me feel as though my heart was knocking against my throat. There wasn't any moisture to spare for tears.

When I had recovered sufficient equilibrium to think about where I was going, I began to worry about the threat to phone the police. I had little faith in Turkish police, and even less in Turkish prisons. Perhaps by this time, having become so thin and weather-beaten, and with my travel-stained clothes and my hair shaggy and needing a cut, I might look to them like a Kurd? Far-fetched though this might seem, weirder things have happened in these parts, where the practice is to act first and think later, if at all. I could see myself being thrown into a police cell, and if I was questioned by anyone as intractable and overbearing as the Jacobite priest, I could be beaten to a pulp before anyone thought to check my credentials.

By this time I had reached the outskirts of Mardin again, and the sight of the police standing around with their guns at the ready decided me to head in the other direction. This was the line of least resistance running downhill towards the plains. I don't think I could have done much more pedalling anyway. But there was no need: all I had to do was stay awake and keep Roberts upright. I freewheeled on and on for about fifteen miles, the slope slowly levelling out, and my knees gradually ceasing their shaking, until I came to a halt at the long straight highway running east-west at the foot of the hills.

There was a filling station at the crossroads, owned by Kurds, a run-down place with piles of rubble behind the disused workshop, amongst which I thought my small tent would be inconspicuous. The owner considered camping too dangerous, however, and offered me a mattress on the roof instead. I could sleep up there with the night-watchman, he said, and showed me that we would be discretely separated by a low wall. Two terrifying dogs were kept up there also, and, as far as I could see, never let down. What with their desiccated droppings and the plethora of old junk and ancient car parts up there, it was no substitute for the venerable saffron cloisters, but it was a port in a storm, and if the police were after me, I doubted they would think to look here. The Kurds' casual and unquestioning acceptance of me was wonderfully soothing after the rejection of my fellow Christians.

Once the sun was down, I went up to the roof with my luggage and the mattress, and made some sort of meal of fruit and nuts and tea. I'd bought bread in Mardin, but I must have dropped it at Dayr Zafaran when I was getting out my ill-received documents; I thought it an odd twist of fortune that it should benefit those who had proved so inhospitable. What I still had, however, were the last drops of whisky I'd bought in Dogubayazit, and as I still retained the faith of my Highland ancestors in this catholicon against all bodily ills, I decided to take it in addition to the antibiotics, a course not advised by doctors.

Within an hour night had transformed the scene of squalor. As the temperature dropped the skies cleared, and stars blazed out of the velvety-blue blackness. I fell asleep in a sense of wonder that such beauty could flower so instantly and over such a place. The sound of rifle fire cracked out intermittently through the night. Once I awoke to the sounds of shouts close by, and the dogs went berserk until they were cursed into silence by the night-watchman curled up under a heap of rags on his string bed beside them. I was so comfortable, cocooned in my sleeping bag, with the panniers stacked close around me to cut the force of the wind that blows relentlessly under these hills — hot and dry by day, cold and dry by night — that I fell easily asleep again, after verifying that the sounds had nothing to do with me.

By the time a grey dawn broke I was up and brewing coffee, feeling a great deal better than I had for some days, and eager to be on my way. The night-watchman, not over pleased at my early start, had to be woken in order to hold back the dogs, and to unlock Roberts from the garage. I tipped him for his troubles, but he would have preferred dollars, he told me, going to great lengths of ingenuity to make this preference known in mime, for he had no English, not even the word dollar. It was all wasted effort alas, as I had no more dollars, and precious little of any other currency by this time, for my journey was almost at an end. An hour's hard slog against the strong desert wind and two hours more in a bus, along the arrow-straight road that has seen the passage of more conquering armies than any other strip of ground in the world, brought me to my final objective, Urfa, a town as ancient as any in the Fertile Crescent.

Urfa entered the annals of recorded history before even the Hittites occupied it, for it was the stronghold of the Hurrites who invented war chariots, with which they were able to wreak havoc in Ancient Egypt. When Alexander the Great came through many centuries later, on his whirlwind conquest of the world, his veterans renamed Hurri Edessa, after their home town in Macedonia. Always in the mainstream of history and conquest, Edessa changed hands between Arabs, Byzantines, Selçuks and Armenians for several hundred years, until in AD 1098, it became briefly the County of Edessa, the first of several Crusader states in the Middle East, when Count Baldwin decided he would rather be its ruler than enjoy the less certain rewards of reaching Jerusalem.

To a Europe emerging from the Dark Ages

Edessa gave the first taste of Arabic culture and scholarship — leading directly to the pointed arch and the emergence of Gothic architecture. When the Holy City of Edessa fell to the Selçuks forty-six years later all Christendom mourned its loss, and the Pope called immediately for a Second Crusade. Imad al-Din Zengi, who ousted the Crusaders from Edessa, was to have a grandson, known popularly as Saladin, who would ultimately succeed in expelling all the Crusaders from the length and breadth of the Holy Land.

There is very little of all this past glory to be seen in Urfa: it has been sacked too often. Two immensely tall Corinthian columns, known as the Throne of Nimrod, tower above the rubble on the dominating rock of the citadel. Other re-used classical columns grace the Ulu Çami, the Great Mosque, whose walls look suspiciously as though they were once part of a great Christian church. Otherwise Urfa seems a hot dusty old-fashioned Ottoman town. The liveliest place there is the extensive shady bazaar where industrious small boys diligently learn their trades, sitting cross-legged in groups before their mentors, hammering away at shoes, or more noisily at metalware pots and pans. But in spite of the absence of monuments, it was here in Urfa that the many threads of history that had twisted themselves into my journey came together, and I found it an immensely satisfying place to sit and think about how it all wove into a pattern like a great web. That I was able to do this in no less significant a place than beside the

Pools of Abraham was yet another bonus.

While it would be perfectly possible to pass through Urfa and gain no inkling of its illustrious past, its connection with Abraham would be difficult to miss. Abraham is almost as important a figure in Islam as he is in Judaism and Christianity, and Urfa believes itself to be the birthplace of the Patriarch. The central complex of buildings at the foot of the great citadel commemorates this belief and is an important focus of Muslim pilgrimage. Various mosques and *madresesi*, from the thirteenth century onwards, including one built over the 'cave of the birth', flank a network of rectangular ponds. The water in these Pools of Abraham churn with thousands of fat 'sacred' carp, which the pilgrims believe they gain merit by feeding, even though there are notices asking them not to do this. There are several legends to account for the special sanctity of the fish and the water, the most popular being that Abraham, refusing to practice idolatrous rites, was thrown into a fire by the Babylonian king, Nimrod, at which point God changed the fire into water, and the quenched coals became golden fish. Interestingly, the spring that feeds these fish ponds was sacred to the Greeks many centuries before Islam, suggesting yet again that the idea of 'the holy' continues, no matter what embodiment it takes.

I worked on my notes in the dusty park surrounding the pools, where café tables were set under leafy trees, and where pilgrims relaxed sipping fizzy drinks and tossing all manner of unsuitable things to the carp. Although the pilgrims were all Muslim, there was the sense of three great faiths meeting here. 'Are we not all people of the Book?' Mohammed is reputed to have said, referring to the shared heritage of Jews, Christians and Muslims, and pointing to the unity they should therefore enjoy.

But it was at Harran, fifteen miles south of Urfa and almost on the Syrian border that I felt I had my own personal encounter with Abraham. Harran stands on the Plain of Jullab, a bleak arid expanse, broken here and there by the conspicuous mounds of ancient settlements. Amongst these hillocks the remains of a wall bearing an inscription of Saladin surround the jumbled ruins of the city which was destroyed by Mongols in AD 1260 and never rebuilt. But although this city of Harran can be dated back to 2000 BC, when a peace treaty was signed there in the temple of the Moon God, Sin, the ruins seem much more recent than the strange mud-brick houses roofed with crude beehive shaped domes that cluster around it. Until recently these 'beehive' villages stretched all along the border, inhabited by semi-nomadic Arabs whose lives have not substantially changed since Biblical times. It was probably just such a place that housed Abraham when he arrived in Harran with his family roundabout the same time as the peace treaty was being concluded in the temple of Sin, as the Book of Genesis records:

. . . And Terai took Abram his son, and Lot his son's son . . . and they went forth from Ur of the Chaldees, to go into the Land of Canaan: and they came into Harran and dwelt there.

Brightly-clad women and girls walked to and from the wells with their donkeys to draw water; others were working in their gardens, and feeding the hens and young animals. Some invited me into their strange little houses and showed how much cooler was the air under the elongated domes. They begged small gifts of lighters, combs or matches, but without over-insistence; they seemed much gentler than the people I'd grown used to in the last few weeks. I gathered that their main livelihood these days came from smuggling sheep into Syria where prices are higher, something Abraham would surely have done well, for none of the Patriarchs seems to have been above a little double dealing or sharp practice.

But Abraham did not remain long in Harran. In the Book of Genesis he comes at the end of the long line of 'the generations of the Sons of Noah' and marks the start of a new age. The Sons of Noah have done as God commanded: gone forth, multiplied and filled the earth. They have built their cities, their temples — and, alas, their Tower of Babel. The human race has failed yet again.

Abraham is charged with a different task. He is to turn his back on security, step outside the bounds of what is safe and familiar and become a wanderer, until his God decides he is ready to inherit a land which is promised to him. Whether this promised land is a small stony country in the Middle East; or what the writer of the Book of Hebrews describes as 'No earthly city'; or something that might seem altogether different, like walking in space, or treading new grounds of thought, depends upon the viewpoint. Abraham, we are told, never reached his goal; for him the journey and the promise had to suffice.

Wandering around the beehive huts of Harran at the end of this particular personal odyssey, with several bare-footed grubby little girls keeping me company and waiting for largesse, I realized once again the special significance the story of Abraham had for me. It was the symbol, the idea of setting forth into the unknown, trusting that whatever the outcome, the cost will prove worth the hazard. It seemed to me that all journeys, no matter how they are undertaken, and whether or not the voyager even leaves his chair, are a sharing in this creative recklessness.

Not that I believe that journeys ever really end, or if they do, then they do so only in order to lead on to another. Standing at the spot where 'Abram took Sarai his wife, and Lot, his brother's son, and all the substance that they had gathered, and all the souls they had gotten in Harran; and they went forth into the land of Canaan . . . ' I wondered how long it would be before I set out once again.

Equipment for the Journey

The bicycle for this journey was made by Roberts of Croydon. It performed like a true thoroughbred, with no vicious habits and with a surprising turn of speed.

Ron Kitching of Harrogate supplied the Suntour components, all of which performed admirably.

Specialized Nimbus tyres proved excellent on all the barbarous roads and tracks, except in thick mud and soft sand. They lasted the entire journey without sustaining a single puncture.

The only piece of equipment that failed was the seat bolt on the 'TTT' seatpin which sheared through on my last day's ride in Turkey. This meant that my comfortable Specialized saddle was no longer attached to the bicycle. Had this happened earlier in the journey it would have been disastrous.

Avocet supplied a very small electronic altimeter/milometer/speedometer for Roberts which gave me a great deal of unexpected pleasure, as well as a lot of useful information. I found it a comfort to know how far I had climbed and how far I still had to go. I could also amuse myself by working out how many Everests (or the equivalent) I had ascended.

The Dog Dazer is made in the USA, and I obtained mine by writing to Dog Dazer, Freepost, London.

My tent was a 'Tadpole' by North Face.

Mountain Equipment supplied my 'Dewline' sleeping bag which at only a pound in weight is an amazing saving over any bag I have used previously, and which, combined with a silk inner bag (which weighs only 4 oz. and can be used separately), was warm enough for even cold September nights in Eastern Turkey.

Thermarest supplied a lightweight three-quarter-length self-inflating mattress, without the comfort of which I no longer even contemplate camping.

The stove I took was the new, very lightweight Epigas burner, which I used with butane/propane mix micro cartridges. Provided I could find sufficient shelter from the wind, this combination was very fast and efficient. A tiny Trangia kettle served as kettle and teapot, and one small aluminium pan served all other purposes for which such a vessel can be utilized — cooking pan, wash basin, candle holder, emergency chamber pot, and so forth.

Stamfords of Long Acre supplied the Kümmerly and Frey map of Turkey. Rohan supplied most of my clothing.

My camera was an Olympus AF-1 Twin.

Film: Kodak Kodachrome Professional.

The whisky was made in Scotland.

I carried all this gear together with the numerous other bits and pieces, like safety-pins, notebooks, pens, poetry books, penknife, first-aid kit, string and travellers cheques in a handlebar bag and four pannier bags made by Carradice of Nelson. These bags are so robust that should I have great-grandchildren who cycle, I'm sure they will still serve admirably for their travels.

THE WILDERNESS WALK
Sheila Bishop

Stifling unpleasant memories of a misbegotten romance in Cleave with Lord Francis Aubrey, Lavinia goes on holiday there with her sister. The two women are thrust into a romantic intrigue involving none other than Lord Francis.

THE RELUCTANT GUEST
Rosalind Brett

Ann Calvert went to spend a month on a South African farm with Theo Borland and his sister. They both proved to be different from her first idea of them, and there was Storr Peterson — the most disturbing man she had ever met.

ONE ENCHANTED SUMMER
Anne Tedlock Brooks

A tale of mystery and romance and a girl who found both during one enchanted summer.

CLOUD OVER MALVERTON
Nancy Buckingham

Dulcie soon realises that something is seriously wrong at Malverton, and when violence strikes she is horrified to find herself under suspicion of murder.

AFTER THOUGHTS
Max Bygraves

The Cockney entertainer tells stories of his East End childhood, of his RAF days, and his post-war showbusiness successes and friendships with fellow comedians.

MOONLIGHT
AND MARCH ROSES
D. Y. Cameron

Lynn's search to trace a missing girl takes her to Spain, where she meets Clive Hendon. While untangling the situation, she untangles her emotions and decides on her own future.

NURSE ALICE IN LOVE
Theresa Charles

Accepting the post of nurse to little Fernie Sherrod, Alice Everton could not guess at the romance, suspense and danger which lay ahead at the Sherrod's isolated estate.

POIROT INVESTIGATES
Agatha Christie

Two things bind these eleven stories together — the brilliance and uncanny skill of the diminutive Belgian detective, and the stupidity of his Watson-like partner, Captain Hastings.

LET LOOSE THE TIGERS
Josephine Cox

Queenie promised to find the long-lost son of the frail, elderly murderess, Hannah Jason. But her enquiries threatened to unlock the cage where crucial secrets had long been held captive.

THE TWILIGHT MAN
Frank Gruber

Jim Rand lives alone in the California desert awaiting death. Into his hermit existence comes a teenage girl who blows both his past and his brief future wide open.

DOG IN THE DARK
Gerald Hammond

Jim Cunningham breeds and trains gun dogs, and his antagonism towards the devotees of show spaniels earns him many enemies. So when one of them is found murdered, the police are on his doorstep within hours.

THE RED KNIGHT
Geoffrey Moxon

When he finds himself a pawn on the chessboard of international espionage with his family in constant danger, Guy Trent becomes embroiled in moves and countermoves which may mean life or death for Western scientists.

TIGER TIGER
Frank Ryan

A young man involved in drugs is found murdered. This is the first event which will draw Detective Inspector Sandy Woodings into a whirlpool of murder and deceit.

CAROLINE MINUSCULE
Andrew Taylor

Caroline Minuscule, a medieval script, is the first clue to the whereabouts of a cache of diamonds. The search becomes a deadly kind of fairy story in which several murders have an other-worldly quality.

LONG CHAIN OF DEATH
Sarah Wolf

During the Second World War four American teenagers from the same town join the Army together. Forty-two years later, the son of one of the soldiers realises that someone is systematically wiping out the families of the four men.

THE LISTERDALE MYSTERY
Agatha Christie

Twelve short stories ranging from the light-hearted to the macabre, diverse mysteries ingeniously and plausibly contrived and convincingly unravelled.

TO BE LOVED
Lynne Collins

Andrew married the woman he had always loved despite the knowledge that Sarah married him for reasons of her own. So much heartache could have been avoided if only he had known how vital it was to be loved.

ACCUSED NURSE
Jane Converse

Paula found herself accused of a crime which could cost her her job, her nurse's reputation, and even the man she loved, unless the truth came to light.

BUTTERFLY MONTANE
Dorothy Cork

Parma had come to New Guinea to marry Alec Rivers, but she found him completely disinterested and that overbearing Pierce Adams getting entirely the wrong idea about her.

HONOURABLE FRIENDS
Janet Daley

Priscilla Burford is happily married when she meets Junior Environment Minister Alistair Thurston. Inevitably, sexual obsession and political necessity collide.

WANDERING MINSTRELS
Mary Delorme

Stella Wade's career as a concert pianist might have been ruined by the rudeness of a famous conductor, so it seemed to her agent and benefactor. Even Sir Nicholas fails to see the possibilities when John Tallis falls deeply in love with Stella.

MORNING IS BREAKING
Lesley Denny

The growing frenzy of war catapults Diane Clements into a clandestine marriage and separation with a German refugee.

LAST BUS TO WOODSTOCK
Colin Dexter

A girl's body is discovered huddled in the courtyard of a Woodstock pub, and Detective Chief Inspector Morse and Sergeant Lewis are hunting a rapist and a murderer.

THE STUBBORN TIDE
Anne Durham

Everyone advised Carol not to grieve so excessively over her cousin's death. She might have followed their advice if the man she loved thought that way about her, but another girl came first in his affections.